Education Is Politics

CRITICAL
TEACHING
ACROSS
DIFFERENCES,
POSTSECONDARY

EDITED BY

Ira Shor & Caroline Pari

Boynton/Cook
HEINEMANN
Portsmouth, NH

Boynton/Cook Publishers, Inc.
A subsidiary of Reed Elsevier Inc.
361 Hanover Street
Portsmouth, NH 03801–3912
www.boyntoncook.com

Offices and agents throughout the world

© 2000 by Ira Shor and Caroline Pari

All rights reserved. No part of this book may be reproduced in any form or by any electronic or mechanical means, including information storage and retrieval systems, without permission in writing from the publisher, except by a reviewer, who may quote brief passages in a review.

The editors and publisher wish to thank those who have generously given permission to reprint borrowed material:

"Teaching and Social Change: Reflections on a Freirean Approach in a College Classroom" by Daniel G. Solorzano was originally published in *Teaching Sociology* (April 1989). Reprinted by permission of the American Sociological Association.

"Teaching Undergraduates About AIDS: An Action-Oriented Approach" by Kimberly Christensen from *Harvard Educational Review*, 61:3 (August 1991). Copyright © 1991 by the President and Fellows of Harvard College. All Rights Reserved.

"Teaching a Course on 'Music and Social Movements'" by Rob Rosenthal was originally published in *Radical Teacher*, Issue No. 52. Reprinted by permission of *Radical Teacher*, Boston Women's Teachers' Group, Inc., PO Box 383316, Cambridge, MA 02238-3816.

"'Commercials in the Classroom?! What Next, Music Videos?' 'Yes.'" by Paul D. Fischer from *Radical Teacher*, Issue No. 52. Reprinted by permission of *Radical Teacher*, Boston Women's Teachers' Group, Inc., PO Box 383316, Cambridge, MA 02238-3816.

"Changing Perceptions, Not Just Channels, in the Heartland: Teaching Television's Teaching" by David B. Owen and Charles L. P. Siley from *Radical Teacher*, Issue No. 50. Reprinted by permission of *Radical Teacher*, Boston Women's Teachers' Group, Inc., PO Box 383316, Cambridge, MA 02238-3816.

"Interrupting Patriarchy: Politics, Resistance, and Transformation in the Feminist Classroom" by Magda Lewis from *Harvard Educational Review*, 60:4. Copyright © 1990 by the President and Fellows of Harvard College. All Rights Reserved.

"Feminists in Action: How to Practice What We Teach" by Rae Rosenthal. Reprinted by permission of the State University of New York Press, from *Left Margins,* by Karen Fitts and Alan Frace (Eds.). © 1995 State University of New York. All rights reserved.

"Keeping Our Activist Selves Alive in the Classroom: Feminist Pedagogy and Political Activism" by Jennifer Scanlon. *Feminist Teacher* 7.2 (1993): 8–14. Reprinted by permission of the Feminist Teacher Editorial Collective.

"Empathy Education: Teaching About Women and Poverty in the Introductory Women's Studies Classroom" by Jennifer Scanlon from *Radical Teacher*, No. 48. Reprinted by permission of *Radical Teacher*, Boston Women's Teachers' Group, Inc., PO Box 383316, Cambridge, MA 02238-3816.

Acknowledgments for borrowed material continue on p. 208.

CIP is on file with the Library of Congress.
ISBN: 0-86709-460-5

Editor: Lisa Luedeke
Production: Vicki Kasabian
Cover design: Catherine Hawkes/Cat and Mouse
Manufacturing: Louise Richardson

Printed in the United States of America on acid-free paper
04 03 02 01 00   DA   1 2 3 4 5

In memory of Paulo Freire, 1921–1997

"This is a great discovery, education is politics! . . . The teacher has to ask, What kind of politics am I doing in the classroom? That is, in favor of whom am I being a teacher? By asking in favor of whom am I educating, the teacher must also ask against whom am I educating . . .

"Through education we can first understand power in society. We can throw light on the power relations made opaque by the dominant class. We can also prepare to participate in programs to change society.

"Our experience in the university tends to form us at a distance from reality. The concepts that we study in the university can work to amputate us from the concrete reality they are supposedly referring to . . .

"I insist on dialogical education starting from the students' comprehension of their daily life experiences, no matter if they are students of the university or kids in primary school or workers in a neighborhood or peasants in the countryside . . . starting from concreteness, from common sense, to reach a rigorous understanding of reality."

—From *A Pedagogy for Liberation*

Contents

Introduction: (Why) Education Is Politics
Ira Shor 1

1 Teaching and Social Change: Reflections on a Freirean Approach in a College Classroom
Daniel G. Solorzano 15

2 Teaching Undergraduates About AIDS: An Action-Oriented Approach
Kimberly Christensen 28

3 Teaching a Course on "Music and Social Movements"
Rob Rosenthal 52

4 "Commercials in the Classroom?! What Next, Music Videos?"
Paul D. Fischer 63

5 Changing Perceptions, Not Just Channels, in the Heartland: Teaching Television's Teaching
David B. Owen and Charles L. P. Siley 71

6 Interrupting Patriarchy: Politics, Resistance, and Transformation in the Feminist Classroom
Magda Lewis 82

7 Feminists in Action: How to Practice What We Teach
Rae Rosenthal 107

8 Keeping Our Activist Selves Alive in the Classroom: Feminist Pedagogy and Political Activism
Jennifer Scanlon 124

9 Empathy Education: Teaching About Women and Poverty
   in the Introductory Women's Studies Classroom
   Jennifer Scanlon   137

10 Human Labor and Literature: A Pedagogy from a Working-Class
   Perspective
   Janet Zandy   145

11 The Inclusion/Exclusion Issue: Including Students
   in Choosing Texts
   Christine Sutphin   160

12 Queer Statistics: Using Lesbigay Word-Problem Content
   in Teaching Statistics
   John Kellermeier   167

13 Disability Studies: Expanding the Parameters of Diversity
   Simi Linton, Susan Mello, and John O'Neill   178

Afterword: How I Got Started:
Student Participation in a (Too) Large Sociology Class
Fred L. Pincus   193

About the Editors   209

Introduction
(Why) Education Is Politics
Ira Shor

Taking Sides

"We must always take sides," said Elie Wiesel in his 1986 Nobel Peace Prize speech. "Neutrality helps the oppressor, never the victim. Silence encourages the tormentor, never the tormented" (Osborn and Osborn 1991, 457).

Wiesel's moral appeal speaks to the life and work of Paulo Freire, who took sides with the subordinates of society ("the power not yet in power," he liked to say). Freire urged educators to teach critically from the bottom up against the myths and inequities imposed from the top down ("the power now in power"). In a Freirean program, teaching critically means inviting students to question the status quo when they study any subject matter. To Freire, critical thinking was not a technical exercise in forms of argument (Paul 1993) but rather an inquiry into the social consequences and personal contexts of any knowledge. Critical thought, from this point of view, is oppositional knowledge making focused on self in society and oriented toward alternatives for change. Thus, in memory of Paulo Freire, here is a book of teachers reporting critical practice in actual classrooms, seeking social change.

The title of this teaching volume is taken from Freire's declaration in *A Pedagogy for Liberation* (Shor and Freire 1987):

> This is a great discovery, education is politics! When a teacher discovers that he or she is a politician, too, the teacher has to ask, What kind of politics am I doing in the classroom? That is, in favor of whom am I being a teacher? The teacher works in favor of something and against something. Because of that, he or she will have another great question, How to be consistent in my teaching practice with my political choice? I cannot proclaim my liberating dream and in the next day be authoritarian in my relationship with the students. (46)

Freire insisted that critical teachers have a special responsibility to align classroom practice with democratic theory, to make the learning process reflect egalitarian ideals. Needless to say, in schools and colleges dominated by top-down authority, bureaucratic testing, Standard usage, Eurocentric canons, rote learning, and masculine discourse (didactic lecturing, agonistic disputation, scholastic mannerisms), it can't be easy to practice a critical, participatory pedagogy. In the 3,000-plus units of higher education in the United States and the 80,000-plus schools that feed students into them, initiating a democratic learning process can be as difficult as offering a syllabus of dissident themes.

The sources of difficulty are too complex to examine in this brief introduction, but the following chapters explore some resistances and obstacles to critical thought and dialogic learning. (See also Willis 1981; Giroux 1983; Oakes 1985, 1990; McNeil, 1986; Nieto 1998.) As I argued in *Empowering Education* (1992), for teachers as well as for students, our prolonged exposure to one-way lectures and other unilateral authority in education, as well as to male and white supremacy in school and society, interferes with our development into critical thinkers and democratic agents who share power, respect differences, make knowledge collaboratively, and build classroom dialogue mutually. In a world neither finished nor humane, obstacles to critical thought are inevitable, given that schooling and all other institutions are controlled by power groups at the top of the social hierarchy. Critical teaching thus starts from an unequal reality that it hopes to transform. This commitment to transformation in and beyond the classroom is a central feature of the practices reported in the upcoming chapters.

Freire and Feminist Pedagogy

The desire for transformation and the critique of inequality are also common ground shared by Freire-based critical pedagogy and feminist pedagogy, two dissident schools of thought with a close and troubled relationship in recent years. (See Ellsworth 1989; Luke and Gore 1992; Gore 1993.) Freirean and feminist pedagogies emerged at about the same time in the United States, just after the activist 1960s, when dissent and participation were ideas whose time had come. From that legendary age of civil rights actions, student protests, antiwar campaigns, a new women's movement (which included proliferating consciousness-raising groups), and environmental agitation, there emerged oppositional projects in Freirean teaching as well as in feminist pedagogy and women's studies, multiculturalism, critical theory, labor studies, and ecology. Some critical educators—including myself and Caroline Pari, the coeditor of this volume—identify with both Freirean and feminist pedagogies. (My own early teaching and publications from the 1970s included a high profile for gender issues, as reported in my 1980 book *Critical Teaching and Everyday Life* [Chicago: University of Chicago Press].) Among feminist educators who identify with Freirean approaches are Jacqui Alexander and Chandra Mohanty, who acknowledged in *Feminist Genealogies, Colonial Legacies, Democratic Futures* (1997) that they drew on Freire's *Pedagogy of the Oppressed* for frameworks on how the ruling elite uses myths of democracy to maintain the status quo. Alexander and Mohanty brought to the theme of "education as politics" a strong grasp of how gender, class, and colonialism intersect:

> We both inherited the belief that education was a key strategy of decolonization, rather than merely a path toward mainstream credentials and upward mobility. In other words, for us, education was always linked to the political

practice of service to community and nation (xii) . . . What kinds of transformative practices are needed in order to develop nonhegemonic selves? (xviii)

However, the differences between Freirean and some feminist tendencies are substantial. The feminist critique of Freirean practice has focused on the universal images of teachers and students found in Freire's work, the abstractness of the language used, the lack of gender analysis, the dilemma of an allegedly "empowering" process that has encountered sturdy resistance in the North, and Freire's use of only the masculine pronoun, especially in his most-read text, *Pedagogy of the Oppressed*. As I will report shortly, some feminist educators have not only objected to the abstract idiom and goals in Freirean critical pedagogy but also to the one-dimensionality in Freire's call for liberation (class-based only) and his undifferentiated reference to "the oppressed" as a unitary rather than as a contradictory and diverse population.

Unlike these difficulties with feminist critiques, Freirean pedagogy has had a more favorable reception among multicultural educators (Ada 1988; Nieto 1996; Auerbach 1992, 1996; hooks 1993, 1994). The higher comfort level between Freire and multiculturalists perhaps originates from the greater poverty in nonwhite communities, which makes Freire's class emphasis more relevant than it is among predominantly white feminists. Then again, perhaps Freire's attention to official violence against the poor speaks directly to minority communities frequently targeted for police abuse. Also, Freire's Third World origins and impoverished childhood give him authentic multicultural and class credentials. His Brazilian roots make Freire a Third World product who traveled north to question metropolitan societies. Still, the mixed feminist reception requires some discussion here, especially because this volume includes a number of feminist articles that cross paths with critical pedagogy.

Conflict and Convergence

In terms of crossing paths, Freirean and feminist approaches are immediately convergent in that both privilege subjectivity and personal experience as sources of curricular themes—"the personal is political" as a feminist orientation and the "generative theme" method of Freire, which seeks issues for problem posing from the students' everyday lives (Maher 1987). Beyond this initial commonality lies a complex of further similarities and distinct differences. In a thoughtful consideration of the Freire-feminist contention, Kathleen Weiler (1991) wrote that "feminist pedagogy as it has developed in the United States provides a historically situated example of a critical pedagogy in practice" (450). Weiler added that "feminist conceptions of education are similar to Freire's pedagogy in a variety of ways, and feminist educators often cite Freire as the educational theorist who comes closest to the approach and goals of feminist pedagogy" (450). Seven years later, Kate Pritchard Hughes, an Australian feminist educator, agreed with Weiler's view of the closeness of the two approaches, in a special memorial issue to Freire published by *Convergence* magazine (1998), in whose pages Jamaican feminist Leith Dunn argued that Freire's notion of conscientization had much to offer women workers in the Third World. Elaborating this Freire-feminist connection, Weiler defined some crossing points that reappear in considerations of the relationship between the two pedagogies:

- visions of social justice;
- a focus on oppression and historical change;
- an emphasis on how dominant discourses affect consciousness and how consciousness can transcend domination;
- a tilt toward defining human beings as subjects and actors in the learning process and in society.

These points of convergence coexist with points of departure and conflict also noted by Weiler and others. As I suggested above, Weiler—and Ellsworth before her—criticized the universal images of students and teachers presented by Freire. Her feminist suggestion here calls for teachers and students to be defined inside a specific locale and process, not portrayed as abstract "liberation" for a generic "oppressed." Weiler calls for the gendering of critical pedagogy to make it speak to and from women's specific experiences. Further, she asks teachers to acknowledge their own subjectivity as a factor in the learning process. Weiler expects critical teachers to define their positions while also recognizing "existing conflicts among oppressed groups themselves" (469).

I agree that teachers should reflect on our positions as educators and individuals, to clarify why and how we teach, facing such conundrums as using our authority while trying to distribute it to students, as well as the fact that male teachers have more authority to distribute than do female instructors (a point about teaching in patriarchy that I will return to below). Further, I agree with Weiler—and Ellsworth—that all students do not share the same oppressions; *oppression* needs to be defined locally at each site, to discover how differences of gender, race, ethnicity, etc. affect a specific group and curriculum. Some students do oppress other students, like men who interrupt women or whites who silence minority issues in class; some students oppress teachers, like male students who refuse to accept the authority of a female teacher; some students resist critical teachers in the name of freedom as they know it, like those students devoted to self-reliant careerism, to competing with their peers with an ideal of "making it on your own." Moreover, some "empowering" teachers oppress students by imposing brilliant critiques of an unrecognizable present followed by "liberatory" visions of an incomprehensible future; these self-absorbed educators with good intentions are often frustrated because students "don't get it." Other teachers are prepared only to address one or two issues, such as race or class, or gender or environmentalism, and can't adjust to the themes of high interest to students. But, then again, some teachers are afraid to go far enough, stopping short at the edge of possible transformations, fearing a limit that has actually dissolved in a process moving faster than they are. Thus, as Weiler and other feminists have suggested, the generic terms of critical pedagogy, such as *liberation* and *oppression,* need to be situated in specific contexts to make them real. Overall, these instructive criticisms were on my mind as I wrote the narrative in my book *When Students Have Power* (Chicago: University of Chicago Press, 1996), in which I tried to account for conflicts among students and contradictions between them and myself.

One of the contributors to this volume, Magda Lewis, identified herself, similarly to Weiler's self-description, as "a White feminist writing and teaching from the traditions of both critical pedagogy and feminist theory" (451). Lewis put Freire's notion that education is politics at the center of her consideration of the Freire-feminist connection:

> As a teacher and a feminist I share the hope for the promise of education as a political project . . . It is my explicit intent in the classroom to raise with students issues of social relations from a critical perspective . . . Yet my frustrations as a feminist teacher arise significantly from the extent to which critical thinking on transformative pedagogical practice fails to address the specifics of women's education as simultaneously a site of desire and threat. (See "Interrupting Patriarchy" in this book.)

"Desire and threat" represent one contradiction situated in women's educational experience, a concrete example of Lewis answering Weiler's call for specificity by gendering "the student." Feminist practice can thus give a complex local identity to critical teaching, which Freire obtained only when he worked with specific groups on his or their home turf (Brazil, Chile, or Guinea-Bissau, for example).

Perhaps a final perspective on the relationship of Freirean and feminist pedagogies can be found in Adrienne Rich (1979), who wrote that "to think like a woman in a man's world means thinking critically" (244). Rich defined critical thinking in powerfully gendered terms that echo the goals of Freirean critical pedagogy:

> refusing to accept the givens, making connections between facts and ideas which men have left unconnected . . . remembering that every mind resides in a body . . . constantly retesting hypotheses against lived experience . . . a constant critique of language . . . And it means the most difficult thing of all: listening and watching in art and literature, in the social sciences, in all the descriptions we are given of the world, for the silences, the absences, the nameless, the unspoken, the encoded—for there we will find the true knowledge of women. (244–45)

Rich urged women to break the silence, to name themselves, and to define a reality resonating female experience—something Magda Lewis suggests in her chapter. Critical teachers of all stripes should feel at home in Rich's call to arms. Consider how her inspiring agenda can be applied not only to sexism, patriarchy, and women's experience but also to race, ethnicity, class, queerness, and other subordinate identities, which will have to define themselves against an entrenched status quo. Consider also how Rich's militant words echo Freire's well-known references to breaking the "culture of silence," to critically "naming the world," and to "illuminating reality."

Freire did conceive his pedagogy in singular "class terms" growing out of his experiences among peasants and workers in impoverished Brazil. Therefore, as feminist educators have proposed, his foundational work from forty years ago needs correction for a theme like gender, among others. Freire himself acknowledged this missing dimension; he also urged educators to avoid copying him and to develop pedagogy suitable for their local situations. This is the daunting task Weiler and other feminist educators have been pursuing, which accounts for the number of feminist articles in this book and for the predominance of women among the original pioneers of critical pedagogy in North America (see Shor 1987).

Freirean/Feminist Pedagogy and Deweyan Education

Freire's original work emphasized class while ignoring gender, but it substantially deepened the critique of undemocratic education begun decades earlier by John Dewey, who defined traditional schooling as the transmission of information and skill already worked out in the past by distant authorities, bearing little connection to students' lives (Dewey 1963, 17). In place of transmission models for "pouring in" official knowledge, Dewey proposed progressive "new education" in the early twentieth century:

> To imposition from above is opposed expression and cultivation of individuality; to external discipline is opposed free activity; to learning from texts and teachers, learning through experience; to acquisition of isolated skills and techniques by drill, is opposed acquisition of them as means of attaining ends which make direct vital appeal. (19)

By "direct vital appeal," Dewey meant that curriculum should begin with items and subjects familiar to students. He proposed a curriculum of scientifically researching the experiential (a "felt problem" close at hand in thought, action, and affect) rather than beginning with the academic, the abstract, or the scholarly (remote materials framed in the special discourse of the teacher). Perhaps herein we can see some early origins for the feminist and Freirean privileging of the subjective, the personal, the everyday "generative theme" in the making of a syllabus. By favoring the experiential, as do Freireans and feminists, Dewey suggested a key democratic principle that would be adopted by both Freirean and feminist critical methods, namely, *collaborative knowledge making from below.* From this principle, some general questions emerge about the politics of education:

- Who decides what counts as knowledge?
- Who controls how, where, and when knowledge is made?
- Where does subject matter come from and what do we do with it?
- How can differences among students cause destructive as well as constructive conflicts?
- How can gender, race, class, ethnicity, physical ability, or sexual preference be posed as subjective problems related to power in society and to academic texts studied in class?

In regard to these questions, in *Empowering Education* (1992), I proposed a "critical paradigm" that saw both teachers and students simultaneously starting out at less than zero and more than zero when a course began, because both bring assets and liabilities to the making of knowledge (see Chapter 8). This critical paradigm is rooted in Dewey's preference for using student perceptions and expressions as the foundational materials for study. It also applies to both Freirean and feminist pedagogies insofar as they too turn to subjectivity as a starting point rather than treating students as cultural deficits who need to be filled with official knowledge.

The definition of students as sources of knowledge and as codevelopers of the curriculum is a democratic choice for making the syllabus from the bottom up instead of from the top down. This choice, a Deweyan/Freirean/feminist one, returns to the opening assertion driving this book, which came from Freire but which is central to feminist pedagogy as well: Education is politics. This is a good point to reframe the issue in some new terms: All teaching is political because all education is what Freire called "cultural action," that is, organized developmental activity for socially constructing human beings into the people who make the world (Freire 1972). Critical pedagogies with feminist or multicultural orientations also constitute cultural action for freedom. But, the obvious ideologies in these approaches should not mislead us into thinking that ideologies are present only when they are obvious. Critical practices are not the only pedagogies saturated with politics. Because all forms of education develop student consciousness one way or another, all teaching is politics. All educators are partisan even if only some are willing or able to articulate the ideologies of their methods, because every teacher presents to students selected materials in a structured learning process that helps form their values. Therefore, every method is political insofar as it uses some materials and methods rather than others to pull student development toward certain values and actions instead of others. Through prolonged exposure to the discourses in curriculum, students take part in cultural action that develops their thought and feeling, their sense of right and wrong, their notions of what is possible and impossible in their lifeworld.

The gravity of this formative cultural action should not be underestimated. The production of student consciousness through curriculum is a deeply consequential and highly supervised undertaking in every society with a school system. The extent of school regulation represents official vigilance over the formation of consciousness. This vigilance exists precisely because *consciousness is a material force in history,* a tool for doing things, a guide to acting in society to make our lives and the larger culture. Education has the potential to orient students toward questioning the status quo, to develop their historical imagination of alternatives and their social activism in favor of changing the system currently in place. Cultural action in schools and colleges is thus fateful for those in power and those not in power, which helps explain the tight grip of authority on the reins of public education at all levels.

Teaching is thus a labor of cultural production whose product is consciousness, which orients us to think, feel, speak, and act in ways that make us into the people we are. Everyday life and society at large are products of human action, so eventually the making of consciousness results in the making of the lifeworld. If this argument makes sense so far in explaining why all education is politics, it follows then that all classroom practices are not mere techniques but rather represent theories and methods for developing students into certain kinds of social beings. To Dewey, to Freire, and to feminist educators like Weiler and Lewis, no pedagogy is a mere technique to get some neutral skills or innocent contents into students. Every method is a value-laden means for making people in the world and making the world in people. Accordingly, dialogic problem posing is not simply a new, more effective technique to achieve nonpartisan literacy and thinking skills among students. Rather, critical dialogue—whether based in feminist, multicultural, queer, or class identities—is committed to education against inequity; it invites students to become social critics who explore alternatives that promote democratic life against regressive forces like sexism, racism, and homophobia.

Power and Education

The essays in this book invite teachers to embrace education as politics and themselves as political change agents, a position that will be hard for many to accept. R. W. Connell (1994) put it like this:

> Educators are uncomfortable with the language of power . . . But schools are literally power-full institutions . . . On the one hand, the school embodies state power . . . On the other hand, the school system has become the main bearer of working-class hopes for a better future, especially where the hopes of unionism or socialism have died . . . To deal with powerful institutions requires power. (134)

Acknowledging and acting on the power inherent in teaching involves some risk, whether from a feminist, multicultural, or class-based position.

Some teachers can handle more risk than others just as a matter of personal psychology. (See *A Pedagogy for Liberation* [Shor and Freire 1987, Chapter 2].) But, there is a political economy of risk and authority insofar as different groups hold unequal social power. As I suggested earlier, teacherly authority varies according to a teacher's gender, race, age, region, physical stature and ability, level of education, terms of employment, and specific discipline. Full-time, tall, able-bodied, veteran, tenured white male professors who teach upper-division majors or graduate courses—especially in science, technology, or business—in elite institutions have the greatest authority in a racial, patriarchal society. Still, as the women's and multicultural movements of the past few decades show; as the feminist contributions in this book demonstrate; and as the female educators (like Elsa Auerbach, Nan Elsasser, Marilyn Frankenstein, Patricia Irvine, and Nina Wallerstein) who first pioneered critical pedagogy in the United States proved, people from less-powerful positions can find the means to challenge inequality and invent democratic alternatives.

A teacher's silence on alternatives to the status quo reduces the risks to the teacher while also denying choices to students. Without critical options to the status quo, a risk-free curriculum presents the world as either fine and finished the way it is or as needing only minor adjustments from tinkering within conventional limits. I suppose the message of teaching without critical alternatives is that history has ended, suggesting to students that little can be done to improve conditions or that *only* a little needs to be done to improve the best of all possible systems. If the system we have is in fact the best and the only one we *can* have, then being sensible means accommodating to the way things are, a model for growing up that invites students to avoid big issues while encouraging them to find their niche by pursuing small private gain against one another (again—self-reliant careerism and "making it on your own"). Such accommodationist politics divide students against one another while letting the status quo off the hook, hiding how the existing order is in fact dysfunctional and inhumane. For example, the United States has more children (21 percent) living in poverty than any other industrial nation, with millions going hungry in a nation that produces a vast agricultural surplus (Bureau of the Census 1997, Table 739; Brouwer 1998, 38–39).

Besides atomizing students into competing careerists and shielding the system's failures from scrutiny, teacherly silence on alternatives is hardly neutral, given that the status quo already operates deeply political enterprises in its schools and colleges, as Connell and others have argued (Giroux 1988; Ohmann 1987, 1996; Spring 1989). "No politics" is actually the politics of ignoring or disguising how the status quo works to sustain inequality. Still, the difficulties of a critical perspective cannot be easily written off. Even Paulo Freire's recognition of the inherently political nature of education did not come early to him:

> There was a time in my life as an educator when I did not speak about politics and education. It was my most naïve moment. There was another time

> when I began to speak about the political aspects of education. That was a *less* naïve moment, when I wrote *Pedagogy of the Oppressed* (1970). In the second moment, nevertheless, I was still thinking that education was *not* politics but only had an *aspect* of politics. In the *third* moment, today, for me there is *not* a political aspect. For me, now I say education has the quality of being politics, which shapes the learning process. Education is politics and politics has *educability.* (Shor and Freire 1987, 61)

This report by Freire on his own evolving awareness reflects levels of consciousness he identified in his educational practice: *intransitive thought,* which sees education and politics as separate, which assumes society itself to be more or less fixed the way it is; *semi-transitive thinking,* which sees political dimensions to education and society and believes in change but addresses problems one at a time in isolation without a transformative perspective on the whole; and *critical transitivity,* which perceives that society and people create each other, that education is embedded in the politics of an unfinished and changeable world, and that single issues or problems are part of a systemic whole. (See Shor 1992, 126–30.) Note here, vis-à-vis the feminist critique of Freirean theory, that these useful distinctions in awareness are not gendered—or raced.

In Freire's case, the 1964 coup in Brazil was a transcendent moment of class warfare, when the economic elite mobilized its potent military and even more potent support in Washington to suppress growing movements of workers, peasants, and students. Freire's subsequent experiences in Chile reiterated the centrality of class conflict in the Third World. From these historical lessons, he concluded that education was neither autonomous nor technical but rather contingently rooted in the political struggles of the age. Freire and critical theorists after him like McLaren (1986) and Apple (1993) have defined education as politically unstable, certainly not fixed or finished. Rather, schooling at all levels is a contentious subsystem in society dominated by authority and reflecting the inequities of the larger culture. Organized and spontaneous resistance from teachers, students, parents, and others disrupts control, though traditional authority dominates the agenda from the top down. From this position, Freire understood that questioning education is questioning the status quo, which is why dissident teachers often fear punishment from those in power—no weekends on tropical beaches, he quipped in *A Pedagogy for Liberation* (Shor and Freire 1987). When challenging the traditional curriculum, then, critical teachers from any position—feminist, multicultural, queer, etc.—are also opposing the larger system that called the official syllabus into being. Teachers who refuse to impose a standard syllabus in any discipline bravely interrupt the ongoing socialization of students and themselves into the status quo. Not encouraging students to fit in while inviting them to question the way things are opens some interesting possibilities and problems, as reported in this book.

Micropolitics and Macropolitics in Education

Every classroom, then, no matter the location, level, or discipline, is a political undertaking for the construction of people and society. The subject matters, texts, tests, assignments, grading practices, rules for speaking and behaving, and teacher commentaries are *micropolitical moments* in the production of student and teacher consciousness. A teacher-centered classroom with a traditional syllabus invites students to develop as authority-dependent people who fit into the top-down power relations predominant in society. A critical classroom rejects positioning students as subordinates who wait to be told what things mean and what to do. When the politics of pedagogy are democratic and critical, students are addressed as authorities asked to share responsibility for their learning and for questioning their society. When issues of gender or race are foregrounded, for example, students are recognized as complex people who may have a contradictory stake in confronting as well as clinging to regressive ideologies that divide them against one another and support the status quo.

Besides the micropolitical choices made by teachers that affect the day-to-day classroom development of students, there are macropolitics as well that are just as influential and need to be mentioned. (See Pincus and Archer 1989; Berliner and Biddle 1995; Tyack and Cuban 1995; Anyon 1998.) These larger domains involve unequal funding and outcomes of elite and mass institutions, segregated districting, biased testing and tracking, inadequate facilities, and bad food. Poor and working-class students get less spent on them in public schools and colleges than is spent on the affluent; community college students achieve less than their senior college peers; school district boundaries are often drawn to segregate kids of different races into separate schools; internal tracking helps segregate students racially within the same school or college; entry testing by colleges favors white students from higher-income homes who grow up familiar with the linguistic codes preferred in formal education; bad food, ugly decor, uncomfortable chairs, and dirty rooms send environmental messages to nonelite students that they don't count and should not expect much now or later from schooling and the larger system.

This book presents practical pedagogy from the micropolitics of teaching and learning in critical classrooms. The authors of the following chapters use diverse themes and practices that question the status quo, connect the academic to the social and the personal, and offer positive orientations to making change. Such efforts to transform traditional methods into critical ones are harder in some times and places than in others, depending on the political climate of the era and the location as well as on the gender, age, class, or race of the students and of the teacher attempting the changes. Coming out of the stridently conservative decades marking the end of the century, the upcoming chapters show what is possible even in hard times. These teachers' ingenuity produced cross-cultural stories of what can be done with some risk and experimentation. Perhaps most of all, they show culturally diverse educators taking sides and refusing to fit students or themselves quietly into the status quo. Honoring the legacy of Paulo Freire, these teacher-authors carry forward Paulo's project of teaching from the bottom up and his dream of making the world less cruel, bringing the future to life in what we do today.

Works Cited

Ada, Alma Flor. 1988. "The Pajaro Valley Experience: Working with Spanish-Speaking Parents to Develop Children's Reading and Writing Skills in the Home Through the Use of Children's Literature." In *Minority Education: From Shame to Struggle*, edited by T. Skuttnab-Kangas and J. Cummins. Clevedon, England: Multilingual Matters.

Alexander, M. Jacqui, and Chandra Talpede Mohanty. 1997. *Feminist Genealogies, Colonial Legacies, Democratic Futures*. New York: Routledge.

Anyon, Jean. 1998. *Ghetto Schooling: A Political Economy of Urban Educational Reform*. New York: Teachers College Press.

Apple, Michael. 1993. *Official Knowledge: Democratic Education in a Conservative Age*. New York: Routledge.

Auerbach, Elsa. 1992. *Making Meaning, Making Change*. Washington, D.C.: Center for Applied Linguistics.

———, et al. 1996. *From the Community to the Community: A Guidebook for Participatory Literacy Training*. Mahwah, NJ: Lawrence Erlbaum.

Berliner, David, and James Biddle. 1995. *The Manufactured Crisis*. New York: Addison-Wesley/Longman.

Brouwer, Steve. 1998. *Sharing the Pie: A Citizen's Guide to Wealth and Power in America*. New York: Owl Books/Henry Holt.

Connell, R. W. 1994. "Poverty and Education." *Harvard Educational Review* 64 (2): 125–49.

Dewey, John. [1938] 1963. *Experience and Education*. New York: Collier.

Dunn, Leith L. 1998. "Freire's Lessons for Liberating Women Workers." *Convergence* 31 (1–2): 50–61.

Ellsworth, Elizabeth. 1989. "Why Doesn't This Feel Empowering?" *Harvard Educational Review* 59 (4): 297–324.

Elsasser, Nan, and Patricia Irvine. 1992. "Literacy as Commodity: Redistributing the Goods." *Journal of Education* 174 (3): 26–40.

Freire, Paulo. 1972. *Cultural Action for Freedom*. Baltimore: Penguin. Originally published as a monograph by the *Harvard Educational Review* in 1970.

———. 1985. *The Politics of Education: Culture, Power, and Liberation*. South Hadley, MA: Bergin-Garvey.

Giroux, Henry. 1983. *Theory and Resistance in Education*. South Hadley, MA: Bergin-Garvey.

———. 1988. *Schooling and the Struggle for Public Life*. Minneapolis: University of Minnesota Press.

Gore, Jennifer. 1993. *The Struggle for Pedagogies.* New York: Routledge.

hooks, bell. 1993. "Transformative Pedagogy and Multiculturalism." In *Freedom's Plow: Teaching in the Multicultural Classroom,* edited by Theresa Perry and James W. Fraser. New York: Routledge.

―――. 1994. *Teaching to Transgress.* New York: Routledge.

Hughes, Kate Pritchard. 1998. "Liberation? Domestication? Freire and Feminism in the University." *Convergence* 31 (1–2): 137–45.

Luke, Carmen, and Jennifer Gore, eds. 1992. *Feminisms and Critical Pedagogy.* New York: Routledge.

Maher, Frances A. 1987. "Toward a Richer Theory of Feminist Pedagogy: A Comparison of 'Liberation' and 'Gender' Models for Teaching and Learning." *Journal of Education* 163 (3): 91–100.

McLaren, Peter. 1986. *Schooling as a Ritual Performance: Towards a Political Economy of Educational Symbols and Gestures.* New York: Routledge.

McNeil, Linda. 1986. *Contradictions of Control.* New York: Routledge, Kegan, Paul.

Nieto, Sonia. 1994. "Learning from Students on Creating a Chance to Dream." *Harvard Educational Review* 64 (Winter): 392–426.

―――. 1998. *Affirming Diversity: The Sociopolitical Context of Multicultural Education.* 3d ed. White Plains, NY: Longman.

Oakes, Jeannie. 1985. *Keeping Track.* New Haven, CT: Yale University Press.

―――. 1990. *Multiplying Inequalities: The Effects of Race, Social Class, and Tracking on Opportunities to Learn Mathematics and Science.* Santa Monica, CA: Rand.

Ohmann, Richard. 1987. *Politics of Letters.* Middletown, CT: Wesleyan University Press.

―――. 1996. *English in America.* New York: Oxford University Press.

Osborn, Michael, and Suzanne Osborn. 1991. *Public Speaking.* 2d ed. Boston: Houghton Mifflin.

Paul, Richard. 1993. *Critical Thinking: How to Prepare Students for a Rapidly Changing World.* Rohnert Park, CA: Center for Critical Thinking and Moral Critique.

Pincus, Fred, and Elaine Archer. 1989. *The Bridges to Opportunity? Are Community Colleges Meeting the Transfer Needs of Minority Students?* New York: The College Board.

Rich, Adrienne. 1979. *On Lies, Secrets, and Silence.* New York: Norton.

Shor, Ira, ed. 1987. *Freire for the Classroom: A Sourcebook for Liberatory Teaching.* Portsmouth, NH: Boynton-Cook/Heinemann.

Shor, Ira. 1992. *Empowering Education: Critical Teaching for Social Change.* Chicago: University of Chicago.

Shor, Ira, and Paulo Freire. 1987. *A Pedagogy for Liberation: Dialogues on Transforming Education.* Westport, CT: Bergin-Garvey/Greenwood.

Spring, Joel. 1989. *The Sorting Machine Revisited: National Education Policy Since 1945.* New York: Longman.

Tyack, David, and Larry Cuban. 1995. *Tinkering Towards Utopia: A Century of Public School Reform.* Cambridge, MA: Harvard University Press.

U.S. Bureau of the Census. 1997. *Statistical Abstract of the United States.* Washington, D.C.

Weiler, Kathleen. 1991. "Freire and a Feminist Pedagogy of Difference." *Harvard Educational Review* 61 (4): 449–74.

Willis, Paul. 1981. *Learning to Labor: How Working-Class Kids Get Working-Class Jobs.* New York: Columbia University Press.

1

Teaching and Social Change

Reflections on a Freirean Approach in a College Classroom*

Daniel G. Solorzano

Editors' Notes: Step by step, Solorzano reflects on his implementation of Freire's problem-posing method with community college students in California who engaged in social activism while exploring their generative theme. His predominantly Chicano students focused on the negative portrayal of Chicanos in the media and organized a successful boycott against films about Latino gangs. Solorzano also points out the increased use of Freire's work in the ten years since he first adopted this pedagogy.

In March 1986, the Brazilian educator and social theorist Paulo Freire traveled to Southern California to hold a dialogue with educators and community organizers who were using—or who considered using—his problem-posing pedagogy. Having employed a Freirean method, I attended the meetings and decided to share my experience with other educators. This paper represents my reflections on the 1978–79 academic year, when I used Freire's problem-posing method with a group of students at a community college.

Freire's Problem-Posing Method

Freire's (1970, 1973) method starts from the premise that all education is political and thus schools are never neutral institutions. He asserts that schools either function to maintain and reproduce the existing social order or empower

---

*Earlier versions of this paper were delivered at the East Coast Chicano Student Forum, Princeton University, November 1986, and at the Annual Meetings of the National Association for Chicano Studies, April 1987. I would like to thank Laura R. Telles, Ronald Solorzano, and the *Teaching Sociology* reviewers for their comments and suggestions on earlier versions of this paper.

people to transform themselves and/or society. Freire argues that when schools domesticate, they socialize students into accepting as legitimate the ideology and values of society's dominant class. According to Freire (1970), schools use the "banking method" to domesticate students. When this approach is taken, students are viewed as passive receptacles waiting for knowledge to be deposited by the teacher. They are taught in a narrative format whereby the teacher communicates with the students in one-way monologues. This approach can lead students to feel that their thoughts and ideas are not important enough to warrant a two-way dialogue with the teacher. Students also are dependent on the teacher for their acquisition of knowledge. Finally, teachers are seen as conduits through which the ideology and values of the dominant social class are transmitted to the students.

When schools liberate, however, students are viewed as subjects willing and able to act on their world. To create a liberating education, Freire developed the problem-posing method, in which a two-way dialogue of cooperation between the student and the teacher is the focus, content, and pedagogy of the classroom.

Freire's method includes three general phases: (1) identifying and naming the problem, (2) analyzing the causes of the problem, and (3) finding solutions to the problem (Freire 1970, 1973; Smith and Alschuler 1976).

In the naming phase, the educator enters the community or social setting. While in the community, she or he learns about the major issues and problems of the area by listening and speaking to the people and observing community life. After gathering the needed information, the educator develops generative codes. These codes are visual renditions—as in pictures, drawings, stories, articles, or films—of the significant themes or problems that have been identified. The codes are at the heart of the problem-posing process because they are used to begin critical dialogue among the participants.

In the second or analytic phase, the educator takes the codified theme and describes and analyzes the causes of the problem through dialogue with students. In the final or solution phase, students—in collaboration with the educator—find and carry out solutions to the problem.

This process of reflecting and acting on one's reality by describing and defining a problem clearly, analyzing its causes, and acting to resolve it is the key element of the problem-posing method. Students are encouraged to view issues as problems that can be resolved, not as a reality to be accepted. Hence students feel that their ideas are recognized as legitimate and that the problem posed can be resolved in a constructive manner. In addition, students and teachers become dependent on each other for knowledge.

The Freirean Approach in the College Classroom

In the fall of 1978 I taught a cross-listed course called "Directed Practice in Social Welfare" at East Los Angeles College in the Sociology and Chicano Studies departments. East Los Angeles College is located about 10 miles east of downtown Los Angeles; in 1978 nearly 20,000 day and evening students attended. About 85 percent were Chicano students, generally from working-class homes in the greater East Los Angeles area. At that time the Chicano Studies department was one of the largest in the country, offering over 50 classes each semester in the day and evening programs.

The purpose of Directed Practice was to involve students in social and political activities in the greater East Los Angeles community. As part of the course, instructors placed students as volunteers in local elementary and secondary schools or in community service agencies. The students worked in the schools or agencies for at least three hours a week and met one day a week in class to discuss their experiences with other students. Although this approach had been shown to be an enriching experience for students, I wanted to integrate a Freirean problem-posing orientation into the class.

Phase I: Naming and Posing the Problem

In Freirean style, I began the semester by engaging the students in a dialogue about social issues of concern to them and discussing how these issues affect their communities. Although such social problems as educational and occupational inequality were identified and discussed, the issue raised most frequently was the youth gang problem in the East Los Angeles neighborhoods. This emphasis was not surprising because gang incidents were, and are, portrayed continually in newspapers, television, and social science texts as a major social problem in the Chicano community (Heller 1966; Trujillo 1974; United States Commission on Civil Rights 1977, 1979). The importance that students placed on this issue also may have been due to the critical and economic success of Luis Valdez's 1978 play *Zoot Suit* (Wilson 1978). The play focused sensitively on the struggles of Pachuco gang youth during the early 1940s in Los Angeles.

By coincidence, in the first week of the fall 1978 semester (September 10) the *Los Angeles Times* ran the first of a three-part series on Chicanos in the mass media (Knoedelseder 1978). This article examined problems on the set of the Universal Studios film titled *Gang* (later renamed *Walk Proud*). The film depicted the story of a young Chicano gang member named Emilio—played by actor Robby Benson—who falls in love with a young white woman named Sarah. At Sarah's insistence and on discovering that his father is white (added at the insistence of Universal Pictures), Emilio leaves the gang (Knoedelseder 1978). The basic story line focused on the film's white characters helping Emilio to see the evil of his cultural (i.e., Chicano) ways. This theme of different cultures clashing was the basis for a preliminary discussion in the class. (Topical class discussions from multiple points of view were central to every stage of the process.)

The initial *Los Angeles Times* articles briefly mentioned another film, *Boulevard Nights*, then in the early production phase for Warner Brothers Studios (Knoedelseder 1978; Wilson 1978). This film had a less offensive story line than *Walk Proud*. It examined intrafamily conflict: an older brother, Raymond, struggles to leave the gang and neighborhood and to become a member of a car club, while his younger brother, Chuco, remains a member of the gang.

Walk Proud and *Boulevard Nights* were not isolated releases. According to another *Times* article, these films—scheduled for 1979 release—represented two in a series of gang films which included the following: *The Warriors* (February), *On the Edge* (May), *The Wanderers* (July), *Defiance* (August), and *The Gangs of New York* (Kilday 1978). Another movie in production titled *America Me*—specifically about a Chicano gang leader—apparently inspired the other projects (Kilday 1978).

Because of these articles, the class spent two weeks on the initial question: "What are some of the images of Chicanos in the mass media?" After reading and discussing the subsequent articles in the *Times* and collecting and discussing other visual and written materials on popular and professional Chicano stereotypes, the class decided that the negative portrayal of Chicanos in the mass media would be the main focus of the semester (see Council on Interracial Books for Children 1977; Martinez 1969; Trujillo 1974; United States Commission on Civil Rights 1977; Wilson 1978; Woll 1977). The students then posed the problem of the negative media image of Chicanos as two additional questions: "Why are Chicanos portrayed negatively in the mass media?" and "Whose interests are served by these negative portrayals of Chicanos?" To answer these questions, the class decided to conduct detailed case studies on the two Chicano gang films, *Boulevard Nights* and *Walk Proud*.

Phase II: Analyzing the Causes of the Problem

After deciding on the problem, the students began to analyze the causes. From the beginning I believed that in order for students to critically understand the nature of any social problem, they had to possess the skills necessary to gather data and have a firm grasp of the theories used to interpret the data. The class decided to gather general information related to Chicanos in the media and Chicano gangs, plus specific information on the films *Boulevard Nights* and *Walk Proud*. To complete this task, students divided into three work groups.

The first group used the library to collect more information on the images of Chicanos in the media from both a contemporary and a historical perspective. They used the *Readers Guide to Periodical Literature, Sociological Abstracts,* the *Social Science Index,* the *Los Angeles Times Index,* and the *New York Times Index.* (Today they could also use the *Hispanic American Periodicals Index* and the *Chicano Periodical Index.*) They also examined such Hollywood trade papers and magazines as *The Hollywood Reporter, Daily Variety,* and *American Film.* In addition, they discovered an excellent Chicano news monitoring service called *COMEXAZ* to gather background information from seven major newspapers in the southwestern United States.

A second group gathered public information data on youth gangs in East Los Angeles from the Los Angeles County Sheriff's Department and the Los

Angeles City Police Department. This group also examined different sociological theories of gang and deviant behavior (see Hernandez, Haug, and Wagner 1976; Mirande 1978; Moore 1978; Morales 1972; and Trujillo 1974). They also gathered first-hand information from youths involved in gang activity. To develop a demographic profile of Chicanos, this group analyzed census data from the 1970 Census publications for the United States, California, and the Los Angeles-Long Beach Standard Metropolitan Statistical Areas (United States Bureau of the Census 1972a, 1972b, 1972c, 1973).

A third group contacted and interviewed representatives of Universal Pictures and Warner Brothers Studios for further information on *Boulevard Nights* and *Walk Proud*. The studio's public relations department gave them a standard press packet on the film's background, shooting schedule, and expected release date. Students also contacted and interviewed Chicano community and professional organizations who were working as technical and script consultants on the two films (Barrios Unidos, Project Ayudate, the Imperials Car Club, and Nosotros). With the help of these groups, students could determine each organization's role in the film's production; some of the groups served as on-site security, while others supplied more technical and professional help. Finally, students contacted and interviewed community and professional groups who were beginning to challenge the negative role of Chicanos in the media, such as the Coalition of Mexicanos/Latinos Against Defamation (Morales 1978).

For two weeks the students analyzed and synthesized the statistical and anecdotal data and the theoretical explanations of the Chicanos' social conditions in the United States, California, and Los Angeles. When they compared their findings with the historical and contemporary image of Chicanos in film and television, it became apparent that the entertainment industry was not concerned with accurate portrayals of Chicano social life. For example, it appeared that the data on Chicano youth gangs were being blown out of proportion. The students' research disclosed that the proportion of Chicano youth in gangs was not the 10 percent claimed by the electronic and print media, but closer to three percent (Morales 1972, 1978). This finding led the students to question the statistics of the Los Angeles County Sheriff and the Los Angeles City Police Department and related police practices regarding Chicano youth and youth gangs in the Los Angeles area.

In addition, through the visual imagery in television, films, newspapers, magazines, and textbooks, the students concluded that Chicanos were stereotyped disproportionately in subordinate and demeaning occupational and social roles such as bandits, thieves, and gangsters. Students also found negative Latino portrayals in films and in magazine and newspaper articles dating back to the turn of the century (Council on Interracial Books for Children 1977; Lamb 1975; Martinez 1969; Trujillo 1974; United States Commission on Civil Rights 1977, 1979; Woll 1977). This popular media portrayal seemed to reinforce the social scientific image of Chicanos as stereotypic social beings whose problems could be traced to a deficient or disadvantaged culture (Heller 1966).

Phase III: Finding Solutions to the Problem

The students concluded that the Hollywood studios were not concerned with projecting a more positive image of Chicanos; their main concern was the profit that this genre of film could generate. Therefore one solution to the problem was to organize some public action against the Chicano youth gang films. The students decided that the action should achieve two goals: 1) to bring the attention of both the Chicano and the non-Chicano community to the problem of negative portrayal of Chicanos in the media, and 2) to stop the further release of media that reinforced a negative image of the Chicano population. After discussion, the students decided to organize a boycott and an information picket against the two films.

In an incident that reinforced the need for organized action, the CBS program *60 Minutes* ran a segment on Chicano gangs in East Los Angeles, titled "The West Coast Story." This program (air date December 10, 1978) was seen as a negative and inaccurate portrayal of life in East Los Angeles, and drew criticism from community and professional organizations (Morales 1978). Dr. Armando Morales, the president of the Coalition of Mexicanos/Latinos Against Defamation, lodged a formal protest with Robert Salant, the president of CBS, criticizing the program's portrayal of Chicano youth. He asked for equal time to present "the ELA gang situation on '60 Minutes' in a more balanced, objective, and factual manner" (Morales 1978). CBS denied his request (Chandler 1978).

This incident reminded the students that they would be fighting a media giant, and that at least a formal campus organization would be needed as a base of support. The students approached MECHA (Movimiento Estudiantil Chicanos de Aztlan), the Chicano student organization of the East Los Angeles College (ELAC) campus, to discuss the project. The MECHA students decided to get involved, and they established the ad hoc Gang Exploitation Film Committee to oversee and support the project.

The Gang Exploitation Film Committee approached and received the support of the MECHA Central Committee of college and high school campuses in the Los Angeles area. In February 1979, the ELAC Committee took a plan of action to MECHA's statewide conference in Sacramento and received the endorsement of the state organization (Gang Exploitation Film Committee 1979). The Committee also took the plan to local community organizations to solicit their support for the boycott. Other MECHA chapters throughout California gathered support in their own areas. During this period a February 1979 article in the magazine *American Film,* titled "The Lowriders of Whittier Boulevard," confirmed our information on other scripts or ideas being considered for films, pending the financial and critical outcome of *Boulevard Nights* and *Walk Proud* (Jeffries 1979).

After examining the information collected on *Walk Proud,* the students felt that this film would be an easier target for the boycott. For unexplained reasons, however, Universal Pictures delayed the release of *Walk Proud* until May 18,

1979. By default, the boycott shifted to March 21, the release date of *Boulevard Nights* (Schreger 1979). Students decided that *Boulevard Nights* symbolized a genre of films on Chicano youth gangs. They were protesting against the gang theme, and *Boulevard Nights* happened to be the first film of that genre to be released.

After a private screening of *Boulevard Nights,* Nosotros, a national Latino organization of media professionals, denounced the film one month before its opening (Warren 1979). (This organization, however, served as technical advisors in script and casting to *Walk Proud; Nuestro Magazine* 1979.)

At the opening of *Boulevard Nights* in West Los Angeles, over 100 students organized a picket line. The mayor of Los Angeles, Tom Bradley, entered the controversy by including and then deleting his name from the list of dignitaries planning to appear at the film's opening. He was to give the filmmaker a city proclamation honoring *Boulevard Nights* as "an instrument of peace" (Warren 1979). In addition, for the first three weeks of the film's run, boycotts and informational picket lines were conducted by local MECHA chapters and community organizations at theaters throughout southern and northern California. During this period television, radio, and newspaper media focused on the problems of Chicano stereotypes in the mass media. After a stabbing and shooting at a San Francisco theater showing *Boulevard Nights,* Mayor Diane Feinstein requested that the film be removed from the theater (Grant 1979a, 1979b). Gang-related incidents also caused the film to be canceled in Pomona (Landsbaum 1979).

Despite the boycott, the picket lines, and generally negative publicity, *Boulevard Nights* had a somewhat successful run. The reviews of the film were mixed; the *Los Angeles Herald Examiner* film critic called it "as Latino in flavor as a Jack-in-the-box taco" (Sagrow 1979). The *Los Angeles Times* critic was kinder, referring to the film "as entertaining and admirable as a use of the medium" (Champlin 1979). An editorial writer for the *Herald Examiner* said, "Were this a book, it might qualify as the Great Mexican-American Novel" (Castro 1979). A *Times* editorial writer called the film a "thoughtful attempt to portray a subculture that Americans have heard much about but know very little." The writer criticized the film, however, for making "no attempt to show the pathetic state of many schools in East Los Angeles . . . it's these schools that help create gang members by turning off young Chicanos with insensitive or ill-trained teachers and outmoded or irrelevant study programs, all of which contribute to high drop-out rates" (Del Olmo 1979). Another *Times* staff writer claimed, "Groups both within the film industry and on its edges are monitoring the gang films . . . there's the question of whether they'll make more . . . no one has announced another gang film." The writer also quoted a Universal Pictures spokesperson, who said, "It's possible that adverse reaction by the splinter groups may very well turn the studios sour about films relating to these groups" (Schreger 1979).

Despite the controversy, Universal Pictures released *Walk Proud* in May 1979. Without explanation, however, the film was not released in any of the major Latino media markets in the southwest United States. Furthermore, none of the other Chicano gang genre movies cited in the *American Film* article were released to the general public (Jeffries 1979).

After the action was complete, the ELAC committee went before the California MECHA organization to report on its successes and failures. It was clear that as an informational tactic, the word on negative stereotypes of Chicanos in the media had been projected to the general public in an organized and documented fashion. Many students also credited the committee with doing something positive about the release of these negative films. It was also clear, however, that *Boulevard Nights* received free publicity; and many people felt that the action brought too much attention to a "B" film. Other students argued that the committee had called negative attention to Latino actors who were only trying to showcase their professional talent, albeit in negative roles. To reinforce this point, the *Los Angeles Times* quoted a Universal Pictures senior vice-president as saying, "In the end, it may very well hurt the job market for (Hispanic) actors and technical people who work in these pictures" (Schreger 1979). The tactical question of whether to take action, or what type of action to take, must be discussed and dealt with if the problem-posing process is to be effective.

Because of the publicity and the action by the studio, the boycott was fulfilling its two major goals: first, to bring the negative image of Chicanos in the media to the attention of both the Chicano and the non-Chicano community, and second, to stop (albeit temporarily) the further release of media that reinforced a negative image of the Chicano population.

Reflections on the Problem-Posing Process

The Hollywood studios' decision to put the Chicano youth gang theme on the back burner was probably based on a sound financial decision. Though the students and the community members could not take full credit for this decision, their actions surely had some effect (see Schreger 1979).

From their interactions with a variety of people, it was apparent that the students developed commitment to and confidence in their own ideas, as well as research, organizational, and communication skills to test those ideas. They had become empowered for the "moment." In that moment they had exposed the larger community to an organized group of people who felt, acted, and succeeded in doing something they considered positive about a genre of films that reinforced the negative stereotypes of Chicano youth. As an educator I can only hope that the students' critical curiosity, their new problem-solving skills, and the related sense of empowerment remain with them as they meet other personal and social problems. If they do remain, the Freirean approach has achieved its major goal of empowering students to reflect and act on real-life problems on a sustained basis.

Moreover, to my knowledge—as of summer 1988—no major motion picture studio has released a major film exclusively on Chicano youth gangs. (Although Chicano gangs are a part of the plot, the major focus of *Colors* [1988] is on black gangs in Los Angeles.) For 10 years the image of Chicanos in major films was largely ignored or remained on the periphery, but in the recent films *La Bamba* (1987), *Born in East L.A.* (1987), *Stand and Deliver* (1988), and *The Milagro Beanfield War* (1988), the major themes and characters are Latino-oriented. The Latino characters range from the narrow and stereotypic to the broad and profound; the messages are relevant and positive. In addition, in recent minor films such as *Zoot Suit* (1981), *The Ballad of Gregorio Cortes* (1982), *El Norte* (1983), and *Latino* (1985), the Latino roles have depth and range; the overall image and messages are relevant, positive, and powerful (Keller 1985). Because of the nature and number of these Latino-related films, this period should be seen as a significant benchmark in Chicano filmmaking.

Critique of the Problem-Posing Process

Several problems emerged both during and after the course. The first problem concerned students who felt uncomfortable with the critical nature of the Freirean pedagogy. As a personal policy, I do not require students to participate in activities to which they feel strongly opposed. Usually I offer alternative ways of meeting the course requirements. In this course, three students reacted negatively to Paulo Freire's radical theory and chose not to participate in any of the political activity. In preparation for each of our discussions, however, I successfully challenged them to bring to the class alternative views on the topics. These challenges supplied important learning exercises for the other students, who later would meet similar skeptics on the picket line and in the press.

A second problem concerned Freire's "action" phase. Because it is the students who decide what actions to take, their range of responses to the problem posed has included the action described in this paper, letter-writing campaigns, and discussions of the problem in class with no outside action. I believe that to understand the problem posed and to empower students, one must take action on the problem and reflect critically on the action taken. Therefore it is my responsibility as the coordinator to challenge students to resist passivity, to take a more active role in their education generally, and to address the specific social problems they have identified. In some of my courses I have failed to do this, but, as most educators know, each class has a different personality and will react to issues differently.

A third problem relates to time; I had the benefit of working with a group of students for two semesters. The action I describe in the paper might not work as effectively in a 10-week quarter or a 16-week semester.

The final problem concerns control of the course; in the Freirean method, the teacher loses much of the control of the classroom. At first I found this situation very disorienting, but as I watched and encouraged students to take control of the course, some of the stability returned.

Despite these problems, the approach described in this paper is a pedagogic method for examining critically and taking action on social problems that students view as significant. Therefore the method can be used—with modifications—in such sociology courses as social problems, social change, and race, ethnic, and gender relations.

Conclusions

When I worked on this project 10 years ago, only a small number of educators were using the Freirean method in college- and community-based settings. Since that time the number has increased modestly to include Shor's work with college students in an English curriculum (Shor 1980; Shor and Freire 1987); Fiore and Elasser (1982) and Holzman (1988) in advanced literacy; Wallerstein's (1983) work with English as a second language for adult students; Hodder (1980) in art education; Frankenstein (1983) in the mathematics curriculum; Moriarity and Wallerstein's (1980) work in teacher training and staff development; Crawford-Lange (1981) in foreign language instruction; and Alschuler (1980) in school discipline. Mackie (1981) is a good source for understanding Freirean pedagogy critically, albeit sympathetically. Freire's most recent collaborative works with Macedo and Shor on the politics of education, adult literacy, and transforming education are up-to-date references on the current state of the method (Freire 1985; Freire and Macedo 1987; Shor and Freire 1987). Also, the publication *Radical Teacher* consistently has information on Freirean pedagogy. Although I'm not sure they still exist, the newsletters *Educacion Liberadora (Liberating Education)* and *Second Thoughts* were excellent sources for people networking in the Freirean method.

Finally, Herbert Gintis (1984) states, "The political economy of learning ... is based on the principle that learning occurs most effectively, and with the greatest positive acceptance on the part of the learners, when the educational environment empowers the learners, and engages them in the active exercise of their individual and collective powers." In this paper I have tried to show that the problem-posing approach has the potential to challenge the problem posed, and to engage, challenge, and empower the students who pose it and the educators who initiate the process.

Works Cited

Alschuler, Alfred. 1980. *School Discipline: A Socially Literate Solution.* New York: McGraw-Hill.

Castro, Tony. 1979. "Los Angeles: A Movie Fights Back." *Los Angeles Herald Examiner,* April 6.

Champlin, Charles. 1979. "Brothers on the Boulevard." *Los Angeles Times,* March 23, Section IV, Page 1.

Chandler, Robert. 1978. Correspondence dated December 29, 1978 to Armando Morales on behalf of CBS Inc. concerning the *60 Minutes* segment "West Coast Story."

Council on Interracial Books for Children. 1977. *Stereotypes Distortions and Omissions in U.S. History Textbooks.* New York: Racism and Sexism Resource Center.

Crawford-Lange, Linda. 1981. "Redirecting Second Language Curricula: Paulo Freire's Contribution." *Foreign Language Annals* 14:257–268.

Del Olmo, Frank. 1979. "'Nights': A View from East L.A." *Los Angeles Times,* March 18, Section IV, Page 1.

Fiore, Kyle, and Nan Elasser. 1982. "'Strangers No More': A Liberatory Literacy Curriculum." *College English* 44:115–128.

Frankenstein, Marilyn. 1983. "Critical Mathematics Education: An Application of Paulo Freire's Epistemology." *Journal of Education* 165:315–339.

Freire, Paulo. 1970. *Cultural Action for Freedom.* Cambridge, MA: Harvard Educational Review Monographs.

———. 1973. *Pedagogy of the Oppressed.* New York: Seabury.

———. 1985. *The Politics of Education: Culture, Power, and Liberation.* South Hadley, MA: Bergin and Garvey.

———, and Donaldo Macedo. 1987. *Literacy: Reading the Word and the World.* South Hadley, MA: Bergin and Garvey.

Gang Exploitation Film Committee. 1979. *A Reader and Information Packet on "Gang" Exploitation Films.* Monterey Park, CA: East Los Angeles College MECHA.

Gintis, Herbert. 1984. "The Political Economy of Literacy Training." *Unesco Courier,* February, Pages 15–16.

Grant, Lee. 1979a. Chicanos Picket 'Boulevard Nights.'" *Los Angeles Times,* March 23, Section IV, Page 19.

———. 1979b. "Producer Hits 'Nights' Closing." *Los Angeles Times,* March 28, Section IV, Page 17.

Heller, Celia. 1966. *Mexican American Youth: Forgotten Youth at the Crossroads.* New York: Random House.

Hernandez, Carrol, Marsha Haug, and Nathaniel Wagner. 1976. *Chicanos: Social and Psychological Perspectives.* St. Louis: Mosby.

Hodder, Geoffrey. 1980. "Human Praxis: A New Basic Assumption for Adult Education of the Future." *Canadian Journal of Education* 5:5–14.

Holzman, Michael. 1988. "A Post-Freirean Model for Adult Literacy Education." *College English* 50:177–189.

Jeffries, Georgia. 1979. "The Lowriders of Whittier Boulevard." *American Film,* February, Page 58.

Keller, Gary. 1985. *Chicano Cinema: Research, Reviews, and Resources.* Binghamton, NY: Bilingual Review Press.

Kilday, Gregg. 1978. "The Gang's All Here." *Los Angeles Times,* September 10, Calendar Section, Page 23.

Knoedelseder, William. 1978. "Filming 'Gang'—A West Side Story." *Los Angeles Times,* September 10, Calendar Section, Page 1.

Lamb, Blaine. 1975. "The Convenient Villain: The Early Cinema Views of the Mexican American." *Journal of the West* 14:75–81.

Landsbaum, Mark. 1979. "Theater Cancels 'Boulevard' Film after Violence." *Los Angeles Times,* March 29, Section II, Page 1.

Mackie, Robert. 1981. *Literacy and Revolution: The Pedagogy of Paulo Freire.* New York: Continuum.

Martinez, Thomas. 1969. "Advertising and Racism: The Case of the Mexican-American." *El Grito: A Journal of Contemporary Mexican American Thought* 2:3–13.

Mirande, Alfredo. 1978. "Chicano Sociology: A New Paradigm for Social Science." *Pacific Sociological Review* 21:293–312.

Moore, Joan (with Robert Garcia, Carlos Garcia, Luis Cerda, and Frank Valencia). 1978. *Homeboys: Gangs, Drugs, and Prisons in the Barrios of Los Angeles.* Philadelphia: Temple University Press.

Morales, Armando. 1972. *Ando Sangrando (I Am Bleeding): A Study of Mexican American Police Conflict.* La Puente, CA: Perspectiva.

———. 1978. Correspondence dated December 19, 1978 to Robert Salant, President of CBS Inc. on behalf of the Coalition of Mexicanos/Latinos Against Defamation concerning the *60 Minutes* segment "West Coast Story."

Moriarity, Pia, and Nina Wallerstein. 1980. "By Teaching We Can Learn: Freire Process for Teachers." *California Journal of Teacher Education* 7:39–46.

Nuestro Magazine. 1979. "Movie Industry Tries to Portray 'Gangs!'?" February, Page 9.

Sagrow, Michael. 1979. "Nights on 'Boulevard' Due Today." *Los Angeles Herald Examiner,* March 23, Section B, Page 1.

Schreger, Charles. 1979. "Gang Movie Stirs Controversy." *Los Angeles Times,* March 28, Section IV, Page 14.

Shor, Ira. 1980. *Critical Teaching and Everyday Life.* Boston: South End.

Shor, Ira, and Paulo Freire. 1987. *A Pedagogy for Liberation: Dialogues on Transforming Education.* South Hadley, MA: Bergin and Garvey.

Smith, William, and Alfred Alschuler. 1976. "How to Measure Freire's Stages of Conscientizacao: The C Code Manual." Unpublished manuscript, University of Massachusetts, Amherst.

Trujillo, Larry. 1974. "La Evolucion del 'Bandido' al 'Pachuco': A Critical Examination and Evaluation of Criminological Literature on Chicanos." *Issues in Criminology* 9:43–67.

United States Bureau of the Census. 1972a. *Census of Housing: 1970, Volume 1, Housing Characteristics for States, Cities, and Counties, Part 6, California.* Washington, DC: United States Government Printing Office.

———. 1972b. *Census of Housing: 1970, Block Statistics, Final Report HC(3)-18, Los Angeles-Long Beach, California Urbanized Area.* Washington, DC: United States Government Printing Office.

———. 1972c. *1970 Census of Population and Housing, Census Tracts, Los Angeles-Long Beach Standard Metropolitan Statistical Area, Parts 1 and 2.* Washington, DC: United States Government Printing Office.

———. 1973. *Census of Population: 1970, Volume 1, Characteristics of the Population, Part 6, California—Sections 1 and 2.* Washington, DC: United States Government Printing Office.

United States Commission on Civil Rights. 1977. *Window Dressing on the Set.* Washington, DC: United States Commission on Civil Rights.

———. 1979. *Window Dressing on the Set: An Update.* Washington, DC: United States Commission on Civil Rights.

Wallerstein, Nina. 1983. *Language and Culture in Conflict: Problem-Posing in the ESL Classroom.* Reading, MA: Addison-Wesley.

Warren, Elaine. 1979. "The Politics of a Gang Film's Premiere." *Los Angeles Herald Examiner,* March 22, Section A, Page 1.

Wilson, John. 1978. "Hollywood and the Chicano." *Los Angeles Times,* September 17, Calendar Section, Page 1.

Woll, Allen. 1977. *The Latin Image in American Film.* Los Angeles: UCLA Latin American Studies Center.

2

Teaching Undergraduates About AIDS

An Action-Oriented Approach

Kimberly Christensen

Editors' Notes: Christensen thoroughly describes the content and pedagogy of an action-oriented undergraduate course she developed about AIDS. Christensen designed her course to move beyond teaching risk-reduction behavior. Her students focused on the political, economic, and ethical issues raised by the AIDS crisis. Christensen helped create a space in which students could express their fears and confusions about AIDS while gaining a sense of shared purpose that would allow them to take action against this disease.

Ten years into the AIDS epidemic, there are few, if any, college campuses that have not been touched directly or indirectly by this crisis. Students, faculty, and administrators across the country have responded to the threat of AIDS with a variety of educational programs, ranging from guest speakers, to safer-sex workshops, to the distribution of condoms.

Located half-an-hour from New York City, the epicenter of the AIDS epidemic, the State University of New York's College at Purchase had been significantly affected by AIDS. We had lost a colleague, a professor of anthropology, to AIDS-related complications in 1988. There were consistent reports of HIV-positive students being harassed by fellow students. Finally, a confidential survey of our campus revealed that, although a large percentage of our student body—particularly gay and bisexual students—was aware of AIDS, only a small percentage of our sexually active students of any sexual orientation was taking precautions to protect themselves from the disease (Fastje, 1990).

In the fall of 1987, a colleague and I proposed at the general faculty meeting that a student/faculty/staff AIDS Task Force be established to educate all segments of the campus community about the epidemic. The faculty meeting unanimously approved the proposal. Since that time, two faculty members and

I have consistently participated in Task Force activities, along with several staff members from the Student Affairs and Campus Life offices and about a half-dozen enthusiastic students. Activities of the AIDS Task Force have included workshops at freshmen orientation, condom and pamphlet distribution in the campus center and dining halls, and a day-long teach-in on AIDS. We also set up VCRs in heavily traveled centers on campus, and played AIDS awareness and prevention videos during lunch hour and dinnertime.[1] We have installed condom vending machines in many campus locations, along with racks of AIDS information pamphlets. We prepared a 90-minute "road show" on AIDS, which visited classes at the request of faculty members. Finally, I prepared an annotated bibliography on the medical, political, and social aspects of the AIDS crisis, which was widely distributed to faculty members.

There is some evidence that the efforts of the AIDS Task Force have been successful. On their own initiative, students have formed support groups for HIV-positive people and for friends and lovers of HIV-positive people. The student newspaper now regularly prints information on AIDS and AIDS prevention, and for a time even carried a regular column on AIDS. Finally, the atmosphere on campus regarding HIV-positive people and People With AIDS (PWAs) has changed significantly. This past semester, two students felt comfortable enough to be interviewed openly as HIV-positive people for the campus paper; to date they have suffered no negative repercussions.

Despite these successes, I felt that our AIDS education efforts on campus were inadequate. In particular, given the sporadic nature of AIDS Task Force discussions with students, it was difficult to convey more than the most superficial knowledge, or to build up enough trust with the students to discuss their complicated feelings around AIDS. For these reasons, I decided in the spring of 1990 to design and teach a full-credit course on the political, economic, and ethical issues raised by the AIDS crisis.

Having lost a dear friend to AIDS, I have been involved in the AIDS activist movement (ACT UP/New York) for over three and a half years. ACT UP is a diverse group of people, many of whom have lost friends or family to AIDS or are themselves HIV infected. Our goals are to increase public awareness of the AIDS crisis, to increase public and private funding for AIDS research, and to combat discrimination against those who are HIV infected. ACT UP's tactics include letter-writing and phone-calling campaigns to public officials; producing and distributing bilingual pamphlets, T-shirts, videos, and other popular AIDS education materials; and demonstrating against government officials and institutions whose policies on AIDS exacerbate the epidemic. ACT UP has had some notable successes. These include the implementation of a "parallel track program" whereby HIV-infected people can get access to experimental AIDS drugs earlier in the process of FDA approval; the high school condom-distribution plan recently adopted in New York City, which began as a project of the ACT UP "Youth Brigade"; and a recent ruling by a New York City criminal court that the distribution of clean needles to drug addicts may be justified in order to stop the spread of HIV.[2] But our efforts to convince our public officials on a federal level to make AIDS a top health priority, to mount a "Manhattan Project" against AIDS, have been less than successful.

Through my own work with ACT UP, I have learned a tremendous amount about AIDS, not only about the medical and technical aspects of the disease, but also about its political and economic context. With the death of my friend, I experienced the sense of powerlessness and horror that often accompany losing someone to AIDS. I also learned that acting to prevent the spread of this disease and working to speed a cure can help one to cope with that sense of loss and powerlessness.

It was this sense of empowerment and commitment that I wished to share with my students. I wanted to create an atmosphere in the classroom in which students would not only feel free to confront and change their own risk behaviors, but would also become actively involved in the fight against AIDS. I wanted them to begin to understand both the viral and societal origins of the AIDS crisis. I wanted students to understand that confronting the AIDS crisis involves more than condom use; that is, that it also involves addressing the structural inequalities and *laissez-faire* public policies that have allowed this epidemic to assume crisis proportions in the United States and abroad. The rapid spread of AIDS in the United States is symptomatic of many deeper problems in our society, including the persistence of racism and heterosexism, an economy that does not provide jobs or adequate income for many of its citizens, an increasingly inadequate health care delivery and finance system, and a "war on drugs" that does little to address the real roots of the drug crisis.[3]

Structure of the Course

In the spring of 1990, I offered a sophomore-level elective course, "AIDS: Political, Economic, and Ethical Issues." John Leppo, a male staff member from the Campus Life office, served as my unofficial teaching assistant. My choice of a male TA turned out to be a real boon to the course, since the young men in the class found it much easier to talk to him than to me about safer sex and related issues. I highly recommend mixed-sex teams for teaching courses of this nature.

The course enrolled over sixty students from the school's fine arts and liberal arts programs. African Americans and Latino/as were more heavily represented than in the student population as a whole, and we had approximately half a dozen older (aged 35–55) students from the local community. Two of these older students were devout Roman Catholic women, whose views on sexual matters were much more conservative than those of the younger students. The class also included several members of the Gay, Lesbian, and Bisexual Union (GLBU), which made for some rather lively discussions. But although the students expressed their widely divergent views, these discussions never became mean-spirited, and actually took on a friendly, teasing quality by the end of the semester. For example, a GLBU member said to one of the older women, "Victoria, I'm about to say something very gay; you may want to block your ears!" Victoria laughed, and made a show of covering her ears with her hands.

I believe that there were several reasons for this tolerant attitude among the students. First, whatever their differences, every student in the class had an earnest desire to learn about and help to end the AIDS crisis. That common commitment, of which I reminded them frequently, saw us through many potentially divisive situations. Second, while moderating and guiding class discussions, I tried very hard to let every student have his or her "say," even if I disagreed strongly with his or her position. Students were free to complain loudly about others' opinions, but they knew that they would never be "jumped on" by the teacher for expressing an unpopular view. The one exception was if a student put forth medically incorrect information; then I would correct the misinformation but allow the discussion to proceed. Third, I believe that journals kept by the students (described in the next section) also helped to "let off steam" about their classmates, thus reducing the level of tension in the classroom. For instance, one of the older women wrote more than twenty pages in her journal about how she felt her religious views were not being taken seriously by the younger students, and how this reminded her of the anti-Catholic bigotry she had faced as a young girl. Similarly, one of the gay male students wrote extensively about how the older woman's homophobia reminded him of his mother's similar attitudes, and how dealing with this fellow student brought up the pain he felt at being kicked out of his parents' house for being gay. In both cases, having an outlet for their feelings allowed the students to deal with each other in a respectful manner.

The Journal

Two ongoing assignments helped establish an atmosphere of reflection and activism in the class: the journal and the service project. My experience in teaching women's studies had convinced me that the journals were an effective way to deal with emotionally charged material. Keeping a weekly log gave students an outlet to express and work through their fears, confusions, and other difficult feelings about the material being covered in class, and about the AIDS crisis in general. I also gave students specific questions to respond to in their journals: for example, "Discuss your reaction to Paul and Roger's gay relationship in *Borrowed Time*" (Monette, 1988) or, "Discuss your reaction to the AIDS-prevention needle-exchange program in Tacoma, Washington" or "Do you believe that Larry Kramer is justified in using the analogy of the Holocaust to describe the AIDS epidemic? Explain."

The journals not only helped students express themselves, which some did beautifully, through poetry and artwork, they also gave me instant feedback about students' reactions to the class material. While many of the students who had taken Women's Studies and other classes with me were familiar with the process of journal-keeping, a few students had trouble getting started, as the following entry indicates:

> After a week of failing to find the "key" to this journal-writing process, some dread at some false starts, I have to begin now. I have not kept a journal in the last seven years . . . because I am embarrassed by the sound of my own "voice." . . . I shudder to think that I am the person such writing contains. . . . So if I am embarrassed when confronting (privately) my own naivete and stupidity, documenting this for others to stumble upon is even more difficult.

I encouraged students who were having trouble starting this assignment to consider using forms of self-expression other than plain prose in their journals; for example one woman who had a "writer's block about AIDS" turned in a journal consisting almost entirely of powerful pen-and-ink sketches representing her feelings about the disease.

When asked to evaluate the helpfulness of the journal in a confidential survey seen only by myself and my teaching assistant, the students rated it highly: an average of 4.3 on a 5-point scale. Many also made comments such as, "It forced me to think! (Damn it!)" and, "When being educated about AIDS, I think I really liked the journal. It helped me express my emotions towards AIDS, which is ultimately just as important as lectures."

The Service Project

To establish and maintain the action orientation of the class, I also required each student to participate in a service project. The students were allowed considerable latitude in designing and implementing their projects. The only requirements were that the student spend at least one hour per week on the project, and that the project contribute in some way to ending the AIDS crisis. To help the students develop these projects and make contacts in the community, I distributed a list of "AIDS Resources" on the first day of class.[4] I also invited representatives from several local AIDS service and activist organizations to give brief presentations about their activities during the first few class sessions.

The variety and creativity the students displayed in their AIDS service projects exceeded my wildest expectations. Rarely during my teaching career have I been as moved as I was by the commitment and courage demonstrated by my students in these projects. Some of the students who took the course now volunteer on a weekly basis with the "AIDS orphan" baby-holding program in Harlem Hospital. Twenty students from the class wrote, choreographed, directed, and performed a professional-caliber theater production about AIDS; their *Divided We Fall: An AIDS Collective* moved me and most of the audience to tears.[5] These same students, some of whom have graduated, are currently making plans to present their production in high schools around New York City. Other students have become AIDS "buddies," and still others are making audiotapes for PWAs who have lost their sight. Half a dozen students organized a successful benefit concert for Community Research Initiative, a local community-based AIDS research program. And during the last class session, one student "came out" as HIV-positive to his classmates; he has since organized AIDS education workshops in his high school, and he recently wrote a piece as an openly HIV-positive person for the school newspaper.

My students were as enthusiastic about the usefulness of the service project as they were about the journal; they rated it 4.4 on a 5-point scale. Their evaluations included comments like, "On a scale of one to five, a ten!" and, "I really enjoyed our service project. It made me feel like I was actively doing something. As my first 'project' concerning AIDS, it was an ice breaker. I want to be more involved now" and, "The service project was AMAZING!"

I believe that allowing the students to design their own projects was a critical factor in the success of this component of the course. Students who were not emotionally ready to be buddies to PWAs, or who did not possess the public-speaking skills to lead AIDS-education workshops, could make posters for AIDS fundraisers or audiotapes for blind PWAs. Each student was allowed to choose his or her own comfortable level of involvement with PWAs, and with service and activist organizations. In my opinion, a large number of options and a high degree of flexibility are critical aspects of any required service projects.

Content and Pedagogy

I divided the course content into three basic sections. In order of presentation, these were:

Awareness/Risk Assessment
The purpose of this section was to help students overcome their fears of PWAs as "the other," and to help them to recognize and change their own risk behaviors. Coming to terms with AIDS on an emotional level was, in my opinion, absolutely necessary for the students. Having already begun to deal with their fears, anger, and other feelings allowed them to concentrate on the biomedical, political, and other aspects of the crisis. Several students told me that connecting to the personal reality of AIDS in this section also motivated them to "plow through" what was sometimes rather tedious and difficult biomedical material.

Biomedical
In this section, students were introduced to the basic vocabulary of HIV infection and opportunistic infections, and were encouraged to learn about current treatment options. Having a basic understanding of the process of HIV infection and of the major treatment modalities was necessary for them to comprehend some of the controversies in the social/political section of the course; for example, an understanding of how HIV infects cells is a necessary precondition for comprehending debates over the FDA's approval or non-approval of various experimental AIDS treatments (see Eigo et al., 1988).

Social/Political

Activities and lectures in this section taught students to analyze AIDS in terms of racism, heterosexism, and other domestic and international forces that have contributed to the spread of this crisis worldwide, and which have impeded progress towards a cure.

Since student involvement was crucial to the success of the course, I used participatory pedagogy as much as possible. Some lectures were needed to introduce very basic concepts and to give us some common vocabulary with which to discuss the epidemic. For example, during the first week I gave a short lecture focused on the medical definition of AIDS, the common opportunistic infections found in male and female PWAs, the epidemiology of HIV infection here and abroad, and the socioeconomic context of the AIDS crisis. The required readings (see the references) also helped the students gain basic biological and social/political information. The following are some of the assigned readings and pedagogical techniques I found useful in the three sections of the course.

Awareness/Risk Assessment

The Names Exercise

I began the first class of the semester by listing on the blackboard the names of my friends and acquaintances who had died of AIDS, and I invited the students to add names to the list. I was surprised when the students, most of them in their teens, filled up the blackboard with names. We then dedicated the class to the memory of those who had died and to those struggling to live with AIDS.

Personal Risk-Assessment Exercise

For the risk-assessment exercise, I passed out file cards and instructed the students to complete the following statements anonymously:

1. I am/am not (choose one) at risk for AIDS because . . .
2. I do/do not (choose one) practice safer sex because . . .
3. Some of the myths of AIDS transmission which I have heard from other students are: . . .
4. I have the following questions about AIDS: . . .

I collected and shuffled the cards and randomly passed them back to the students. I read the questions aloud and asked students to volunteer to read the answers on the cards they were holding. The entire class then commented on these anonymous answers and on each other's knowledge of AIDS. I intervened only when medically incorrect information was being given. I found this exercise to be a powerful pedagogical device for students; it forced them to confront their own risk behaviors and to see that they too could be at risk for AIDS. I would recommend that anyone who is interested in developing AIDS education curricula consider using a similar exercise.

These two exercises enabled me to see that as educators, sharing our experiences with AIDS with our students can encourage them to come to terms with the disease. However, it is only after we have confronted our own fears and anxieties about AIDS that we can help our students to confront theirs.

Guest Lectures
Two early guest lectures were crucial in establishing the tone for the class: one by a mother who had lost her son to AIDS and another by a PWA.

Local chapters of Parents and Friends of Lesbians and Gays (PFLAG) are an excellent source of well-informed, committed speakers about AIDS. A mother of an AIDS patient from the New York City PFLAG spoke honestly and movingly to our class about her and her husband's struggle to understand and accept their son's being gay, and about his battle to live as fully as possible from the time of his AIDS diagnosis to his death.

A PWA friend of mine from ACT UP/New York also visited the class early in the semester. He spoke to the class honestly and with humor about a whole range of experiences common to many PWAs: fear and pain about his medical condition, the frustration of dealing with the medical and social service bureaucracies, and the strength he has gained from his activist work on behalf of PWAs. Many students told me later that they "turned a corner" after his visit: AIDS was no longer an overwhelming and abstract fear; while still frightening, it had become a real disease being fought by someone they had met.

Required Readings
The first reading assignment in this section was Paul Monette's *Borrowed Time: An AIDS Memoir* (1988). Monette's book is a moving personal account of the death of his lover, Roger, from AIDS, in October of 1986. I assigned this book both to draw students into the emotional reality of AIDS and to force them to confront and deal with any homophobia they might feel.[6] The students were as moved as I was by Monette's work. One man in the class had lost his lover to AIDS two years earlier, and had spoken about it to only a few people. He wrote:

> Often I found myself remembering intimately the feelings Monette was relating, reliving my experiences with the treatments and the doctors, the denial and the mask of unfounded hopes. So much feeling which I have repressed for so long now beginning to surface. Wednesday, Thursday, Friday were crying days. . . . The first night when I started the book, I could not sleep. All curled up in my bed though I wasn't cold, I cried till I fell asleep, crying for Paul Monette and his lover, crying for S. and myself.

One of the older women in the class wrote:

> I am now close to the end of *Borrowed Time*. I no longer see the two gay men. I see two people so desparetly [sic] in love. So pathetically in love. It is heart wrenching. The more Paul clings to Roger, the more I want to take my husband in my arms just for comfort and the feeling of security. Death must come

to all of us, but—why must it be so painful to some? . . . to take away some of life's most precious gifts ever so slowly. Energy, sight, dignity.

Many of the students in the class, a significant number of whom were from low-income families, said that they sometimes felt "distanced" from the story by Roger and Paul's obvious and ostentatious wealth (e.g., the references to "the Jag," and their ability to afford experimental treatments and 24-hour nursing care). Nonetheless, the class rated the book highly, 4.0 on a 5-point scale, and all but three students recommended that it be required reading the next time I taught the course.

The second book in this section was Randy Shilts's *And the Band Played On* (1987). I had ambivalent feelings about assigning Shilts, due to his sensational descriptions of gay male life. But I also felt that his documentation of government and media apathy in the early years of the AIDS crisis was crucial. The students' feelings about the book mirrored my own. One young woman wrote:

> I've been trudging my way through Shilts's *And the Band Played On;* for the same reason, I have a lot of trouble getting through it. Much of what he said was valid (i.e., the governments [lack of] response to AIDS etc.) but I could have lived without all the gossip.

Another simply said: *"And the Band Played On,* and on, and on, and on . . . "

Shilts's book was the one item on the reading list that the students recommended against using in the next class. When I teach the class again, I plan to use instead Bruce Nussbaum's *Good Intentions: How Big Business and The Medical Establishment Are Corrupting the Fight Against AIDS* (1990). Nussbaum, a writer for *Business Week,* makes many of the same points about government and corrupt management, but does so without "all the gossip."[7]

Other readings for this section included *Making It: A Woman's Guide to Sex in the Age of AIDS* (Patton & Kelly, 1988), which was an invaluable addition to the safer-sex role-play exercise (see below), and several articles on the personal experience of being HIV-positive or having AIDS, which I copied from *The Body Positive* (Slocum, 1989), *The PWA Newsline,* and other sources. Since two of the primary texts for this section, Monette and Shilts, focused on gay White men, I concentrated on finding articles by and about women and/or people of color (see, for example, Pearson, 1990; Rieder & Ruppelt, 1988; Terson, 1989; Whitmore, 1988).

Safer-Sex Materials and the Role-Play Exercise

Two exercises facilitated class discussion of the sometimes difficult subject of safer sex. First, my teaching assistant and I collected every unusual and humorous safer-sex material we could find, including fluorescent-green condoms, chocolate-flavored lubricant, and red-white-and-blue dental dams. The hilarity that erupted in class when we produced these items helped break the ice and begin a serious discussion of the obstacles to practicing safer sex.[8]

For the role-play exercise, I divided the class into three groups and asked them to break down into pairs. I then announced that the pairs within these three groups would play the roles of heterosexual couples, gay male couples, and lesbian couples. Their assignment was to negotiate safer sex, with one partner trying to convince the other, who thought that protection was unnecessary. After ten minutes, the convincer and the "convincee" switched roles and repeated the negotiations. Three volunteer couples, one from each sexual orientation group, were then asked to replay their negotiations before the class.

This exercise, predictably, brought gales of giggles from the students, but the discussion it generated was very enlightening. The students unanimously agreed that the subject of AIDS and safer sex should be broached before one gets into a potential sexual situation. By the time they were in the situation I had set up for the role play (back in the apartment alone together), rational discourse was very difficult. I believe this role play makes an important point, and I plan to continue to use it in future classes.

Most of the students also realized that they had trouble actually saying the words required to negotiate safer sex. As one woman put it, "If you ask him to put 'whazit' on his 'thingee,' you're not going to get very far." The difficulty these students—most of whom were sexually active—had in vocalizing simple anatomical words like "penis," "vagina," and "semen" illuminated the sexual shame that still lurks below the surface of our so-called sexually liberated culture, shame that greatly complicates safer-sex negotiations.

The reactions to the roles of convincee and convincer differed significantly by gender and by sexual orientation. Several of the heterosexual men said that they felt they were being "accused" of being gay, bisexual, or IV drug users when women raised the issue of AIDS and condom use. A few heterosexual women said they felt they were being accused of promiscuity when a male partner raised the issue. Women of all sexual orientations said that fear of abandonment, of losing the relationship, was the major reason they "gave in" and had unsafe sex. But one heterosexual woman stated that negotiations about safer sex were a good "test" of a relationship; if a man did not respect her enough to protect her health, then he was not worth worrying about!

We also discussed strategies that could be used on partners who were reluctant to use protection. These included bringing up the experience of a friend who had contracted HIV or died of AIDS, inundating the reluctant partner with pamphlets and other AIDS information, and, in a tight spot, claiming to have a medical or birth-control problem that requires the use of condoms. One woman suggested, "Tell him you forgot to take your pill or that you have a yeast infection. Then you have a *real* discussion with him in the morning!" One last strategy, which was semiseriously proposed, was "blaming it on the teacher"—that is, telling the reluctant partner, "I'm taking this AIDS class, and the prof says it's important to practice safer sex." (I assured the students that I would be happy to act as their excuse for safer sex, though I was not sure how much weight this would carry in the heat of passion!)

Biomedical

Two colleagues of mine from the biology department opened this section of the course with a guest lecture on the basic biology of the immune system and of the HIV infection. Their lectures built on the material covered in the assigned readings, taken from *The Science of AIDS: Readings from Scientific American* (1984).[9]

Due to the difficult nature of this material, I spent several class sessions recapitulating and answering their questions. I found reviewing questions in small groups helpful, particularly if science majors were divided among the groups. Also useful was the popularly written section on HIV infection found in the *Treatment Decisions Handbook* (Bohne, Cunningham, Engbretson, Fornataro, & Harrington, 1989) published by ACT UP's Treatment and Data Committee.

One scene from the student's production *Divided We Fall* also made me consider using art to reinforce learning of the basic biomedical material. The dancers wore T-shirts, each one labelled as either a component of the immune system (e.g., T4 cell or macrophage, two types of white blood cells vulnerable to HIV infection), or as a component of the HIV virus (e.g., gp-120, a surface protein of HIV, central to the cell infection process).[10] The beautifully choreographed piece visually demonstrated the process of HIV infection of an immune system cell, and subsequent viral reproduction within that cell. I am hoping to adapt this idea into a role play with students playing the parts of various components of the immune system the next time I teach the course.

Guest Lecturers

After the students had gained a basic understanding of the biomedical basis of AIDS, two guest speakers—from our local PWA Health Group and the American Foundation for AIDS Research (AmFAR)—explained some of the controversies surrounding current research efforts and government procedures regarding AIDS drugs.[11]

The representative from our local PWA Health Group shared with the group his criticisms of the current FDA procedures for drug approval in cases of terminal illness. He related how the illness and subsequent death of his lover of nine years had moved him to become involved in smuggling unapproved AIDS drugs into the United States from Japan, Germany, and Israel. No one in the class questioned his right to engage in this activity, despite the fact that it is illegal. The students were impressed with his courage, but they also criticized the Health Group for not putting more effort into reaching lower-income PWAs and PWAs of color.[12]

The speaker from AmFAR discussed the lack of equitable access to experimental AIDS drugs. Most experimental trials are conducted at major research universities; thus, HIV-positive people and PWAs who do not live near urban centers are often excluded, as are those who do not have private physicians to help them fill out the paperwork. In addition, many experimental drug trials blatantly exclude HIV-positive women,[13] and many more subtly discriminate against HIV-positive African Americans and Latino/as.[14] The speaker explored the promise that small, community-based AIDS research clinics, such as the New York Community Research Initiative, hold for improving access to potentially life-saving experimental medications.

Midterm Exams on Biomedical Section

I gave the students individual take-home exams on the biology of the immune system and HIV infection. The questions included the following:

1. Carefully define AIDS. What do PWAs actually die from?
2. Briefly explain the epidemiology of AIDS in the U.S. and abroad.
3. (a) Explain the basic structure and replication process of HIV; (b) Explain how the major classes of white blood cells function in a normal immune system; (c) Explain some of the ways in which HIV infection is thought to interfere with normal immune response.

In general, the students did fairly well on this section of the midterm. Understandably, those with more background in the natural sciences did better; in fact, one biology major's answers were so concise and beautifully illustrated that I plan to use her answers as a handout next year. But the vast majority of students made it clear that they had absorbed enough information about the immune system and HIV infection to comprehend discussions of treatment modalities, vaccine strategies, and so on.

I also asked the students to divide into groups of approximately six people, and gave each team a copy of a "group exam" that was to be discussed, answered, and turned in as a team. The primary purpose of these group exams was to encourage discussions about issues raised in the initial "awareness" section of the course. Questions in this section of the midterm included the following:

1. Your best friend from high school tells you that he or she just tested HIV-positive. Explain in detail what information, including referrals, you would give him or her.
2. Discuss some of the obstacles to negotiating and practicing safer sex.
3. Discuss some of the changes which would have to be made to effectively deal with the AIDS epidemic here on campus, in New York City, and in the U.S. (for extra credit, discuss global policies).

I was pleased with the answers to these group exam questions, many of which displayed creativity and a great deal of thought. In response to Question 1, several teams produced detailed plans of action for the imaginary friend, which included phone numbers for the local HIV-positive support groups and local physicians specializing in AIDS, and other practical data. The questions to Question 3 were also especially impressive; one team even created a detailed proposal for AIDS education on campus, complete with budget estimates. Another team's suggestions for a "flashy, humorous" AIDS education pamphlet for the campus has been adopted by the AIDS Task Force.

Social and Political Context

During the final section of the course, I emphasized five factors that have created fertile ground for the spread of AIDS:

Homophobia/Heterosexism

From the beginning of the AIDS crisis, the reactions of the media and government have been decisively influenced by the fact that the first patients identified with AIDS in the United States were gay. (In fact, AIDS was first, erroneously, called "Gay Related Immune Deficiency," or GRID.) The apathy of the heterosexual public over the fate of gay men and the relative political powerlessness of the gay/lesbian/bisexual community allowed the media and government officials to virtually ignore the disease during the first critical years. As Shilts points out, over 21,000 Americans were already dead from AIDS before President Reagan uttered the word in public, in May of 1987. It is simply inconceivable that an infectious disease could have killed 21,000 White, middle-class, *heterosexual* Americans without becoming a major national priority for education and research.

Racism

The continued virulence of racial discrimination in the labor market, the political sphere, and elsewhere has greatly exacerbated the spread of AIDS. The consequent higher levels of poverty among people of color have often limited their access to timely, high-quality health care and, hence, to early AIDS diagnosis and treatment. Racism and insensitivity have resulted in a lack of culturally sensitive and language-appropriate AIDS education materials. For example, although Latino/as are disproportionately represented among the HIV infected, much crucial AIDS prevention and treatment information is simply not available in Spanish. Most of the information available has been translated from English, rather than written in the idioms of the Puerto Rican, Chicano, and other Latino/a communities. The situation is even worse for Asians and other language minorities. Finally, given the large percentage of current PWAs in the United States who are gay and/or people of color, racism has greatly contributed to the relative indifference with which this crisis has been treated by virtually all levels of government.

The Drug Epidemic

The federal government's War on Drugs has overemphasized interrupting the supply of drugs, while giving too little attention to addressing the conditions that give rise to drug use in the first place. For instance, over two-thirds of the monies allocated recently to fight the War on Drugs were earmarked for interdiction and imprisonment, with only one-third allocated to education and treatment. Conditions such as joblessness and homelessness, which contribute to drug use, are rarely addressed at all.

The Crisis in Health Care
The United States and the Republic of South Africa are the only industrialized countries in the world without some form of national health care. Thirty-eight million Americans, a disproportionate number of them people of color, have no health insurance whatsoever and rely upon the emergency rooms of public hospitals for their medical care. An additional fifty-six million are seriously underinsured (V. Navarro, cited in Morris, 1990). This lack of access to health care and health education greatly exacerbates the spread of HIV in these populations.

Male Bias
The medical research establishment in this country has traditionally viewed White males as the norm for clinical drug trials and other forms of medical research. In the case of AIDS, this focus on White males has rendered women largely invisible, except as "vectors" of transmission to men and to "innocent" children. The current medical definition of AIDS, formulated by the Centers for Disease Control (CDC), is based largely upon symptomology in males and ignores pelvic inflammatory disease and other gynecological opportunistic infections.[15] For women, this has led to serious under-diagnosis of AIDS, a consequent lack of proper medical care, and an inability to qualify for necessary social services (ACT UP/New York Women and AIDS Book Group, 1990).

Required Readings
Readings for this section were rather extensive, and were divided into topic areas.[16] Readings for the subsection on racism included: Renee Sabatier's *Blaming Others: Prejudice, Race, and Worldwide AIDS* (1988); "People of Color and AIDS" (1989) and "Media Network's AIDS/HIV Media Screenings" (1990) by Ray Navarro; and "Fighting HIV in Communities of Color" by Michael Slocum (1989).[17] *Blaming Others,* which explores the dynamics of blame and misunderstanding in the discussions of the origins of HIV, and also the myth of fundamental "differentness" of African AIDS, was well received by the students. They gave it the highest ratings of any text, 4.6 on a 5-point scale, and made comments such as, "Good info! Helps put things into perspective!" and "I wish we could have spent more time on this one. It helps people confront their prejudices and fears." All but one student recommended its use in the next class.

Required readings for the subsection on women and AIDS included selections from *AIDS: The Women* (Rieder & Ruppelt, 1988); "Reproductive Freedom: An Urgent Issue for Lesbians, Gay Men, and People Affected by AIDS" (Wheatley et al., 1989); and "Women: The Missing Persons in the AIDS Epidemic" (Anastos & Marte, 1991).[18] The students found *AIDS: The Women,* a compilation of personal accounts by women PWAs and women caretakers of PWAs, moving, and rated it 4.5 on a 5-point scale. Comments such as "Excellent!" and "Very emotionally moving!" were typical.

The readings for the final section of the course, "AIDS Activism," included David Leavitt's "The Way I Live Now" (1989) from *The New York Times Magazine,* a debate on needle-exchange programs from *The Amsterdam News* (Curtis et al., 1988; Joseph, 1988), a *New York Times* article on the use of theater in AIDS education efforts (Rich, 1988), Sue Rochman's piece on AIDS education in a woman's prison (1989), and Larry Kramer's *Reports from the Holocaust* (1989).[19]

Kramer's book, a scathing attack on the lack of media and government response to the AIDS crisis, elicited strong and mixed reactions from the students. One student said:

> Some of the writing in *Reports* was outrageous—but then Larry Kramer is outrageous! . . . I'm very glad you put this book in the reading list. I'm positive I would never have bought such a book on my own—I would have missed out on a great deal of information and never gotten to appreciate a fine writer and a sensitive (if abrasive) human being.

And another wrote:

> Again, very informative. . . . It went into depth about how people, as a whole, can just sit by and do nothing. How this country does not respond—to this day. . . . How when he went to Washington how each one passes the buck—no one's responsible. . . . People (with AIDS) must see large bureaucracys [*sic*] as monsters. Larry Kramer sounds totally frustrated with these people—and justifiably so.

Others were not so enthusiastic about Kramer's perspective:

> Why doesn't he address the AIDS problem: women and children and people of color in his book? Why doesn't he address the surrounding areas of racism and classism in this book? Aren't they, along with homophobia, the real things perpetuating AIDS . . . in NYC?. . . . Larry Kramer is doing just what we need not to do—we mustn't distance ourselves from the mutual struggles. All minorities must fight for freedom to live the way we choose, freedom to love the way we want, freedom to earn a living and maintain a reasonable personal lifestyle. Larry is doing just what he does not want others to do—he is dividing us.

The numerical evaluations of Kramer's book were similarly divided. Many rated it 5.0, a fair number 1.0, with an average around 4.0. Six students recommended against using this book again—more than for any other assigned book—but more also strongly supported its use, with comments such as "Crucial!" and "Vital!"

Pedagogy for the Social/Political Context Section

Some lectures were necessary in this section, such as my lectures on the percentage of Americans covered by health insurance, and on the relative merits of the U.S. health insurance system versus the health coverage plans of other industrialized countries.[20] However, most of the social and political material was covered by assigning questions for small group discussion. These questions included the following:

1. Why are the participants in AIDS clinical drug trials overwhelmingly White and male, even in areas where PWAs are disproportionately Black and Latino? Is this a problem? Why? What could be done to change this situation?
2. Why has the War on Drugs not been terribly effective? What kinds of changes would have to occur to truly end the drug epidemic?
3. Discuss the strengths and weaknesses of a national health care plan, such as Canada's, compared with the current U.S. system.

Two videos were also valuable in this section. First we viewed *Bleach, Teach, and Outreach,* a short film on intravenous drug use and AIDS, which provoked a lively discussion on the pros and cons of needle-exchange programs for AIDS prevention.[21]

Next we screened a video by the New York City Human Rights Commission's AIDS Discrimination Unit, *The Second Epidemic,* which dramatized how the stigma against PWAs actually exacerbates the spread of AIDS.[22] In addition, a speaker from the Commission described her work on behalf of PWAs who are victims of AIDS-related discrimination.

The primary point I hoped to make in the social/political section was that the AIDS crisis did not arrive full blown as a scourge from above, but, rather, that social, political, and economic inequality provided the conditions under which HIV infection could reach epidemic proportions. To address the AIDS crisis successfully in all communities, we must also address the stigmatization and institutionalized inequalities that have allowed this epidemic to occur.

At the end of this section, I gave a take-home final exam, which included questions such as the following:

1. Carefully define racism. Discuss the impact which racism has had on the course of the AIDS epidemic.
2. What changes do you believe would need to be made in the U.S. health care system (and health care financing system) to effectively deal with the AIDS epidemic?
3. Do you believe that pregnant women with AIDS should be permitted to enroll in experimental AIDS drug trials? What about asymptomatic HIV-positive women? Explain your position.

I was generally pleased with the quality of students' answers in the final. The question about racism, for example, elicited several thoughtful answers. For example, one woman explored in detail the impact that educational funding derived primarily from property taxes has on the quality of education in White communities versus communities of color. She concluded her essay with this:

> Only when people in low-income communities of colour [sic] have the educational tools and supportive services to really become part of the economic mainstream in this country will they be able to turn away from the hopeless oppressions of the ignorance, poverty, and drugs, which lead to AIDS. Only when the entrenched governmental institutions address their racist policies regarding equality in educational and economic opportunities, will people in these communities be able to respond effectively to the AIDS crisis.

Another woman simply wrote:

Re: Racism and AIDS: It really pisses me off that:

—access to health care is dependent upon ability to pay;

—people of color don't have the same access to clinical trials as White, middle-class men;

—we buy their theories of the origins of HIV because they agree with what we want to believe (e.g., HIV came from Africa) without ever examining the evidence;

—we assume that people of color invariably contracted HIV through IV drug use, as if there are no gay people of color (and as if heterosexual transmission were non-existent).

The answers to the remaining questions also indicated that the students had taken these issues seriously, and had a basic understanding of the sociopolitical forces that have exacerbated the spread of AIDS.

Closure

During the final class session, students volunteered to give reports on their service projects. Two students showed an AIDS education videotape they had made. The two women, Carla and Anne, took a video camera to a local shopping mall on several successive Saturdays, and randomly interviewed young people there about their knowledge of AIDS. Carla and Anne then presented the interviewees with correct information on AIDS transmission and prevention, including pamphlets produced by a local AIDS service agency, and continued to film while the shoppers began to assimilate and react to this information.

The state of knowledge of the young people reflected in the video was even worse than we had expected. The majority of these young people, in 1990 suburban New York, said that AIDS was a "gay disease," and that, being heterosexual, they were at no risk. Several of the young men bragged about their unsafe sexual practices. Others expressed concern about transmission through mosquito bites, the use of public toilets, and other risk-free behaviors. When confronted with correct information, many were quite startled. The following reaction, by a woman in her late teens, was typical: "What! You mean I could still get AIDS even though my boyfriend and I have been going steady for ten months?"

Obviously the interviewees in the tape gained valuable information about HIV transmission. Carla and Anne and the students who viewed the video learned a great deal about the dismal state of AIDS education in suburban New York high schools.

We then ended the class with two participatory exercises, which were designed to end the class on a hopeful and action-oriented note:

Future Action

I wrote on the board, "What am I going to do to end the AIDS crisis after this course is over?", left plenty of chalk, and left the room for ten minutes. When I returned, the board was filled with comments, ranging from "Demand that my boyfriend wear a rubber!" to "Work on my homophobic feelings" to "Write a letter to my Congressperson demanding more funding for AIDS research" to "Join the Purchase AIDS Task Force."

The Names Exercise Revisited

I reproduced the list of "Friends who have died of AIDS" from our first class meeting, but also added a new list: "Friends who are struggling to live with HIV infection/AIDS." After their involvement with the service project, the students' second list was much longer than the first. After the list was seemingly complete and filled two blackboards, an HIV-positive student walked up to the board and added his own name. After a collective intake of breath on the part of the students, he was drowned in hugs and promises of support. It seemed a fitting way to end the semester.

Conclusion

Judging from both the student evaluations and informal feedback, this course was a success both in imparting information and getting students to seriously reflect on and change their own risk behaviors. I believe that the primary reason for this success was our ability to create a real sense of community in the classroom. The students' inevitable confrontations with their own mortality, with assessing their own risk, and with the difficult ethical and political questions posed by the AIDS crisis occurred not only in isolated dorm rooms, but also in a supportive classroom setting. The students felt free to express their fears and angers, to ask their embarrassing questions, and to work through their own bigotries and prejudices.

Another important factor in the course's success was its role in helping the students begin to overcome their sense of powerlessness and desperation with respect to AIDS, emotions that are more pervasive among students than might be suspected. The service project, the repeated appearance of open PWAs, and the general action-orientation of the class were crucial elements here.

The realistic fear of HIV infection that we, as educators, bring to our students must be coupled with a sense that they *can* do something about AIDS—in their own lives and in society. This sense of shared purpose allows them to move beyond fear-of-AIDS paralysis—to hear themselves, each other, and HIV-positive people and PWAs—and begin to take action against AIDS. This was perhaps expressed most eloquently in the journal of the man who had lost his lover to AIDS:

> How different now this all is for me. How easily and freely I write now; how social I've become. And how has all this come to pass? I think that this class has had alot to do with these changes. First, because AIDS became something that I could talk about. Not only was the taboo on how it has affected me personally removed, (I've been able to talk about S.'s and my lives with people from class . . .), but now I've also got objective ways of discussing AIDS as a political issue, an ethical issue, etc. with people. And this gives me some power over how AIDS effects [sic] my life.
>
> Which is another change: my involvement . . . My face hasn't been hidden behind a book all semester . . . But more [important] than talking and hanging out is making things happen . . . Here I mean particularly the [AIDS education] T-shirts I printed and sold. I amazed myself with that project. I'd never silk-screened before in my life . . . And then M. got the Students' Union to commit the money to the project, and suddenly I was committed not just to myself and the idea, but to other people who were as enthusiastic as I was . . . What a lot of barriers to have broken.
>
> All of these things became meaningful to/for me, and also helped me to define me, become part of my identity on campus: He's the guy who made those AIDS activist T-shirts. I am learning how meaning develops out of usage, action. That's how words derive their meaning, and lives too. I found also that my life was getting meaning from involvement with people, with a community. . . . It wasn't until I started interaction this semester with people here [on campus], and with ACT UP that I found this need for meaning actually satisfied. What a remarkable and wonderful change this is.

Students need supportive spaces in which they can freely discuss their fears and confusions about AIDS, as well as avenues to put their energies to constructive use. It is up to us as educators to create such spaces for them.

Notes

1. A complete video bibliography can be found in the appendix to *Women, AIDS, and Activism* (ACT UP/NY Women and AIDS Book Group, 1990).

2. See Ronald Sullivan, "Needle Exchangers Had Right to Break Law, Judge Rules" (1991).

3. Heterosexism is the belief that everyone is heterosexual, which is often accompanied by homophobia, the fear and/or hatred of lesbians, gay men, and bisexuals. Heterosexism is embodied in institutions (such as in hospital visiting policies, the IRS tax code), as well as in the beliefs of individuals, media, and government officials.

4. These included the New York City Department of Health's *AIDS: A Resource Guide for New York City* (1991). Many governments in urban areas now publish similar guides.

5. *Divided We Fall: An AIDS Collective* was created and directed by Arlene Xavier.

6. Another work which would serve these purposes is Carol Maso's *The Art Lover* (1990), which was published since I first taught the class. Maso's book is a touching account of the death of her best friend from AIDS.

7. Erica Carter and Simon Watney's *Taking Liberties: AIDS and Cultural Politics* (1989) explores the cultural perceptions and prejudices that lie behind this inaction. Though too advanced for most undergraduates, it is a helpful resource for the teacher and for upper-division students.

8. For more information on the effectiveness of condoms in preventing HIV transmission, see "Condoms and Spermicides: How Much Protection?" in *World Population Reports* (World Health Organization, 1989).

9. Teachers should exercise care in selecting articles from *The Science of AIDS*. Some, such as the introductory piece, "The AIDS Epidemic" by Robert Gallo and Luc Montagnier, are comprehensible by most undergraduates. Others, such as William Haseltine and Flossie Wong-Staal's "The Molecular Biology of AIDS," are very difficult for students without a science background. In addition, Max Essex and Phyllis Kanki's piece on the origins of HIV in Africa is highly controversial (see Sabatier, 1988). And, of course, the epidemiology and treatment information must be updated by the instructor. Eve Nichols's *Mobilizing against AIDS* (1989) is a possible alternative text.

10. Non-technical definitions of these and other terms regarding the basic biology of AIDS can be found in the appendix to ACT UP/NY's *Women, AIDS, and Activism* (1990) and in further detail in Mark Harrington's *Glossary of AIDS Drug Trials, Testing, and Treatment Issues* (1988).

11. See, for example, Harrington's "Anatomy of a Disaster: Why is Federal AIDS Research at a Standstill?" (1990) and his *Critique of the AIDS Clinical Trials Group* (1990).

12. John James's *Treatment News*, a monthly newsletter, is a good source of information on experimental drugs for AIDS.

13. Many trials totally exclude HIV-positive women "for the protection of the fetus," even if the woman is not currently heterosexually active or agrees to use reliable birth control. Some trials have mandated sterilization for women participants, but not for men. This is particularly horrendous, given the history of the U.S. government-sponsored sterilization abuse in communities of color, and the fact that 75 percent of women PWAs are African Americans or Latinas (see Committee for Abortion Rights and against Sterilization Abuse, 1988; Davis, 1983).

14. For instance, for reasons not yet identified, HIV-positive African-American men seem to be less likely than HIV-positive White men to carry "p24 antigen," a subcomponent of HIV, in their blood. Clinical trials that use measured p24 antigen levels as a criterion for entry will therefore *de facto* discriminate against African Americans, even if there is no conscious intent to exclude.

15. An official definition of AIDS requires not only a positive HIV antibody test, but the presence of one or more of a number of "indicator" diseases. In extraordinary cases, the diagnosis may be made when HIV antibody testing is unavailable, inconclusive, or thought to be erroneous. The Centers for Disease Control twice (in 1985 and 1987) expanded the list of such "indicator diseases." But critics charge that those opportunistic infections that will infect women (e.g., cervical cancer and resistant pelvic inflammatory disease) and HIV drug users (e.g., bacterial endocarditis) are still not included in the definition. Some of the most common "indicator diseases" include, but are not limited to: PCP (pneumoncystis carinii pneumonia), Kaposi's Sarcoma, toxoplasmotic encephalitis, cytomegalovirus infection of the eyes or bowels, intestinal cryptosporidiosis, extrapulmonary crytococcosis (including crytococcal meningitis), HIV encephalopathy (dementia), MAI/MAC infection (macrobacterium avium complex), oral or esophogal candidiasis (thrush), and PML (progressive multifocal leukoencephalopathy).

16. Readings relevant to the section on homophobia/heterosexism (Shilts, Monette, etc.) have been covered earlier in the course.

17. An excellent article on racism and AIDS, Harlon Dalton's "AIDS in Blackface," is now available in an anthology edited by Nancy MacKenzie, *The AIDS Reader* (1991). Several other important articles are also collected in this reader, which I intend to assign as a required text the next time I teach the class.

18. Since I taught the class, the ACT UP/New York Women and AIDS Book Group has published *Women, AIDS, and Activism* (1990), which contains analyses of the impact of AIDS on many different groups of women—heterosexual women, lesbians, mothers, prostitutes, prisoners, and women of color, as well as numerous personal testimonies by HIV-positive women. I plan to assign readings from this collection the next time I teach this course.

19. Douglass Crimp and Adam Rolston's recent *AIDS Demographics* (1990) discusses ACT UP's use of visual imagery and other art in the fight against AIDS.

20. David Morris's "America's Health Care System is Ailing" (1990) is a helpful reference on this point.

21. *Bleach, Teach, and Outreach* was filmed and directed by Ray Navarro and Catharine Saalfield. It is available for loan from Gay Men's Health Crisis in New York City.

22. *The Second Epidemic,* produced by Amber Hollinbaugh, is available for distribution from the AIDS Discrimination Unit of the New York City Human Rights Commission.

Works Cited

ACT UP/NY Women and AIDS Book Group. (1990). *Women, AIDS, and activism.* Boston: South End Press.

Anastos, K., & Marte, C. (1991). Women: The missing persons in the AIDS epidemic. In N. MacKenzie (Ed.), *The AIDS reader.* New York: Meridian Books.

Bohne, J., Cunningham, T., Engbretson, J., Fornataro, K., & Harrington, M. (1989). *Treatment decisions.* New York: ACT UP/NY.

Carter, E., & Watney, S. (Eds.). (1989). *Taking liberties: AIDS and cultural politics.* Bristol, Eng.: Serpent's Tail.

Committee for Abortion Rights and Against Sterilization Abuse. (1988). *Women under attack: Victories, backlash, and the fight against sterilization abuse.* Boston: South End Press.

Crimp, D., & Rolston, A. (1990). *AIDS demographics.* Seattle: Bay Press.

Curtis, J. L., Rangel, C. B., Flake, F., et al. (1988, October 15). Why it musn't be tried. *Amsterdam News,* p. 15.

Davis, A. (1983). *Women, race, and class.* New York: Vintage.

Eigo, J., Harrington, M., Long, I., McCarthy, M., Spinella, S., & Sugden, R. (1988). *FDA action handbook.* New York: ACT UP/NY.

Fastje, J. (1990). *The effects of AIDS upon sexual behavior among college students.* Unpublished senior thesis, State University of New York, Purchase.

Harrington, M. (1990, March 13). Anatomy of a disaster. Why is federal AIDS research at a standstill? *The Village Voice,* p. 15.

Harrington, M. (1990). *A critique of the AIDS Clinical Trials Group.* New York: ACT UP/NY.

Harrington, M., Eigo, J., Kirschenbaum, D., & Long, I. (1988). *Glossary of AIDS drug trials, testing, and treatment issues.* New York: ACT UP/NY.

James, J. *AIDS Treatment News.* (April 1986–ongoing). [Newsletter].

Joseph, S. (1988, October 15). Needle exchange experimental program: Why it must be tried. *Amsterdam News,* p. 15.

Kramer, L. (1989). *Reports from the holocaust.* New York: St. Martin's.

Leavitt, D. (1989, July 9). The way I live now. *The New York Times Magazine,* p. 16.

MacKenzie, N. (Ed.) (1991). *The AIDS reader: Social, political, ethical issues.* New York: Meridian Books.

Maso, C. (1990). *The art lover.* San Francisco: North Point Press.

Monette, P. (1988). *Borrowed time: An AIDS memoir.* New York: Harcourt Brace Jovanich.

Morris, D. (1990, March/April). America's health care system is ailing. *Utne Reader,* p. 20.

Navarro, R. (1990). Media Network's AIDS/HIV media screenings [Special issue]. *Media Network News, 3*(1).

Navarro, R. (1989). People of color and AIDS. In L. Chou, R. Elovich, C. Goodman, et al., (Eds.), *Target City Hall: An AIDS activist's guide to New York City in 1989.* New York: ACT UP/NY.

New York City Department of Health. (1991). *AIDS: A resource guide for New York City.* New York: Author.

Nichols, E. (1989). *Mobilizing against AIDS.* Cambridge: Harvard University Press, 1989.

Norwood, C. (1988, July). Alarming rise in deaths: Are women showing new AIDS symptoms? *Ms.,* p. 65.

Nussbaum, B. (1990). *Good intentions: How big business and the medical establishment are corrupting the fight against AIDS.* New York: Atlantic Monthly Press.

Patton, C., & Kelly, J. (1988). *Making it: A woman's guide to sex in the age of AIDS.* Ithaca, NY: Firebrand Books.

Pearson, M. (1990, April). Mother Pearson of "Mother's Love." *The Body Positive,* p. 19.

People With AIDS Coalition. (July 1985–ongoing). *PWA Coalition Newsline.* New York: Author.

Rich, F. (1988, August 1). Actors confront AIDS on stage and off. *The New York Times,* p. C1.

Rieder, I., & Ruppelt, P. (Eds.). (1988). *AIDS: The women.* San Francisco: Cleis Press.

Rochman, S. (1989, March 17). In an unlikely place, women offer each other AIDS education and love: The story of ACE (AIDS Counsellors and Educators) in Bedford Hills Prison. *Gay Community News,* p. 7.

Sabatier, R. (1988). *Blaming others: Prejudice, race, and worldwide AIDS.* Washington, DC: Panos Institute.

Slocum, M. (1989, November). Fighting AIDS in communities of color. *The Body Positive,* p. 15.

Staff of *Scientific American.* (1989). *The science of AIDS: Readings from Scientific American.* New York: Freeman Co.

Shilts, R. (1987). *And the band played on: Politics, people, and the AIDS epidemic.* New York: St. Martin's.

Sullivan, R. (1991, June 22). Needle exchangers had right to break law, judge rules. *The New York Times,* p. B1.

Terson, A. (1989, November). All about Alice. *The Body Positive,* p. 8.

Wheatley, M., McCarthy, M., Karp, M., & Glover, T. (1989, September 17). Reproductive freedom: An urgent issue for lesbians, gay men, and people affected by AIDS. *Gay Community News,* p. 5.

Whitmore, G. (1988, January 31). Bearing witness. *The New York Times Magazine,* p. 14.

World Health Organization. (1989). Condoms and spermicides: How much protection? *World Population Reports* (Series L, No. 8). New York: Author.

Worth, C. (1989, July 9). Handle with care. *The New York Times Magazine,* p. 12.

3

Teaching a Course on "Music and Social Movements"
Rob Rosenthal

Editors' Notes: Activist and sociologist Rob Rosenthal invites his students to investigate the role of culture on social movements by studying the influence of music on politics. Through several class projects, students examined lyrics, political movements, the recording industry, and mainstream music. Rosenthal alerts us to the problems that can occur with this kind of course, such as the heterogeneity of the students' majors, attitudes toward past movements and music, and political cynicism. But he also suggests ways to alleviate these problems.

For the past five years I've been teaching a course on "Music and Social Movements" at Wesleyan University, a small private school in Connecticut with a long tradition of progressive students. Many, particularly those drawn to the social sciences, are interested in social movements; nearly all, like students elsewhere, are interested in music for its entertainment value at the very least.

When I began teaching this course, my basis of knowledge was mainly my own experiences as a performer and producer of social movement music. But as I began rummaging around in the fields of cultural studies and ethnomusicology, as well as the sociology of music, I discovered an explosion of literature relevant to the topic written in the past few years [1] (particularly as baby boomers ascended in the academy). The problem became how to bring focus to readings and classes.

Focussing requires first thinking through the most elementary question: Why teach this course? Part of the reason, of course, is simply love of the topic. Those of us who grew up in the civil rights or anti-war movements tend to link music to some of the most meaningful moments of our lives. Even today, walking down the supermarket aisle and hearing 1001 Strings play "Blowing in the Wind" stirs memories.

But there are more pedagogically correct reasons as well. I'm often amazed at how little most students know about the social movements which have played such a large role in shaping our society: labor, civil rights, New Left/countercultural, and women's, for instance. What they do know of these movements (typically a little about the latter two, a bit about the civil rights movement, virtually nothing about the labor movement) often comes from films and music. Music therefore is a very convenient window into the topic, a way (to be honest) of hooking in students to allow them to explore an alternative way of understanding the history of the country.

But further, as a sociologist and activist, I'm interested in what contributes to the rise and growth of a social movement, and the less studied question of what traces such movements leave behind after their institutionalization or apparent demise (Flacks 1988; Eyerman & Jamison 1991). In particular, we really still know very little about the role of culture. Let me suggest five (not all mutually exclusive) possibilities:

1. Culture is necessary for the rise and growth of a movement. In simplistic terms, without "We Shall Overcome," the civil rights movement would not have been sustained;

2. The converse: Culture is not necessary for the rise and growth of a movement. Without "We Shall Overcome" (or any movement songs, plays, etc.) the movement would have accomplished about as much as it accomplished anyway;

3. Movements inevitably produce movement culture. If there had been no "We Shall Overcome," "We Shall Not Be Moved" would have become the anthem of the civil rights movement. If there had been no Bob Dylan, Phil Ochs or Jane Blow would have played that role. If there had been no civil rights songs, there would have been civil rights dances, or paintings, or wall newspapers;

4. Culture substitutes for movement activity. If there had been less time spent singing, writing, and listening to music, the civil rights movement would have accomplished far more. For instance, Northern white liberals listening to Pete Seeger sing Civil Rights songs in his famous 1963 Carnegie Hall concert may have felt they had thereby discharged their moral responsibilities. They might otherwise have sent greater contributions to SNCC, or actually gone down to the South to help with voter registration, or organized against racism in their own communities. (Of course, possibility (1) would imply that their efforts were spurred by this concert.)

5. Certain types of culture actively inhibit the development of movement activity. For instance, for over fifty years theorists have been arguing whether Theodor Adorno (1990) was right to say that the *form* of popular music — formulaic, repetitive, in general not requiring any active participation by the listener — encouraged traits conducive to passivity (if not fascism) regardless of whether the lyrics of such songs were "progressive."

Confronting these possibilities (and any others students raise along the way) is one focus of the course as I give it. Another is to confront what are probably the basic questions for those my colleague Dick Flacks and I refer to as "movement musicians": if music (and culture generally) does have some political impact, what is it, and how does it happen?

Mention movement music and the picture most people see is civil rights workers singing "We Shall Overcome" as they're attacked by police or whiling away time in jail. Virtually all students of music and movements agree that music plays a function illustrated by this picture which I characterize as "cheerleading," or (because Dick hates that term) "spirit maintenance," or "reaffirmation." That is, music lifts the spirits of those who are already actively involved in a movement.

Yet there are many other functions music might play, functions movement musicians and others have at various times argued music *was* playing. In our 1997 work Flacks and I discuss a number of these: education, mobilization, internal criticism, "totalization" (Hampton 1986), and fundraising. But there are certainly theorists, such as the late R. Serge Denisoff, a pioneer in this field, who argue that "[t]here is little, if any, concrete or empirical evidence that songs do in fact have an independent impact upon attitudes in the political arena" (Denisoff 1983, 149). In a sense, much of the class becomes a debate over whether music can do anything beyond buoying the spirits of the converted (an important function not to be slighted, of course); and if so, when has it and under what conditions?

As I teach it, the course includes lectures, discussions, and student projects. Discussions seem to work best when (1) at the end of each class I give out some suggestions of themes and questions we might discuss at the next class so students come with ideas already formed; and (2) I provide some base of shared knowledge prior to the beginning of discussion, particularly when the music and/or movement being discussed is not something most students are already familiar with.

I assign two projects. The first is a paper on the topic of "Do lyrics matter?" Students pick five songs they think are generally well known and ask five friends to tell them as many lyrics and as much of the "meaning" as they can of each song. Based on their data, they try to generalize about whether lyrics are really heard by listeners, whether the meaning assigned to a song is based on the lyrics or other factors, and what factors (in the music, in the listener, in the setting the music's heard in, and so forth) are most important in establishing meaning in the minds of an audience.

The other project is a final paper on any topic they're interested in which has some reasonable connection to the class. Among the topics in recent years: How digital music will change movement music, the Harlem Renaissance, Joe Hill, the role of jazz in the civil rights movement, the Nazis' use of music, oi (the music of skinheads), riot grrrls, Paul Robeson, straight edge, rave culture, gangster rap's marginalization of women and women fans' responses, and the political uses of "The Star Spangled Banner." Students make an oral presentation to the class a few weeks before the final paper is due, and are expected to incorporate class feedback in their final drafts.

A Sample Syllabus

Of course each instructor feels most comfortable with his or her own syllabus, but for those who would like to have something to play off, here's a summary of what I do.

Section 1: What is a social movement?
Particularly since the class draws heavily from both music and sociology majors, students enter the class with very different backgrounds. I use short articles from Freeman (1983), McAdam (1994), and Eyerman & Jamison (1995) to ensure that everyone understands what a social movement is, how social movement theory progressed from explanations which stressed individual and irrational behavior toward structural explanations, and how the current attempt to understand how individual and structural factors interact (e.g., McAdams' work [1988] on "micromobilization contexts") points to the importance of understanding the role of culture in the social movements.

Section 2: Academic visions
We briefly explore the differences between "folk" and "pop," and then discuss a number of academic views concerning pop music: that it is inevitably counter-oppositional (Adorno 1990); anti-intellectual (Riesman 1990); intrinsically oppositional (Fiske 1989); or oppositional under certain circumstances (Frith 1987, 1991; Street 1986). I conclude with postmodern approaches (Hebdige 1979, 1988; McClary 1991).

These perspectives differ most obviously in how active they take the audience to be. Are we simply robots, programmed by pop music as we are by the conditions of our labor in industrial capitalism (Adorno)? Do we instead pick and choose among the musical possibilities offered us (Street), many of which (as in the 60s) are oppositional due to the groups that created and nurtured them (Fiske)? Or, in the most extreme opposition to Adorno, are we co-creators of the product, constructing meanings as we choose from the pop music presented (Hebdige)? Students are always initially resistant to Adorno, who is easy to write off on minor details such as his clear ignorance of jazz, but whose basic point regarding how meanings are conveyed through *the form itself* cannot be lightly dismissed; they always end up captivated by the challenge he presents to the music they love.

Section 3: Functions of music for social movements
Once we get past reaffirmation, what other functions might music play for social movements? Activist musicians themselves (or those writing about them)

seem to think they can do (and have done) much more. Analysts on both the Left (Gleason 1972) and Right (Allen 1972; Huck 1972) have argued that music can "educate" or "brainwash" (depending on the perspective of the analyst) previously uncommitted or indifferent audiences. Activist musicians have consciously attempted to use music to mobilize those who are partial to a movement but not yet involved, including the Almanac Singers' attempts to get workers to join the CIO, the SNCC Freedom Singers tours of Northern campuses which inspired many college students to come South for Freedom Summer, and the efforts of Red Wedge in England to spur activity among supporters of the Labour Party. Wayne Hampton (1986) has argued that musicians—even more than their music—have served as "totalizing agents" around which movements can form and mobilize, with audiences attributing to the star the qualities they assume the movement is about.

Songs have also been intended to communicate criticism within movements, for instance Phil Ochs' "Links on the Chain," which (fraternally) criticized the labor movement in the mid-1960s for not endorsing and aiding the civil rights movement, or Queen Latifah's "U.N.I.T.Y," which (sororitally?) criticizes sexism within the hip-hop community. Finally, while the mega-events of the past twenty years have been widely criticized for trivializing or actually impeding the growth of movements, a number of writers argue that on balance they have helped with several of these functions (education, mobilization) while raising badly-needed funds for movement organizations. We try to examine the evidence for each of these claims (and in doing so encounter the difficulties in obtaining and analyzing evidence in this field) and assess whether, when, and under what conditions these other functions have been served.

Section 4: The dilemmas of movement music

Whatever the functions a piece of music might play for a movement, some "technical" questions arise. The first is whether lyrics even matter (hence the first assignment), i.e., to what extent are lyrics known and to what extent do they convey "meaning" to listeners. A second, somewhat related, question is whether some forms of music are more appropriate to conveying political ideas than others. For instance, singer/activist Leon Rosselson has argued that songs need to encourage quiet contemplation of the issues to do any good; Jesse Lemisch has argued that Leftists should write in *whatever* form of music is most popular at the time, and the drawbacks of a form (say the difficulty in hearing lyrics—let alone contemplating them quietly—in punk) should be struggled with rather than seen as a reason to use a different form (e.g., the "folk music" of Pete Seeger and Seeger-wanna-bes). As far back as 1940s, the Almanac Singers wrestled with the same kinds of questions; Bruce Springsteen is apparently wrestling with them today.

Another set of dilemmas concerns the relation of the artist to formal organizations, both social movement groups and ruling governments. We first examine what the relation of the artist to the movement might be and attempt to grapple with conceptions of what it *should* be. For instance, we look at the issues of party discipline and censorship: should the artist be held to a party line when others are, or does the nature of artistic work demand freedom of expression? Similarly, we examine whether artists should be expected to do the same organizing tasks everyone else does: If so, when will they have time to work on their art? If not, will they be able to authentically speak for the group?

Such questions of freedom and control are also intrinsic to the relation of artists to states. At various time and in various places, governments have used music (Germany under the Nazis), repressed some forms (jazz in the Soviet Union at various times), promoted music generally (Holland in the 1980s), promoted particular types, especially indigenous forms in danger of extinction (Canada and Sweden in the 1980s), or left music largely to the market (the United States with some obvious exceptions). Students grapple with what stance they think governments should take toward music and culture in general.

Section 5: The recording industry
This leads naturally to an examination of the role of the market in general, and the recording industry in particular, in shaping what music becomes available to consumers, including movement members. Particularly after reading the classic work by Peterson & Berger (1972)—which demonstrates how music that grows from cohesive communities, political and otherwise (and indeed radical musics of all kinds), has tended to surface periodically on small independent labels, only to be swallowed up by the major recording companies and then watered down to "cross over" to a mainstream audience—students are tempted to dismiss all commercialized music as inauthentic, diluted, and politically suspect. But reading pieces by Garofalo (1992) and Goodwin & Gore (1995) invariably leads to more nuanced discussions in which both negative and positive affects of commercialization are weighed, and important distinctions are drawn (for instance, between "cultural imperialism" and "transculturation").

Section 6: Case studies from U.S. history
The lessons we've learned from these discussions are then applied to a series of case studies from the United States: the labor and proletarian movements 1850–1950; the civil rights movement; the New Left and the counterculture; the modern women's movement; and hip-hop (including: is that a movement per se?). Here I find it very useful to assign some short history of each movement as well as readings about the music itself. I've used the American Social History Project's *Who Built America* (1992) for a number of units, but any short, succinct history will do.

Section 7: Mainstream music in the U.S.
It's obvious that movements often use music, but there's also a strong effect of movements *on* music, including mainstream music (which is part of the argument about seeing movements in terms of what they leave behind that Eyerman & Jamison and Flacks have made). For instance, I show my students Jimi Hendrix in the film *Monterey Pop,* and then *Jimi Plays Berkeley* to show

the enormous difference in his act (how it's mounted, how it sounds, how it's received, how it's framed by the filmmakers) just three years later as Peace, Love and Understanding has given way to militancy and revolution in the movement.

Section 8: Other countries
There is a fascinating literature about the use of music in recent radical and revolutionary movements in other countries. A number of writers even claim music and musicians have played *central* roles in momentous political events, for instance in Argentina (Vila 1992) and East Germany (Wicke 1992). Discussions here generally revolve around the questions of how much of this is applicable to the United States, and what we can learn from these events.

Section 9: Student reports
As outlined above, each student gives an oral report (as well as handing in a paper) on any related topic he or she has cleared with me.

Section 10: A return to theory
Based on their own projects and the case studies, we return to the theoreticians we read in the opening weeks and reevaluate their work.

Section 11: Methodological questions
Work in this field is in its infancy largely because it is so difficult to come up with a methodology for examining the key questions. How do we know if people really had their minds changed by hearing "The Message"? In this last unit, we discuss which methodologies we trust most, while I beg them to come up with some new ideas for my own work as well as their own.

A Few Problems to Watch Out For

In general this course has worked well for me, but there have been some problems along the way, including:

(1) Heterogeneity of students
Heterogeneity of students in terms of personal backgrounds and musical tastes, I've found, is very enriching for the class. To their credit, students in my courses have been very respectful of each other's musical tastes, and at least somewhat willing to learn from each other.

But a more difficult mix to deal with is the split between music and social science majors, who bring very different bodies of knowledge to the course. For instance, many music majors don't know what a social movement is; many social science students have no idea what we mean by the "hook" of a song. The danger is that the two groups end up talking past each other, or even worse, one group dominates and the other becomes passive.

It's imperative that the instructor remember that each group needs help understanding basic concepts that the other group takes for granted, and intercedes in discussions whenever the technical language of one group is preventing others from being able to take part.

(2) Attitudes towards past movements and music
Here there are two contrary dangers. One is a dismissal of old music, which sounds "cheesey" to students. My first year I played Paul Robeson singing some spirituals, and their eyes just glazed over. The next class I found myself apologizing for boring them, when I came to my senses and realized I should be confronting this attitude rather than enabling it.

So far I've used two weapons against this tendency. The first is to clearly alert them to the dangers of being "era-centric." Our job, I tell students, is to understand why whatever music we're listening to was considered the very hippest music there was by some group at some time. The second is to provide context, both musically and sociologically, for any music I play. Readings and lectures must be informed by this need; films are of great help with this as well.[2]

But there is also the converse danger: reverence and romanticization of the old days, particularly the 1960s. For many reasons (not the least of which is just the sheer numbers of the baby boom generation), the music and the politics of the 60s lie heavily on the current student generation. Knowledge and appreciation of the past is a virtue, but this can become undue deference and a sense of inferiority which is crippling to self-development and the creation of new movements.

(3) Cynicism re politics
I'm constantly astounded by how cynical many students today are about politics and the possibility for real change. Many invoke the 60s in support of that cynicism: if that large a mass movement couldn't change the world (and what does that mean to them?), it can't be done. But their cynicism extends far beyond the distrust of "Establishment" politics found in the 60s to include social movements themselves. For instance, in discussions of the relations between musicians and the movements they're tied to, the notion that musicians who are members of political groups should be subject to group beliefs or discipline in any way is totally repugnant to them (and certainly that argument should be considered, but that's not the point here). In cases like this, I like to turn the tables on them: Form them as the Central Committee of a political group and see what they feel they can and should expect from musician members. But the larger problem of cynicism is best countered, I've found, by their learning about movements that have made a difference, not only in the United States' past, but around the world in the present.[3]

(4) A lack of focus (as detailed in the beginning of this article)
And here it is the professor who generally is responsible. Especially those of us who love this music tend to think that just telling people who don't know about it is a service in itself—and it may be, but there's *too damn much* of it out there

to just lob anything that comes to mind at them. (As Tom Lehrer once said—satirically—of the Spanish Civil War, "They may have won all the battles / but we had all the good songs!").

A Closing Tip

As I look back through the notes filed in my "revisions" folder that I've scribbled over the past five years, I find one note appearing time after time: make use of *their* music. Though a class that combines music and social movements seems to have guaranteed sex appeal, students still need to feel that it says something to them about their current lives, that it's not "just history." Despite what I've just said about the need to get them to appreciate music of different eras, it seems crucial to use or refer to some modern music (or at least music they're already familiar with) in as many classes as you possibly can (which means *you* need to learn *their* music as they learn the music you love). I've found it very helpful to have students bring in their own music and speak to why they like it; it doesn't have to be overtly political music to help them learn to look at what messages are contained and how "meaning" emerges from music generally.

In a *New Yorker* article reflecting on the death of Kurt Cobain, Alex Ross wrote:

> The attempt to carry out social engineering through rock lyrics is an impossible one. Rock and roll has never been and will never be a vehicle for social amelioration, despite many fond hopes. Music is robbed of its intentions and associations as it goes out into the great wide open; like a rumor passed through a crowd, it emerges utterly changed. (1994, 102)

Conversely Eyerman & Jamison have argued that:

> In the 1960s songs contributed to a political movement, and were often performed at political demonstrations and collective festivals. Singers and songs were central to the cognitive praxis of these social movements, indeed, they may be central to all social movements in their formative states. (1995, 451)

We are still at a very early point in our understanding of what music contributes to a social movement and how social movements affect music, and social and political life in general. The field is wide open, and this, along with the intrinsic interest of the subject, provides an exciting opportunity for students to become immersed in working out tentative answers to difficult questions.

Notes

1. Among the many works published since 1970 that touch directly or indirectly on the subject, I recommend looking at: R. Serge Denisoff & Richard A. Peterson, *The Sounds of Social Change;* John Street, *Rebel Rock;* Robin Denselow, *When the Music's*

Over; Simon Frith and Andrew Goodwin, *On Record;* Ronald Edsforth and Larry Bennett, *Popular Culture and Political Change in Modern America;* Dick Hebdige, *Hiding in the Light* and *Subculture;* Wayne Hampton, *Guerrilla Minstrels;* Tricia Rose, *Black Noise;* Reebee Garofalo, *Rockin' the Boat;* Robert Walser, *Running with the Devil;* Robbie Lieberman, *My Song Is My Weapon;* and Ray Pratt, *Rhythm and Resistance.* Full bibliographic information may be found in the references.

2. Among the films I've shown in my course are *We Shall Overcome, Crossover Dreams, Matewan, Monterey Pop,* and *Jimi Plays Berkeley,* but the possibilities are virtually endless.

3. A fine source of articles about recent movements using music around the world is Reebee Garofalo's *Rockin' the Boat,* which includes articles on movements on six continents.

Works Cited

Adorno, Theodor. 1990 [1941]. "On Popular Music," in Simon Frith and Andrew Goodwin, *On Record.* NY: Pantheon, 1990.

Allen, Gary. 1972 [1969]. "More subversion than meets the ear." *American Opinion* 12 (February 1969): 49–62. Reprinted (pp. 151–166) in Serge R. Denisoff and Richard A. Peterson, *The Sounds of Social Change.* New York: Rand, McNally.

American Social History Project. 1992. *Who Built America, Volume II.* New York: Pantheon.

Denisoff, R. Serge. 1983. *Sing a Song of Social Significance.* Bowling Green, Ohio: Bowling Green State University Popular Press.

Denisoff, R. Serge, and Richard A. Peterson. 1972. *The Sounds of Social Change.* New York: Rand, McNally.

Denselow, Robin. 1989. *When the Music's Over.* London: Faber & Faber.

Edsforth, Ronald, and Larry Bennett. 1991. *Popular Culture and Political Change in Modern America.* Albany: State University of New York.

Eyerman, Ron, and Andrew Jamison. 1995. "Social movements and cultural transformation: Popular music in the 1960s." *Media, Culture & Society* 17:449–468.

———. 1991. *Social Movements: A Cognitive Approach.* University Park, PA: Pennsylvania State University.

Fiske, John. 1989. *Understanding Popular Culture.* Boston: Unwin Hyman.

Flacks, Richard. 1988. *Making History.* New York: Columbia University.

Freeman, Jo. 1983. "On the origins of social movements," in Jo Freeman (ed.), *Social Movements of the Sixties and Seventies.* New York: Longman.

Frith, Simon. 1987. "Toward an aesthetic of popular music," in *Music and Society,* Richard Leppert and Susan McClary (eds.). New York: Cambridge University.

Frith, Simon. 1991. "The good, the bad, and the indifferent: Defending popular culture from the populists." *diacritics* 21 (Winter 1991): 102–115.

Frith, Simon, and Andrew Goodwin (eds.). 1990. *On Record.* New York: Pantheon.

Garofalo, Reebee (ed.). 1992. *Rockin' the Boat.* Boston: South End.

———. "Understanding Mega-Events." 1992. Chapter 1 in Garofalo (ed.), *Rockin' the Boat*.

Gleason, Ralph J. 1972 [1969]. "The Greater Sound." *Yale Drama Review* 13 (Summer 1969): 160–167. Reprinted (pp. 137–147) as "Cultural revolution" in Denisoff and Peterson, *The Sounds of Social Change*.

Goodwin, Andrew, and Joe Gore. 1995 [1990]. "World beat and the cultural imperialism debate." *Socialist Review* 2013 (July/September 1990). Reprinted (pp. 121–131) in Ron Sakolsky and Fred Wei-Han Ho (eds.), *Sounding Off*. Brooklyn, NY: Autonomedia.

Hampton, Wayne. 1986. *Guerrilla Minstrels*. Knoxville: University of Tennessee.

Hebdige, Dick. 1988. *Hiding in the Light*. New York: Routledge.

Hebdige, Dick. 1979. *Subculture, the Meaning of Style*. New York: Metheun.

Huck, Susan. 1972 [1970]. "The great kid con." *Review of the News* (February 11, 1970), pp. 17–24. Reprinted (pp. 167–172) in Denisoff and Peterson, *The Sounds of Social Change*.

Lieberman, Robbie. 1989. *My Song Is My Weapon*. Chicago: University of Illinois Press.

McAdam, Doug. 1994. "Culture and social movements." Pp. 36–57 in Enrique Larana, Hank Johnston, and Joseph R. Gusfield (eds.), *New Social Movements*. Philadelphia: Temple.

———. 1988. "Micromobilization contexts and recruitment to activism." *International Social Movement Research* 1:125–154.

McClary, Susan. 1991. "Living to tell: Madonna's resurrection of the fleshly," in McClary (ed.), *Feminine Endings*. Minnesota: University of Minnesota.

Peterson, Richard A., and David G. Berger. 1972. "Three eras in the manufacture of popular music lyrics." Pp. 292–303 in Denisoff and Peterson, *The Sounds of Social Change*.

Pratt, Ray. 1990. *Rhythm and Resistance*. Washington: Smithsonian Institution.

Riesman, David. 1990 [1950]. "Listening to popular music." Reprinted in Frith and Goodwin, *On Record*.

Rosenthal, Rob, and Richard Flacks. 1997. *Playing for Change*. Minneapolis: University of Minnesota.

Rose, Tricia. 1994. *Black Noise*. Hanover, NH: Wesleyan University.

Ross, Alex. 1994. "Postscript: Kurt Cobain." *The New Yorker* 70(10): 102.

Street, John. 1986. *Rebel Rock*. New York: Blackwell.

Vila, Pablo. 1992. "*Rock Nacional* and dictatorship in Argentina," in Garofalo, *Rockin' the Boat*.

Walser, Robert. 1993. *Running with the Devil*. Hanover, NH: Wesleyan University.

Wicke, Peter. 1992. "The times they are a-changin'," in Garofalo, *Rockin' the Boat*.

4

"Commercials in the Classroom?! What Next, Music Videos?"

Paul D. Fischer

Editors' Notes: Fischer uses a Freirean approach to media literacy and, in this article, describes an in-class exercise in which he shows a series of commercials. Shown out of their ordinary context, the commercials help raise consciousness of advertisement as part of students' everyday life and their roles as consumers, while also raising questions about the status quo, gender roles and behaviors, star quality, and corporate-based consumer culture.

An experience I had teaching an Honors composition seminar (twice) on "American Youth Culture Since the Second World War" led to the creation of an in-class exercise using a video of commercials and a music video. While trying to convey the importance of certain elements of popular culture from my most formative years, specifically the significance of each new Beatles release, a learner quipped, "Aaaaah, John Lennon just sells shoes." Immediately I flashed on the then current Nike ad which uses the song "Revolution" in its soundtrack, and learned several new things. First, that it is incredibly difficult to successfully invoke or recreate for learners cultural conditions prevailing at the introduction of non-contemporary popular culture. Second, that the rapidly shifting and reconfiguring realm of the popular can drastically change the image of popular artists for those encountering them later in, or even after, their active careers. Third, that using contemporary popular culture materials demands that teachers show respect for the media environments and content in learners' everyday lives. And fourth, that exercises using contemporary popular culture materials provide opportunities for learners to articulate their perceptions of everyday life which can catalyze new knowledge for themselves, their peers, and their teachers.

Teaching first-year college composition as a Teaching Fellow while working on my Ph.D. in American Culture Studies, I had an unfettered opportunity to grapple with these issues in the Honors seminar I taught in my third and last years of funding ('94–'95). Being a white male, well into my thirties at this point, I made strong efforts to not privilege my perspective and opinions. Attempting to develop a paradigm of liberatory pedagogy that derives from the work of Paolo Freire, I endeavored to raise more questions than I answered, hoping the learners' growing background about youth in postwar America would lead them to answers of their own.

The class consisted of traditional midwestern college freshmen (all but one were caucasian). Learners were pointed to sources on the 50s, 60s, and 70s to explore and expand established interests. They brought information into discussions on the Baby Boom and Madison Avenue's discovery of youth as a market, the Generation Gap, Women's Liberation, Gay Liberation, the Vietnam War, Watergate, and more. We viewed two hours of the PBS documentary "Making Sense of the Sixties," and screened the films "Over the Edge," and "Pump Up the Volume" which provide similar story lines set in the 70s and 80s respectively. We discussed the differences between them and what has changed further in the 90s.

Initially, my pleas that Lennon himself had no input on the way his song was used seemed to fall on deaf ears. Even explaining that Michael Jackson held the publishing rights and had to make a substantial donation to the United Negro College Fund in Lennon's widow's name to placate her did not soften the perception that making money was the artist's highest priority. It was with this stimulus that I devised a classroom experience that would confront learners with commercial appearances by artists in whom they had greater emotional investments. With the financial underwriting of a donor (about $400), I procured a custom-made tape consisting of commercials featuring pop music stars. (There are businesses on both coasts which provide "off air" tapes of this sort.)

This essay details the video exercise in critical thinking about popular culture that I devised, adaptable to many grade levels from its origin with college freshmen, and some of the rationales underlying its construction. The exercise, described below, requires learners to interrogate the everyday structures of American culture as it relates to themselves and the category youth. It presents learners with a videotape of eleven commercials for a range of products featuring the stars of popular music. The tape includes The Rolling Stones, The Who, and Steve Winwood for beer, Tina Turner and Aretha Franklin for automobiles, Genesis for an airline, Elton John for a clothes company, and Robert Palmer, Robert Plant, and Madonna for soft drinks. Thanks to the popularity of the "classic rock" radio format, many of these singers were familiar to and often liked by the learners. Some were already an integral part of their world.

The ads featuring the Stones were said to be ads for their "Steel Wheels" tour, but few viewers took note of that. The Who is featured in an ad promoting their Los Angeles performance of "Tommy," but again most saw it as a beer ad. Winwood's ad for Michelob showcases his song "What the Night Can Do," which was rumored to have been written with that campaign in mind. Tina Turner appears in her only ad for Chrysler, as a straightforward spokesperson. They felt she'd fill that role for a decade but apparently consumers couldn't picture her driving a minivan. Franklin belts out Chevrolet's "Heartbeat of America" theme against tightly edited heart-tugging schemes featuring red, white, and blue. The members of Genesis are shown contradicting themselves in a self-deprecating way. Elton John is shown singing lyrics from "Sad Songs Say So Much" changed to "Sasson Says So Much" probably the crassest exploitation of creative output included. Robert Palmer sings "Simply Irresistible" in front of a line of seemingly interchangeable models as in his videos. Robert Plant's Coke ad features the song "Tall Cool One," leggy models, and what one learner termed an "exploding, orgasmic Coke bottle." The reel closes with Madonna's two minute "Like a Prayer" ad for Pepsi, the one which aired only once and was at the center of a controversy involving Rev. Donald Wildmon's threatened product boycott.

The video exercise is used to produce the first written work in the class. After beginning the term with a session or two of getting acquainted activities (which includes self-disclosure by the teacher of all data requested of learners) and detailing the syllabus and achievement requirements, I end a session with the nine-minute videotape and about fifteen minutes for learners to craft written reactions. Prior to viewing the tape I explain that it consists of eleven short segments and would like a paragraph or two of explanation of the learners' strongest reaction to one of them, whether positive or negative.

I collect the written reactions and compile them into a handout to be used in the next class session as a catalyst for discussion. The learners' reactions are grouped by the commercial they respond to and the authors are not identified. Time is given for the class to read through the handout, then each commercial is discussed based on the reactions in hand and additional concerns raised by class members. In this way every class member's view is shared (albeit anonymously) with their peers, and the discussion highlights a range of both positive and negative views of the ads and the appearance of celebrities in them. Having used this exercise in numerous classes now, I have noticed an interesting aspect of learners' reactions to the tape: through the first three or four ads the class remains fully engaged with the monitor, but as the fifth and subsequent ads roll, fidgeting begins and their focus on the screen eases despite the fact that some of the more visually engaging pieces are in the second half of the tape. By the end of the nine minutes, some seem noticeably uncomfortable. I do not chalk this up to brief attention spans so much as the fact that most learners have never seen commercials outside their everyday context. This provides a real opportunity for scrutiny of the commercial corporate orientation of contemporary media.

The "normal" experience of commercials is in groups of three or four during television programs. As the additional ads unspool, learners are confronted with these messages at face value, for what they are, finely crafted persuasive sales communications. This heightens audience consciousness of the fact that marketers position them as consumers, and youthful ones at that. While a minority of reactions are positive descriptions of "good, successful" commercials, most raise problems. Some take issue with ads "talking down" to them, others with the way women are portrayed, still others call attention to the believeability of stars as spokespeople, and a few discuss possible negative impacts on the stars' images and careers. As facilitator of the discussion I attempt to use the written reactions to spark sustained exchanges between the class members, remaining silent whenever possible.

Many times the discussion among learners has elicited the response, "I'd never thought about that before." When this occurs, I tend to think of the exercise as a success, because someone (or several someones) has found it necessary to think about commercials in new ways. Some have had their consciousness raised about how they accept sales messages as an integral part of life. Others have reacted more to matters of content—gratuitous use of the female form to associate products with popularity, conventional ideas of beauty and sexuality, which are routinely critiqued as sexist. At the level of first-year college classes, many learners have not yet begun to question traditional gender roles and behaviors. With peers who have done so as a catalyst, however, some begin to do so out of class, having heard their views. When connections like this are made between classroom content and everyday social activities and alliances, the exercise takes on a liberatory dimension.

Learners also regularly use the phrase "selling out" to negatively characterize the practice of taking money for commercial appearances, song usage, and endorsements. I ask the person(s) using the phrase to define it, usually attracting several contributors to that process. The most common dimension raised in these definitions is the appearance of artists making commerce more important than creativity and communication with the fans. Some feel the artists have "lowered" themselves by appearing in these messages. Some raise discussion of the impact on the artist's image, but need to be drawn out about what they mean. I have often found myself asking, "What is it they have to sell out?" to tease out responses here. A common response brings in the esteem fans have for the artists and the previous impact their creative output has had on learners' thoughts and feelings. At this point the discussion is on the verge of explicitly exposing the commodification of learners' passions, desires, and emotional/intellectual investments in popular music, but many lack the vocabulary to satisfactorily explain themselves. Further, most young learners lack sufficient background on the subcultural origins and "countercultural" traditions of this music to articulate the contradiction represented by these artists becoming corporate mouthpieces. Once these issues have been identified by the learners, the instructor can easily add examples from preceding decades, contextualizing these commercials as the most current manifestation of an ongoing struggle to co-opt and assimilate rebellious voices in the lyrics. In doing so, teachers are given an opportunity to demonstrate vocabulary and concepts which can add depth and precision to learners' subsequent writing on this and other topics.

Toward the end of the class period I expand the topic from the specific ads to the practice of using celebrities as product endorsers generally. I close the session by making the points that these practices really became prominent in the nineteen eighties, a unique aspect of their experience of Youth, and that they have to develop new responses and coping skills. Using the Super Bowl as an example of how audience size is a key factor in setting ad rates and endorsement compensation, I remind the class that what advertisers really pay for is access to audiences. Meaning that, in addition to selling their work and appearance, the stars are selling the established relations with their fans too. I then screen a music video that was, for a time, banned by MTV. It is Neil Young's "This Note's for You," which parodies several commercials with high profile music endorsers and opens with the lyric:

> Ain't singin' for Pepsi
> Ain't singin' for Coke
> Don't sing for nobody
> Makes me look like a joke
> This note's for you . . .

I urge the learners to ponder the motivations behind the MTV ban and end the class.

This exercise endeavors to establish precedents for a democratic dialogic model in the classroom which will prevail for the balance of the term. Breaking the ice by making everyone's voice "heard" and allowing exchanges among and between learners to progress and to be unchecked sets an important tone early in the term. The use of contemporary everyday materials is geared toward contextual skill development. All points of view are actively encouraged and supported, while the instructor endeavors not to impose his authority. This has worked with varying degrees of success, but always manages to acquaint learners with their peers' thinking and range of concerns. It also begins to problematize corporate/mass/consumer culture and the role individuals are expected to play in it. Decontextualizing commercials is an important first step in denaturalizing learners' relationships with commercial media.

Making analysis of elements of their out-of-school lives a source of success in school creates opportunities for learners to make those boundaries permeable in other and more frequent ways. Sharpening the critical abilities of increasingly self-reflexive learners surely fits David Lusted's definition of pedagogy expressed in *Screen* (1986):

> What pedagogy addresses is the process of production and exchange in this cycle, the transformation of consciousness that takes place in the interaction of three agencies—the teacher, the learner, and the knowledge they together produce. (3)

This definition of pedagogy takes an interesting turn on the notion of agency in the production of meaning, giving agency to the collaboratively produced knowledge. Such knowledge can powerfully act back upon its creators, causing them to alter future behaviors.

One area that the contemporaneous generation of young learners regularly encounters that is foreign to many of their teachers is video music. With MTV (Music Television network on cable) coming into existence in 1981, many learners today do not even consider the nature of a world without it. Many teachers, on the other hand, have no experience going through adolescence with predetermined visual input added to the experience of popular music. Further, since about that same time, corporate merchandisers of consumer goods have been using popular music stars in their advertising messages. This practice would have been abhorrent to many such artists in earlier decades, but to many young learners, is simply the way things have always been. To some, reasons for objecting to this practice are a mystery.

Using an approach to contemporary popular culture materials informed by cultural studies can give learners a sense of the importance of their own experiences, knowledges, lives and their views about them. Though some initially resist having cherished items plucked from the realm of entertainment to be made objects of study, most quickly begin to express insights unavailable to their instructors and relish the positive regard their perceptions and expertise earn from peers and teachers alike.

As a student of cultural studies I support analyses of institutions which highlight inequalities of power related to race, gender, class, ethnicity, age, sexual preference, etc. as platforms for critique. While acknowledging the presence of marginalization and oppression in contemporary society, I try to refrain in my teaching from casting any gender, political, or other group as villain, though I do tend to problematize definitions of American life and culture which foreground capitalism rather than democracy. Most often I stress depersonalization as a negative to be addressed in discussions of contemporary mass culture. I try to evoke from learners a sense of critical literacy that goes far beyond the ability to read and write. Stanley Aronowitz sketched the outlines of this project in the late nineteen seventies when he wrote: "If writing is to become part of the critical process, deconstruction of mass audience culture is the first priority.... The job of the teacher is to legitimate mass culture in order to criticize and transcend it" (467).

I would qualify that by saying that it is incumbent upon the teacher to encourage learners to use the tools of media criticism, popular culture analysis, and cultural studies to criticize and transcend mass culture for themselves. When the validity of their insights and strength of their observations and arguments leads to academic success and enhanced self-confidence, the liberating potential of such exercises is quickly realized. In these exercises, the tasks of classroom life are shown to be engaged with learners' everyday lives and that their individual points of view provide them with valid points of departure for critical analysis and academic success. In the process, the non-spectacle world can take on added depth and become a true site for cultural action. This makes the process liberating—as opposed to mere banking—in Freire's sense.

Problematizing learners' relationships with commercial media fits what critical pedagogue Ira Shor calls "extraordinarily experiencing the ordinary," a part of contextual skill development. By linking teaching and development of introductory academic skills (e.g., writing) with critical examination of aspects of everyday life, learners as subjects quickly feel the power of their subjectivities. In flexing their subjectivities, learners can shrug off the passive consumerist positioning often engendered by consumption of contemporary mass media. In critically analyzing contemporary popular culture in this way, some experience the thrill of conscientization, the essence of Freire's radical pedagogy. I view this exercise as an example of how media presentations crafted and intended for youth can be critiqued by young learners to enhance their subjectivities and increase their media literacy.

Beginning with everyday materials and means of communication with which learners are to some degree expert provides a good jumping off point for confident analysis and criticism. What I try to help create is what McLuhan called "civil defense against media fallout" (267), a skeptical critical attitude toward the media and their content. Promoting critical thinking and effective self-expression with elements of everyday life as objects of scrutiny satisfies my desire for "relevance" beyond the classroom. I believe that the tools of criticism of media and what is considered "popular" are valuable to all living in mass societies, not just those seeking careers in media-related industries.

Urging learners to make critical interventions in the "real world," to take cultural action designed to promote and perpetuate democracy is education for political literacy, conscientization, and justice. That this would surely be controversial and labeled part of the "culture wars" by the political right only makes this struggle more imperative. All education springs from a view of the future—when that view is insensitive to constantly changing contemporary conditions, teaching that the future will be substantially like the past, it disserves its most important constituency, the young. All of the above is part and parcel of getting recalcitrant, bureaucratic institutions to respond to changing cultural conditions in the societies they serve by building upon existing structures to begin the process with a minimum of institutional opposition. Youth culture as a topic can be an important catalyst for liberatory education in America in the twenty-first century and will have to be aggressively defended as a form of resistance to domination.

Works Cited

Aronowitz, Stanley. "Mass Culture and the Eclipse of Reason." *American Media and Mass Culture: Left Perspectives*. Ed. Donald Lazere. Berkeley: U. of California Press, 1987.

Freire, Paulo. *Pedagogy of the Oppressed.* New York: Continuum, 1993.

George, Diana, and Diana Shoos. "Issues of Subjectivity and Resistance: Cultural Studies in the English Classroom." *Cultural Studies in the English Classroom.* Eds. James A. Berlin and Michael Vivion. Portsmouth, NH: Boynton/Cook, 1992.

Lusted, David. "Introduction—Why Pedagogy?" *Screen* 27:5 (1986): 2–14.

McLuhan, Marshall. *Understanding Media: The Extensions of Man.* New York: New English Library, 1964.

Shor, Ira. *Critical Teaching in Everyday Life.* Boston: South End Press, 1980.

Weiler, Kathleen. "Freire and a Feminist Pedagogy of Difference." *Harvard Educational Review* 61:4 (1991): 449–474.

5

Changing Perceptions, Not Just Channels, in the Heartland

Teaching Television's Teaching

David B. Owen and Charles L. P. Siley

Editors' Notes: Using critical pedagogy, Owen and Siley focus their teacher-preparation course on media literacy. The course includes sections on TV advertising, TV genres, children's TV, and an exploration of television's relationship to American culture. The authors hope that their students develop critical distance from TV and teach TV to their future students with an approach that illuminates television's power and prejudice.

How does one convince college students who grow up in the conservative culture of America's heartland that they need to rethink their lives radically? Further, how does one do this in a public university that is increasingly committed to technology transfer and corporate R & D and advertises itself as an educational institution which primarily trains its students to fit into the world of work? As instructors in such an academic environment with such traditional students, we have struggled with various pedagogies through the years, searching for a way to teach a liberating curriculum and devising strategies that would increase the student's sense of her or his own intellectual empowerment and promote a more critical and sophisticated cultural awareness.

Currently we are teaching a course on television analysis to a group of students who are preparing to be teachers. Our course combines an analysis of television with the development of a critical pedagogy for teaching the media in public primary and secondary schools. The purpose of this paper is to share with other academics our tentative successes and to outline the approach we have developed for overcoming our students' reluctance to think about the ideological and practical implications of their own culture. Our paper is divided into three main sections. The first gives the circumstances and background of the course, the second describes the course's goals and structure, and the last treats the pedagogic means we use.

I

We teach at Iowa State University, a public university with 21,000 undergraduates who come primarily from Iowa and adjoining states. The majority of them are from small, rural communities almost exclusively white, with north European traditions, especially German and Scandinavian. We have some suburban students from metropolitan areas and a few minority students, most of whom come from out of state. Very few students have had any personal exposure to labor and working-class traditions; the great majority, both men and women, are politically and socially conventional and uncommitted, usually leaning toward conservative. By and large they unreflectively accept their educational preparation as primarily *vocational* and instrumental and as of limited benefit in developing a personal, critical perspective on themselves, their goals in life, and the culture they live in. As with students around the country, ours work at jobs too many hours outside of school, thereby reducing time for thoughtful reading and reflection and for attending and learning from extracurricular and cultural activities. Their educational experience is narrow; one might even call it, in some sense, impoverished.

On the other hand, since most of these undergraduates are from Iowa, which traditionally has the nation's highest ACT scores, they come generally prepared academically to do college work. Additionally, they subscribe to the work ethic, which means that they tend to come to class, do assignments, and get their papers in on time. They take school seriously, if only for vocational purposes.

The students in our class are preparing to be elementary and secondary public school teachers—most of them hope this will be close to where they grew up—and they represent a general cross-section of the undergraduate student population. Their approach to courses in teacher preparation, like ours, is similar to that in other courses: they look for "cookbook" techniques that they can take from the course to apply impartially in their chosen field.

The strength of these students is that, for the most part, they genuinely care about what happens to children and are worried about the conditions under which the latter grow up today. They perceive that the traditional nuclear family is collapsing and not providing children the guidance and protection they experienced. They hear about increasing violence in the society that children both experience and create. They are also aware of extensive problems of drug and alcohol abuse, of AIDS, and of "children having children." They sense vaguely a general decline in job opportunities and decrease of social mobility, fearing that they might not achieve their parents' level of economic success. In short, what allows us to connect what happens in class to the reality of the world outside the university is their genuine worry about the problems children face, and this provides the bridge by which they come to recognize that classwork can be meaningful and empowering in their own lives.

Our choice of television as the medium to focus on in the course was suggested by the ever-growing data which points to its importance as an educational force in contemporary American society. Almost every large-scale analysis of education from the 1960s on to the most recent U.S. Department of Education's *Strong Families, Strong Schools*[1] mentions the central importance of children's television viewing as one of the most powerful factors—and possibly *the* most powerful—in developing their definitions of self and connection with the world. These reports have repeatedly called for the study of the impact of television on education in this country, but as yet these concerns have only been infrequently addressed by educational research, departments and colleges of education, and teachers' professional organizations. If television is largely responsible for forming the children who populate our nation's classrooms, should not we, as educators, be training future teachers both to understand and to teach others about the formative power of the medium?

The intent of our class is twofold. First, we want to help our students learn to view television critically, to see how the screen reflects the guiding hegemonic ideologies of consumerism and of prejudice based on gender, race, and class, as well as to recognize those "openings" in the programming which allow for constructing alternatives to that ideology. Second, and even more important, we also want students to invent ways, through their own pedagogic strategies, to pass on to *their* students the critical perspective they have acquired in our class. Experience has led us to revise our teaching methods for developing such a critical pedagogy. Rather than confronting students with traditional progressive materials and rhetoric, which often assume a dialectic of opposition, we have chosen to start with our students' own conceptions and to tease out of them the contradictions that are inherent in "conventional wisdom." Given the background of students, we have had to face their antipathy toward using the unfamiliar, and to them alienating, language of radical social critiques. For example, instead of imposing attention on the idea of a "false consciousness" when discussing the effects of advertising, students themselves come to recognize over time that the "average" individual shown in ads is not average but, indeed, a "construction"—and they introduce this word themselves—of the advertisers, who cast their audience into a form which, without intervention, the audience is not.

In other words, when we focus on root institutional and cultural problems, we encourage the students to discuss as explicitly as possible the contradictions inherent in the society without using the language normally associated with the analysis of those contradictions. We have found that in this fashion, students who are unfamiliar with the political traditions or language of social democracy slowly come to embrace the results of their *own* analysis and begin to understand the relationships between themselves and the institutions which mold their knowledge of the world they lived in.

II

The media class we teach is a sophomore course which is a required class for students in a new, experimental, teacher-preparation program. It comes after a semester overview of the historical, philosophical, and sociological foundations of education and an extended practicum experience in the schools, and it precedes courses in teaching methods and student teaching itself. The general purpose of the course is to sensitize students to television's educational power and its influence on children and youth, especially on the definitions of self, the set of values, and the social behaviors that children bring with them into classrooms.

As we have designed it, the course accomplishes three things. First, it introduces students to the history, technology, and aesthetics of television. Here they learn the "nuts and bolts" of what makes up television shows—how lighting, sets, camera, acting, and script all fit together on screen—as well as the distinctions among various television genres and the basic vocabulary needed to discuss this video world. Second, it leads these future teachers to understand and create curricula for *their* future students which will help them become active viewers of television, not just passive "couch potatoes." Third comes what is to us the most important component of the class: the cultivation in our students of a critical awareness of how television shapes attitudes regarding gender, race, class, and consumerism and what the consequences of these ideologies are for the culture. This third part is designed to encourage students to extend their understanding from the medium of television to the society at large with all of its social, economic, and cultural dynamics. This movement outward from the particular to the general has led us to organize the course on a sequence from advertising through news and children's programming to other genres like soaps, sitcoms, and primetime drama. The progress is from the more obviously manipulative and purposive to the more subtle, indirectly controlling shows which often mask themselves as "mere entertainment." The end purpose of the progression is to recognize that all commercial television is suffused with the hegemonic ideology of late 20th century capitalism and attempts to foreclose alternate points of view.

We designed the class to be interactive, keeping our lecturing to a minimum and emphasizing student participation. For example, most class periods turn around analyses of specific television programs that students themselves have selected, edited, and presented to their classmates. Presentations to the whole class are made by students individually, in pairs, or in small groups. When a group of students has a presentation, they have to meet outside of class to prepare their materials and ideas. We have found this not only encourages cooperative learning but also increases participation and a sense of community in the classroom itself. Presentations are not just lectures with students instead of professors talking at the class; rather, presentations are interactive, with a great deal of give and take between presenters and audience. Frequently, students write informal critiques, analyses, and evaluations of the presentations.

We have discovered that when we let students select and present the majority of the course materials to the class within a framework that we have initially set up, bolstered and informed by readings and our suggestions, they take the class more seriously, analyzing problems they believe are important and coming to conclusions that are truly theirs.

As for the class itself, we divide the term into four sections. The first is on advertising. We begin the first day by examining magazine advertisements for a variety of products like Revlon make-up, Budweiser beer, Dodge cars, Guess jeans, and so on, discussing them for their emotional appeals and social implications. By using still photographs we can focus on a fixed image rich in detail and on an accompanying text, both as yet unencumbered by the complexities of soundtracks and images in motion. Students register surprise at how dense and controlled *all* the details in the image are and how focused the ads are on shaping the viewers' emotions and consumption. This is a good way to start because it is relatively simple, is something that students can easily grasp, and can be analyzed in great detail in the short period of time offered by a class period. We provide some suggestions for how to analyze and discuss these ads and assign reading materials which will increase their understanding of how advertising shapes and manipulates. The class then spends two weeks selecting ads on television they want to analyze, recording them on VCRs, and bringing them to class for discussion. Class discussion focuses on the complexity of technical details with which advertisers carefully shape the response of their audience. By starting here, students are able to lay bare the commercial workings at the heart of television and not just recognize but truly accept that commercial nature of the medium. Moreover, this allows us to introduce the idea of commercialism and all that ideologically accompanies it as a central characteristic of the medium in America and to touch on the idea of television as a means by which the larger culture reproduces its consumerist ideology, gender and race positioning, and class distinctions.

The next section provides an overview of the basic television genres. In it, the class examines three broad areas: news and information; drama, including soap operas, police and medical shows, and primetime dramas; and entertainment, especially sitcoms, talk shows, MTV, and simulations such as "911." The students treat these broad areas in different ways. They begin by assuming that shows like news and information programs provide information about matters over which they have little control and, therefore, require little analysis and personal involvement (other than sports and weather, of course). The drama shows they view as being "serious" insofar as the latter deal with a personal perspective—as distinct from a social one—on problems such as violence, economic difficulty, AIDS, abortion, divorce, and so on. Finally, entertainment they perceive to be "just fun," something merely to pass one's time without need for reflection and without important consequences for viewers. Our comments in discussions challenge these preconceptions by helping the students to discover the highly problematic nature of their initial responses and to develop a more informed and nuanced reading of the agendas that underlie such television programming.

An unusual feature of our class is that we are working exclusively with a group of future public school teachers. Consequently, a significant section of the course looks not only at what is formally known as "children's television" but also at the shows children are in fact watching, many of which are included in the genres listed in the preceding paragraph. This section has a double purpose. The first is to get our students looking at and thinking about what *their* future students are watching today, most particularly how the culture of television shapes, even controls, children's behavior and desires. Second, our students explore what they have learned both by interviewing real children — they are taking a practicum the same semester as our course in which they work with children in local schools — and by creating exemplary lesson plans for using children's own experience of television in order to get them reflecting about television and their experiences with it.

The fourth and final section of this course moves outward intellectually; extending beyond the specific issues and genres examined heretofore, it begins to explore the relationship of television to the culture at large. It is at this point in the semester that we expand on the critical habits we have encouraged and explore the consequences of the specific conclusions the students have themselves developed concerning television's purposeful nature, connecting them to the larger social, economic, political, and cultural issues of America today. We find students are here willing to struggle with the more sophisticated, critical readings, ones using the more customary academic critical language, because they have begun to entertain the plausibility of the viewpoint those readings express.[2] By now, students are more ready to begin to recognize the educative and ideological power television has, to begin to look "through" the screen at the realities of the larger society, and to assess how television constructs a "view" of the world based on a highly "directive" ideology which is often at odds with their experience of the world.

III

Given the logical structure of the course described above, let's now turn to the pedagogical, especially the psychodynamic, character of our approach. We are deeply committed to avoiding the traditional power structure in the classroom which tends to impose the teacher's "knowledge" on the student. We prefer to mix readings, which we as a class discuss, with classroom presentations, again guided by our participation, and to keep lecturing as such to an absolute minimum. We believe that truly empowered students are ones who have developed themselves through a reflective, critical process of self-discovery. Therefore, in this course we wanted to use students' own experiences of television and to cultivate their reflection, investigation, and discussion of what they were seeing. However, our experience has shown us that, like thinking habits, old viewing habits die hard. This means that the first thing we must do in the course is get the students to step back from the screen, to develop some critical distance from what they see. That is why we start with a section on the aesthetics of television production, focusing on the particulars of what appears on the screen—lighting, composition, relationship of dialogue and image, soundtrack, all of those technical elements which make up television-as-viewed. We use advertising as our subject matter because it provides the smallest meaningful unit to examine. Because of their short length, ten to sixty seconds, and relatively freestanding character, ads provide a complete narrative which can be more comprehensively analyzed than a similar-length video clip taken from a longer show. An additional value in starting with advertisements is that they embody directly the commercial nature of the entire medium. When we explicitly introduce the ideology of commercialism here, students are willing to accept an analysis based on economic manipulation of the audience. After all, ads are about selling and buying things, and all viewers know that. This perspective, consequently, readily accepted at the beginning, extends naturally into the less obviously commercial genres as the course progresses.

Our next step is to take the viewing techniques which we have introduced and guide our students in applying them to shows they have habitually watched but are now encouraged to view in an unhabitual manner. The purpose here is to let students use their newly acquired understanding of television techniques to discover new meanings in what they watch and to make those new viewing skills habitual. We begin this section with news and information.

Because students already think of news as subject to debate—an attitude derived from high school history and journalism classes?—as potentially propaganda, as "ideological" (though they certainly would not use that term), it is easy to begin our discussion of television genres here. Students look at various news formats, such as local news, morning national news, evening news, and news specials, prepare analyses, including illustrative video clips, and bring them to class for general examination and discussion. In this process, they come to recognize how extensively the techniques used in making advertisements are used in making news shows. They also discover the various narrative structures used by both. This leads them to start talking about how "constructed" is what had initially appeared to be more "objective," and it lays open or exposes the biases—economic, social, and cultural—inherent even in such seemingly bias-free programming as news shows.

For example, in this last spring's class a student group presented and analyzed a video clip from ABC's national evening news showing a reporter standing in front of a open-air market in Sarajevo which he said had recently been shelled by besieging forces in the surrounding hills. The report included pictures of bodies and people mourning the casualties. In their analysis students began asking questions about the source of the clips on casualties because they detected a difference in picture quality between the reporter sequences and the casualty footage, demonstrating their new visual sensitivity as a basis for critiquing what they were being shown. A week later, they brought to class a follow-up story which suggested that the defenders of Sarajevo, knowing an American news crew was filming in the city, had *themselves* fired the mortar rounds into the crowded market. In spite of their growing visual sophistication, the students were, nonetheless, shocked not only by the city's defenders' cynical manipulation of the news but also by the news organization's construction of a "reality" which the newscast presented as definitive though it was, in fact, simply a fabrication. Most of the revelations our students experience are not this clear and dramatic, but this anecdote characterizes the growing critical awareness of how extensively television manipulates what students had previously taken to be more or less a straight-forward presentation of "truth."

In addition, we always insist that students include the associated advertisements in the analysis of whatever programs they have selected. They begin to talk about the visual flow of programming, where advertisement blends into news story which blends back into advertisement again, and so forth on and on, back and forth. They begin to recognize that there is a relationship between program, content, commerce, and audience. For instance, in the Sarajevo story, we as instructors introduced the question of whether Peter Jennings is selling us something in the same way that the preceding car commercial and succeeding fast food ad are selling us something. Students began to question what the difference is between the inserted casualty footage and the inserted advertisement. In this process of questioning we have found that narrative is a key element because it connects the dynamics of advertising with the dynamics of the news and makes both more than just a listing of "facts." When television tells us stories, aren't we in the audience expected to draw the "proper" moral, for instance, in the original Sarajevo news story, that the defenders are the "good guys" and those shelling civilians the "bad guys"?

In the next section, on drama, we explore more extensively the whole idea of narration, especially in a story told with a "moral," that is, with a "lesson" in the telling that the audience should "learn." In drama, we have tended to focus on soap operas and primetime police and medical shows like "NYPD Blue" and "ER." Since these shows tend to focus on an urban, diverse population, they are particularly instructive for our specific student population, most of whom come from homogeneous rural and small-town settings. Narrative allows us to introduce issues of gender, race, and class in an informal way and to discuss how television drama relies on stereotypes which disguise as much as they reveal the realities of contemporary life. At this point in the semester, we have found that students themselves begin to recognize spontaneously issues of stereotyping in the shows they have selected and to discuss the contradictions between what they see on the screen and what they experience in their lives. The seriousness of the issues highlighted by urban settings, issues like AIDS, violence, racism, sexism, social inequalities, and so on, encourages the students to treat those dramas seriously. They begin to think about these issues and many of them discover aspects of them in their own, quite different, personal circumstances. This is one of those Gramscian moments when one can use the very instrument of cultural hegemony to reveal and criticize that culture's ideological assumptions. Students often begin to see that a relationship does exist between what they see on television and what is going in their culture, and that television is neither just a "mirror" of that culture nor merely just a harmless escape. This growing recognition allows us to explore our third area and helps students see that "entertainment" may not be just entertainment.

To be frank, we have found the section on entertainment the most difficult to teach in the sense that students are least apt to recognize spontaneously that these shows are anything more than just a transient and ideologically free recreation. It appears to them that a show like "Home Improvement," for example, is merely an innocuous way to pass a half hour. Therefore, getting the students to recognize that sitcoms, simulations, and talk shows by and large also reveal the same attitudes about sexism, racism, and economic inequality that appear more explicitly in the advertisements, news, and drama shows becomes the main pedagogic issue we deal with in this section. Because drama and the various entertainment shows seem to reflect the common, everyday experience students have or imagine they might have in the circumstances depicted in the shows, we can connect the critical issues discussed in class to the larger society, thereby opening up possibilities in our final section, which we will discuss below.

A unique feature of our class is that since we are teaching future teachers, they have a compelling interest in studying "children's" television: Saturday-morning cartoons, after-school programming, and the array of shows on public television. In contrast to most media classes, therefore, we devote a whole unit to an examination of children's television. In our course, this is the turning point at which students really connect the more theoretical, analytical perspective of the first half of the class with the serious consequences in viewers' lives. Because they have been working with children in schools as part of a practicum that runs concurrently with our course, they have become increasingly aware of how powerful television is in the lives of children and of the disparities between television executives' and public officials' assertions that television is harmless entertainment and their experiences of children's language, free play, attitudes, and behavior in the classrooms they are observing. When our students begin to witness for themselves the influence such television characters as the Power Rangers or the (now-dated) Ninja Turtles have on recess activities, which often include violent behavior, the level of aggression their students sometimes exhibit towards them as teachers and toward each other, plus the general level of distractedness of the students they observe, the lesson sinks in. Now comes the opportunity to assign them the task of making up lesson plans for teaching children of the age they intend to teach about television. We find in the oral and written responses to this assignment that our students have begun to change their attitude toward television substantially. Television has become a problematic social force, not just harmless entertainment. Through the children, students find themselves compelled to reflect on their *own* standing in relation to television and to begin to consider television's place in contemporary American life.

The last three weeks of the semester we spend exploring the broad issues of the relationship of television to the culture at large. Here we find the students are more receptive to the Newcomb reader,[3] with its academic essays more explicitly critical of both television and society. Since by this point the students have themselves pointed out how much of advertising is problematic, how constructed apparently objective news is, and how exploitive children's television has become, they are prepared, at least, to entertain the possibility that these problems are a reflection of systemic cultural problems such as prejudice and inequities of wealth and power. Because they have begun to see the contradictions inherent in specific television programs and the operation of power and ideology, they are receptive to discussion of such contractions and issues of power and ideology on a broad level. It is at this point that we begin to introduce them to the formal language and approaches of academic social criticism. Students find that ideas they have generated themselves, especially those related to the broad concept of the contradictions of capitalism, have been systematically developed in a body of writings with specialized language which heretofore would have been meaningless as well as alienating to them. They begin to use terms like "capitalism," "hegemony," "alienation," and "class," as well as concepts related to discrimination based on gender, race, and class. Thus, we end the term at what could be considered the beginning: students are now open to giving serious thought to a formal, rigorous cultural critique of their experience and their environment. Unfortunately, we are not able to follow up with a second course that would cultivate this new awareness systematically. Still, we like to believe that we have made a beginning, for, as the ancient phrase went, "The beginning is more than half the whole."

Such, then, is our answer to the question we began with as we first conceptualized and taught this introductory course in television analysis. Essentially, that question was, How do you cultivate a progressive perspective in students whose background has habituated them in conventional views and whose institutional setting does not encourage critical thinking? This article presents what we have learned so far. It is not definitive, and we continue to change what we do as we learn from our students better ways to help them see the circumstances of their lives.

Notes

1. U.S. Department of Education, *Strong Families, Strong Schools* (Washington, D.C.: U.S. Government Printing Office, 1994–ERIC Document ED 371909). For an historical overview of the debate regarding television's influence on children's development, including various public commissions' reports, see Newton N. Minow and Craig L. LaMay, *Abandoned in the Wasteland: Children, Television, and the First Amendment* (New York: Hill and Wang, 1995).

2. It is at this point in the semester that we can use some of the more complex readings from Horace Newcomb's 5th edition of his *Television: The Critical View* (New York: Oxford University Press, 1994). Earlier in the course we used only a few of the essays from Newcomb's collection, instead assigning pairs of readings grouped around various topics from the much less formal and intellectually demanding reader created by William Barbour, *Mass Media: Opposing Viewpoints* (San Diego, CA: Greenhaven Press, 1994). For children's television, students read the mildly critical Edward L. Palmer analysis, *Television & America's Children: A Crisis of Neglect* (New York: Oxford University Press, 1988).

3. See note 2 above.

6

Interrupting Patriarchy

*Politics, Resistance, and Transformation
in the Feminist Classroom*

Magda Lewis

Editors' Notes: Taking us into her classroom, Lewis shows how she developed a feminist pedagogy of critical transformation out of student resistance to feminist politics. Through her stories, she explores the psychological, social, and sexual dynamics of the feminist classroom. Lewis offers a unique perspective of the gendered classroom and describes ways she subverted the status quo of interaction between women and men that reaffirmed women's subordination. These experiences helped her develop an interpretive framework for creating a counter-hegemony from her teaching practice. But Lewis suggests that we look at how our feminist practice/ politics can feel less threatening to students before we expect them to develop counter-hegemonic stances.

In Canada, the fall of 1989 marked a particularly hostile environment for women on university campuses. On my own campus the events surrounding our "NO MEANS NO" campaign drew national attention. "NO MEANS NO" was an educational campaign organized by the Gender Issues Committee of the undergraduate student government (Alma Mater Society) aimed at alerting young women, particularly first year women, to the forms and expressions of date rape. The reaction of a faction of the male students was to respond with a "sign campaign" that made explicit their belief that women's refusal of male sexual demands could appropriately be countered with violence ("No means tie me up") or with their own definitions of women's sexual deviance ("No means dyke"). To the extent that the signs were accompanied by active verbal threats and physical intimidation, many women experienced the threatening atmosphere as misogyny.

My campus was not on the only one experiencing what appeared to be an increasing backlash to a feminist presence inside the academy. As women academics across and between campuses shared stories of violation, more and more examples of misogyny surfaced. Our isolation and small numbers (women still comprise a very small fraction of academic faculty) precluded any possibility of collective action (Brodribb, 1987; McCormack, 1987). In the face of an academic community complicit in its complacency and unwilling to acknowledge its own oppressive practices born of the sexual subordination of women, we were atomized and held inside the private spaces of our own violations. And yet, despite the isolation of our struggles, we worked with our students to create an intellectually and emotionally supportive environment for them (Lewis, 1990a).

It was within this context that we witnessed with horror the spiraling momentum of woman-hating explode, in the early evening of December 6, 1989. Fourteen women at the Université de Montréal were massacred by a gun-wielding young man who had convinced himself that women, transposed in his own sad head into the phrase "you bunch of feminists," were the cause of his own personal misery.[1]

This incident focused, on several levels, my concerns about teaching and learning as a feminist in the academy. The historical context of our individual and collective experiences as intellectual women enabled me to see that what the media identified as the "idiosyncratic" madness of this young man actually reflected infinitely receding images of male power transformed into violence—a polished surface facing the mirror of masculine privilege. Because of our identification with a politic that makes explicit our critique of women's subordination as a function of masculine privilege, my students' and my own safety were in question. This was not the single act of a deranged mind, nor the outcome of peculiar conditions on that specific campus. That the events at the Université de Montréal could have happened on any campus in this country—indeed, any campus on this continent—became a tangible reality (Malette and Chalouh, 1990).

I am haunted by the image of young women—not unlike the women I teach—lined up against the wall, while their perplexed, perhaps helpless, male colleagues and male instructor vacated the classroom. I am haunted, too, by the words (reported in the media) of that young woman whose vain efforts to save herself and her women classmates were captured when she screamed at the gunman: "You have the wrong women; we are not feminists!"

The words "you have the wrong women; we are not feminists!" provides a backdrop for the question I raise: How might we bring about the social changes we desire without negating women's perspective on our reality, or turning it, yet one more time, into a self-perpetuated liability? More specifically, how might I create a feminist pedagogy that supports women's desire to wish well for ourselves when for many women the "good news" of the transformative powers of feminist consciousness turns into the "bad news" of social inequality and, therefore, a perspective and politics they want to resist. More than resistance, which, drawing on Willis (1977), I characterize as the struggles against social forms that are experienced as oppressive, transformation is the fusion of political perspective and practice. Transformation is the development of a critical perspective through which individuals can begin to see how social practices are organized to support certain interests, and the process whereby this understanding is then used as the basis for active political intervention directed toward social change with the intent to disempower relations of inequality.

In short, my agenda in this paper is to understand the basis from which I might fashion a viable feminist pedagogy of transformation out of student resistance, not to patriarchic meaning-making but to feminist politics.

Using my experiences in Foundations 490, in this article I continue to raise the dilemmas I face as a feminist teacher. I explore the possibilities and limits of feminist teaching and learning in the academy under conditions that directly contradict its intent (Lewis & Simon, 1986; Lewis, 1988a, 1989, 1990a). Foundations 490 is a sociology of education course I teach in the faculty of education at Queen's University. While it is not one of the core Women's Studies courses, it is cross-listed in the Women's Studies Programme Calendar. For this reason the course often draws students from a wide range of disciplines. The specific title of the course, "Seminar in Social Class, Gender and Race in Education," is explicitly descriptive of the course focus. In the course outline I tell students that the theoretical framework we are using draws on critical and feminist theory and method. More specifically, the course proposes to "examine and develop a critical understanding of the implications for children's educational experiences of the effects of social class background, sex/gender differences and racial background." It also proposes to "locate school practices as part of the larger social context within which schools exist."

The course format is a seminar which incorporates class discussion around assigned readings and student presentations. The class presentation component requires students to articulate the social meaning of a cultural artifact or practice of their choice. Students examine how the artifact or practice reflects the social/cultural context out of which it has arisen. The purpose of the assignment is to help students develop their skills in raising questions about our culture, which they had previously taken as a given. My intention is also that, through the exercise, they might see differently how sexism, racism, class differentiation, homophobia, and so on, are embedded in concrete cultural products and social practices.

I begin the course with an introductory lecture that outlines to the students what I intend that we take up during the coming term and the perspective from which my analysis proceeds. By doing this I attempt to incorporate many aspects of women's lives articulated within feminist politics.

The course is attended by both female and male students, although women tend to outnumber the men four to one. This, in part, is accounted for by the fact that student enrollment in faculties of education is still largely skewed in favor of women, who comprise approximately 70 to 75 percent of the undergraduate teacher education component. Because the majority of students in Foundations 490 are women, in this paper I use the general designation "student" to refer to women or to the students in general. When I refer to the men in the classroom I shall use the qualifier "male."

While in this paper I explore the context of my teaching practice and the politics of the classroom, it is not my intention to offer prescriptive and generic feminist teaching strategies abstracted from the particular situations of feminist classrooms. Although it might be possible to employ suggestive approaches, we cannot artificially construct pedagogical moments in the classroom to serve as moments of transformation toward a critical political perspective. Nor can we predict how such moments will be responded to when they arise in particular situations, given the personal histories of the students and instructors involved.

Rather, I believe questions about the politics of feminist teaching have most specifically to do with how we identify those pedagogical moments whose transformative power lies precisely in the understandings we bring to the gendered context of the classroom. Ruth Pierson (1987) provides a clear and comprehensive definition of feminism, which frames the intent of my own teaching from a feminist perspective:

> One identifiable characteristic of feminism across an entire spectrum of varieties has been the pursuit of autonomy for women. Integral to this feminist pursuit of independent personhood is the critical awareness of a sex/gender system that relegates power and autonomy to men and dependence and subordination to women. Feminists start from an insistence on the importance of women and women's experience, but a woman-centered perspective alone does not constitute feminism. Before a woman-centered perspective becomes a feminist perspective, it has to have been politicized by the experience of women in pursuit of self-determination coming into conflict with a sex/gender system of male dominance. From a feminist perspective the sex/gender system appears to be a fundamental organizing principle of society and for that reason it becomes a primary object of analysis. (p. 203)

From this perspective I raise the psychological, social, and sexual dynamics of the feminist classroom as a site where, I believe, the political struggle over meaning must be seen as the focus of our pedagogical project. It is a context in which a serious intrusion of *feminist pedagogy* must concern itself, as Rachel Blau DuPlessis (1985) suggests, not with urging our women students to "resent the treatment of [their] sex and plead for its rights" (p. 33)—a project that acts to reaffirm women's subordination and encourage our exploitation—but to examine and question self-consciously the conditions of our own meaning-making and to use it as the place from which to begin to work toward change.

In taking up the psychological, social, and sexual dynamics of the feminist classroom, in this paper I propose to examine the violence/negotiation dichotomy environment as a feature of women's educational experience. In this context, I share the strategies I employ in specific instances as a feminist teacher to subvert the status quo of classroom interaction between women and men. Finally, in the conclusion I suggest a specific framework that articulates the terms of feminist teaching.

Theoretical Framework

In the largely unchallenged practices of the school setting marked by patriarchic privilege (Corrigan, 1987), for women the dynamics of contestation born of knowledge are more complex than is often implied in the resistance literature. By paying close attention to practices in the classroom, forms of discourse, directions taken in discussion, the subtleties of body language, and so on, it is clear that, for women, a dichotomy between desire and threat is reproduced and experienced inside the classroom itself.

The salience of this dichotomy for women is suggested by Kathleen Rockhill (1987) in her powerful and moving article, "Literacy as Threat/Desire: Longing to be SOMEBODY," in which she articulates women's contradictory reality as an educational dilemma. For the women in Rockhill's study, the knowledge and power made potentially available through becoming literate contradictorily also repositioned them in such a way that it threatened familial, conjugal, and ultimately economic relations. Rockhill explains:

> It is common today for education to be ideologically dressed as the pathway to a new kind of romance for women, the romance of a "career," a profession, a middle-class way of life; the image is one of a well-dressed woman doing "clean" work, important work. As such, it feeds her yearning, her desire, for a way out of the "working class" life she has known (Steedman, 1986). It is precisely because education holds out this promise for women that it also poses a threat to them in their everyday lives. This is especially true for women in heterosexual relationships when their men feel threatened by the images of power (independence and success) attached to education. (p. 315)

In the feminist classroom, the contradiction that women experience is compounded by the way in which feminist politics challenges the everyday lives they have learned to negotiate.

The complexities of student resistance to the intentions of schooling have been documented before, and indeed such accounts provide much of the data for the theoretical framework of critical pedagogy. Paul Willis's classic work, *Learning to Labour* (1977), influenced by the theoretical work of Bowles and Gintis, Althusser, Bourdieu and Passeron, and Gramsci, was one of the first. Willis's study dealt exclusively with the experiences of male students. He included women only in their relations as girl friends and mothers. In this context, it is interesting to note the irony of the title of the more recent book by

Dale Spender and Elizabeth Sarah, *Learning to Lose* (1980), a study of the experiences of girls in school.

In its classic form, critical pedagogy emphasizes that student resistance to the experiences of institutionalized education is forged from the contradictions they perceive between the dominant discourse of school knowledge on the one hand and their own lived experiences of subordination and violation on the other. According to resistance theory, students struggle to mark themselves off against the dominant discourse of the school through the enactment of practices that reaffirm and validate their subjectivities as specifically classed, raced, and gendered social actors.

It is my explicit intent in the classroom to raise with students issues of social relations from a critical perspective. But I am also a feminist who has worked for many years in feminist politics across a variety of sites. My family life, my involvement with grassroots community organizations, and my intellectual work are informed in concrete ways by the politics of feminist analysis. By extension, the politics that informs my everyday life infuses my relations with students, generates the readings for the course, and suggests my classroom teaching style and practice. Yet my frustrations as a feminist teacher arise significantly from the extent to which critical thinking on transformative pedagogical practices fails to address the specifics of women's education as simultaneously a site of desire and threat.

Based on my own experiences, I know that a feminist perspective could offer understandings the students might develop and bring to bear on their own experiences (Lather, 1988). Yet I also realize that attending to feminist politics and cultural critique in the classroom requires difficult emotional work from them and from me. I know that new understandings are often experienced painfully, and that lives are transformed.

All of this has happened in Foundations 490. Yet, the forms through which such transformations have taken place are not those that I anticipated—or perhaps hoped for. As a teacher and a feminist I share the hope for the promise of education as a political project: That through the offer of a theoretical framework—analysis and critique—students would eagerly join in my enthusiasm to work for social change in their personal and public lives. Clearly there are times when women immediately embrace the intentions of feminist teaching because it helps them make a different sense of their experiences. But just as often students struggle with these new understandings as they explore the space between the public and theoretical agenda of the course and the privacy of their everyday lives, where complex negotiations across gender often take their most salient form.

In the academy, women find themselves inside institutions whose practices and intentions are historically designed to keep them outside its concrete and theoretical frames. For women students, negotiating masculine content and practices often means that they have to absorb as well as struggle to survive the violations of their subordination. My students often find more simple and, therefore, more powerful words through which to express my meaning. The legacy of the violations women experience in the academy are apparent in the following conversations:

> I don't speak in class anymore. All this professor ever talked about was men, what they do, what they say, always just what's important to men. He, he, he is all I ever hear in class. He wasn't speaking my language. And whenever I tried to speak about what was important to me, whenever I tried to ask questions about how women fit into his scheme all I got was a negative response. I always felt I was speaking from inside brackets, like walls I couldn't be heard past. I got tired of not being heard so I stopped speaking altogether.

> I often tried to bring up examples of famous women in class because I thought it was important that people should acknowledge that women had done some things too. But no one ever knew who I was talking about. There was this assumption that if someone was a woman she couldn't possibly have done anything famous. The most important thing that happened to me in high school was that one of my history teachers had a picture of Agnes Mcphail pinned above the blackboard in the classroom. We never talked about it directly but for me that became a symbol of a woman. Sometimes I got really disgusted in some of my classes but I would think of that picture in that history class and that helped me to feel less alienated.

> In history we never talked about what women did; in geography it was always what was important to men. The same in our English class, we hardly ever studied women authors. I won't even talk about math and science . . . I always felt that I didn't belong . . . sometimes the boys would make jokes about girls doing science experiments. They always thought they were going to do it better and it made me really nervous. Sometimes I didn't even try to do an experiment because I knew they would laugh if I got it wrong. Now I just *deaden* myself against it, so I don't hear it any more. But I feel really alienated. My experience now is one of total silence. Sometimes I even wish I didn't know what I know.

For me, as a feminist teacher, such statements are not only painful but revealing. The remarks suggest that the politics of my teaching should focus not on teaching women what we already know but on finding ways of helping all of us articulate the knowledge we gain from our experience.

As a beginning point I agree with the claim of Giroux and Simon (1988):

> We are not concerned with simply motivating students to learn, but rather *establishing the conditions of learning* that enable them to locate themselves in history and to interrogate the adequacy of that location as both a pedagogical and political question. (p. 3, emphasis added)

Yet a feminist pedagogy cannot stop here. For women, the cultural, political, and ultimately historical discourse of the everyday, the present, and the immediate are conditions of learning marked by the varied forms of patriarchic violence (Brookes, 1988; Belenkey, Clinchy, Goldberger, & Tarule, 1986; McMahon, 1986). Pedagogy, even radical pedagogy, does not easily translate into an education that includes women if we do not address the threat to women's survival and livelihood that a critique of patriarchy in its varied manifestations confronts.

The dynamics of the classroom context when students engage a feminist analysis presents the most challenging aspects of feminist teaching (Lewis, 1988a). In what follows I explore the psychological, social, and sexual aspects of this context.

Psychological Dynamics in the Feminist Classroom

For women, tension in the feminist classroom is often organized around our historically produced nurturing capacity as a feature of our psychologically internalized role as caretakers (Lewis, 1988b). The following example is a case in point. Recently, in reference to a set of class readings dealing with peace education, my introductory presentation spoke to the connections between patriarchy, violence, and political economy. As I finished, one of the first students to speak was a young woman. She said, "As you were speaking I was wondering and worrying about how the men in the room were feeling. What you said made sense to me, but I felt uncomfortable about how the men took it." A couple of other women nodded their agreement. Such a protective posture on the part of women on behalf of men is a common drama played out in many classrooms.

Similar responses to feminist critique are not specific to mixed-gender classrooms. The absence of men in the classroom does not significantly diminish the psychological investment women are required to make in the emotional well-being of men—an investment that goes well beyond the classroom into the private spaces of women's lives, which cannot easily be left at the classroom door. The response women bring to feminist politics/analyses arises from women's social/political location within patriarchic forms, which requires that men be the focus of women's attentions. Examples range from general claims that men are also isolated and contained by patriarchy in what is required of them within the terms of masculinity, to more specific references to personal family relations aimed at exempting intimate male relations from the general population of men. The sharing of household duties is often used as an example, although the articulation of details of this shared housework is often vague. Young women growing up in physically violent and sexually violating homes know a more brutal side of the caretaking imperative.[2]

Whether or not men are bodily present in the classroom, women carry the parameters of patriarchic meaning-making as a frame from within which we struggle to articulate our own interests. How women live this experience is not specific to mixed-gender classrooms. While it is my observation that the practice of a woman-as-caretaker ideology is more obvious in the presence of men, this ideology holds sway whether or not men are present as long as women believe their interests to be served by maintaining existing relations.

This formulation is not intended to subsume the experiences of all women and men under seamless, hegemonic constructs articulated through dominant expressions of femininity/masculinity. I use Alison Jaggar's (1983) formulation of Gramsci's notion of hegemony: A concept "designed to explain how a dominant class maintains control by projecting its own particular way of seeing social reality so successfully that its view is accepted as common sense and as part of the natural order by those who in fact are subordinated to it" (p. 151). In this respect, hegemony is accomplished through an ongoing struggle over meaning not only against, but for the maintenance of, power. Lesbians and gay men experience the social constructs of femininity/masculinity differently than women and men whose emotional and psychic investment is in heterosexual relationships. However, especially in professional schools, where students' aspirations for future employment often govern their willingness to challenge the status quo, pressures to conform to the dominant social text are shared by lesbians and heterosexual women alike (Khayatt, 1987). Because lesbians and gay men often remain voiceless within such classroom dynamics, the relations between the women and men in the classroom remains a site that supports only practices that construct women's social acceptability as caretakers of men.

In the mixed-gender classroom, much of the caretaking takes the form of hard-to-describe body language displayed as a barely perceptible "moving toward"; a not-quite-visible extending of the hand; a protective stance accomplished through eye contact. However, as the young woman's question of concern has shown, just as often it is explicitly articulated. In the feminist classroom, such caretaking responses on the part of women toward men are ones that, as feminist teachers, we easily recognize and anticipate. We must choose words carefully and negotiate our analyses with the women students in ways that will not turn them away from the knowledge they carry in their experiences.

Following the young woman's comments, many of the men seemed to feel that what she said vindicated their feelings of discomfort with the way in which I was formulating the issues. Some of the men expressed this through verbal support of the woman's concern over their emotional well-being. They showed a strong inclination to redirect the discussion toward notions of world violence as a *human* and not a gendered problem. By doing so, the men attempted to reappropriate a speaking space for themselves, which they saw to be threatened by my analysis. Even more troublesome for me was the pleasure some of the men seemed to take in encouraging women to take up the caretaking on their behalf and in how the women seemed to be brought up against one another in the debate that followed. The question of whether or not feminist critique constituted a confrontational stance by women against men was the substance of the debate between the women and the men and among the women. Some of the men offered verbal support for women who agreed with them and a rebuttal of those who did not. However, the more subtle forms of pleasure-taking are difficult to describe. We do not have language that can adequately express the social meaning of the practice of relaxing back into one's chair, with a barely there smile on one's face while eyes are fixed on the object of negation. One of the reasons feminist films are a source of exceptionally powerful critique is because they can display how violation works at the level of the non-verbal (Lewis, 1990b). Yet such practices are unmistakable in their intent. The non-verbal is a social language that women—and all culturally marginal groups—have learned to read well and that does its sad work on women's emotions.

That such a dynamic should develop among the students was not a surprise. I know that, within the terms of patriarchy, women have had no choice but to care about the feelings of men. Women know that, historically, not caring has cost us our lives: intellectually, emotionally, socially, psychologically, and physically. I see this played out over and over again in my classes, and in every case it makes women recoil from saying what they really want to say and simultaneously leaves men reassured about their right to speak on behalf of us all.

For me, this dynamic presented a pedagogical dilemma. How could I question particularities of our present social organization, which requires women to work as caretakers of men not only in economic/material relations but in emotional/psychological ones as well? Furthermore, how was I to do this in ways that did not reproduce the women's strong inclination to protect the men from what was *felt* to be an indictment of men in general and the men in the classroom in particular? Specifically, how could I help them focus on social organizational practices rather than on the man sitting next to them in the classroom?

I asked them to think of instances when we might expect men to reciprocate for women the kind of caretaking practices and ego support that women are expected to extend on behalf of men. Most specifically, I asked the women if they had ever been in the company of a male friend/partner/family member/stranger who, upon seeing our discomfort at the common public display of misogyny in such examples as billboards, had ever offered support for how uncomfortable and violated such displays must make us feel. By asking students to focus on the personal, I felt that it might be possible to reposition the women and men in a social configuration that did not take a gendered hierarchy and its attendant practices for granted. Not only the women, but the men as well, admitted that they had never had such an experience. More to the point, there was general agreement that the possibility had never even occurred to them.

Through our discussion, it became clear that as a collective social practice, for men, attentiveness to other than one's self is largely a matter of choice, whereas for women, it has been a socially and historically mandated condition of our acceptability as women. This provided, for some of the students in the class, a moment of critical reflection and transformation. It also offered a framework from which to envision a set of social relations not based fundamentally on inequality. For men such transformation often appears as a willingness to listen. Less eager to talk, they sometimes acknowledge that they can see themselves on the privileged side of the gender divide and admit that they had not previously given it a lot of thought. These acknowledgements are often fairly brief and to the point: "I had never thought of it that way" is a common response. Whether or not men carry their new understanding into their public and private lives outside the classroom is unclear. If they do, they have not shared it with me. For women, transformation often means a more active process. At times, younger women have asked to bring male friends to the class with them. More frequently, students have reported that they have asked their male friends or partners to read some of the course material. And some women have reported major changes in their family life, either in terms of renegotiated practices—mostly pertaining to household responsibilities—or in a decision to end a relationship. I do not want to suggest that every student in every class experiences these transformations. Progress is slow and often tentative as students struggle with the implications of their new understanding.

By shifting our focus from the topic of discussion (the political economy and masculine forms of world violence) and refocusing on the dynamics in the classroom at that moment, we made it possible to ask what cultural/political forms might articulate caretaking as a reciprocal process between women and men. This teaching strategy is central to my pedagogical agenda: identifying the moment when students might be most receptive to uncovering how they are invested in their own meaning-making practices.

Social Dynamics in the Feminist Classroom

For many students, the social context of the feminist classroom is another sphere of tension. For the women students, the content and processes of feminist curricula and teaching can result in the class version of consciousness raising. "Feminist method," says Catharine MacKinnon (1983), "is consciousness raising:"

> the collective critical reconstitution of the meaning of women's social experience, as women live through it. . . . Consciousness raising . . . inquires into an intrinsically social situation, into that mixture of thought and materiality which is women's sexuality in the most generic sense. It approaches its world through a process that shares its determination: women's consciousness, not as individual or subjective ideas, but as a collective social being. . . . The process is transformative as well as perceptive, since thought and thing are inextricable and reciprocally constituting of women's oppression, just as the state as coercion and the state as legitimizing ideology are indistinguishable, and for the same reason. The pursuit of consciousness becomes a form of political practice. (p. 255)

Reading Catharine MacKinnon has convinced me that the politic of consciousness raising has earned a bad name precisely because it is a profoundly effective practice. There is a long history to the fear of women coming together and, in that space, sharing the personal stories that become metaphorical bases for generating a theory of women's subordination (Daly, 1978). The dominant forms of discourse are aimed hegemonically at preventing women from engaging in discussions that lead toward consciousness raising; the threat of social sanctions defuse the vitality of storytelling. Telling our stories of violation and subordination in the presence of those whose advantages are highlighted and challenged by such sharing, or doing so in the presence of those who hold the discursive power to subvert the act of consciousness raising as a feminist method is, for many women, a contradictory outcome of their experiences in the feminist classroom.

I believe the following exchange demonstrates this point well. Recently, a student was making a class presentation on the topic of violence against women. A few minutes after the beginning of her presentation, a frustrated young man demanded to know why we had to talk about women and men all the time, and why the presenter did not offer "the other side of the story." This example confirms other experiences indicating that students, particularly those who benefit from the present social arrangements, often find it difficult to engage in the self-reflection required to question the unequal and violent social relations in which we ourselves are social actors.

As a feature of classroom dynamics, the unpacking and uncovering of deeply submerged social practices of domination/entitlement experienced by the "other" as subordination/oppression, which we carry in and on our gendered bodies, in our verbal expressions, in the privilege (or lack of it) of having choice, can itself become another source for experiences of oppression. For women, as for other subordinate groups, it is the fact of "knowing" that is seen to be an act of insubordination; exposing that knowledge, speaking it in public space, claiming language through which to articulate our knowledge, refusing to believe that the dominant discourse speaks for all, as it speaks on behalf of patriarchic interests, is used as the justification for continued violation.

In part, patriarchy disempowers women by marginalizing their experiences of violation in an ongoing discourse that legitimates only those ways of making sense or the telling of only those kinds of stories that do not make men "look bad" (MacKinnon, 1987, p. 154). The usage of language, for example, which exchanges "wife battering" with "family violence," as a way to redirect our focus away from masculine practices is a case in point.

One way male students sometimes wish to displace the sense women make of our experience is to refocus the discussion in directions that are less disquieting for them. In the instance mentioned above, I understood the young man's demand—the tone of his voice left no doubt that it was a demand—to be an attempt to redirect the discussion away from his own social identity as a male who, whether he acknowledges it or not, benefits from the culturally, legally, and politically encoded social relations of patriarchy (MacKinnon, 1987). Yet men can no more deny the embodiment of their masculine privilege than any of us can deny the embodiment of our entitlement if we are White, economically advantaged, heterosexual, able bodied, and carrying the valued assets of the privilege of Euro-American culture. As is suggested by Biddy Martin and Chandra Mohanty (1986), "the claim to a lack of identity or positionality is itself based on privilege, on a refusal to accept responsibility for one's implication in actual historical or social relations, or a denial that positionalities exist or that they matter, the denial of one's own personal history and the claim to a total separation from it" (p. 208). Furthermore, to the extent that sexism, racism, and social class inequalities represent social systems within which we either appropriate or struggle against particular personal relations, those who embody positions of privilege are often not attracted to an articulation of their interests in the terms required by self-reflexivity.

On this occasion, I judged that, by providing for the possibility of self-reflexive critique, I might avert the tendency of such debates to degenerate into expressions of guilt and victimization that would destroy the creative potential of a feminist political discourse that speaks not only to women but to men as well. I also felt that how I presented my response was crucial. Whatever my response was, it had to be possible for women to see it as a model for how they might also take up similar challenges to their own meaning-making in ways other than to demand their right to do so—precisely the point of debate. My challenge was to create the possibility for students to be self-reflexive.

The young man's demand for the "other side" of the story about men's violence against women created the space I was looking for. In classrooms, as in other social/political spaces, women and men come together unequally (Lewis & Simon, 1986). In such a context, a pedagogical approach that fails to acknowledge how such inequality silences serves to reinforce the powerlessness of the powerless. I knew from my own experience that under such circumstances, asking women to "speak up" and intervene on their own behalf would have reproduced exactly that marginalization that the young man's demand was intended to create. Clearly, I needed to employ another strategy.

The power of teaching as dramatic performance cannot be discounted on this particular occasion. Following the question, I allowed a few moments of silence. In these few moments, as the question and the dynamics of the situation settled into our consciousness, the social history of the world was relived in the bodies of the women and men around the table. What is the "other side of the story" about violence against women! What could the women say? Faced with the demand to articulate their *reality in terms not of their own making,* the women visibly shrank into their chairs; their breathing became invisible (Rockhill, 1987a). In contrast, whether I imagined it or not, it seemed to me that the men sat more upright and "leaned into" the response that began to formulate in my head. It seemed clear to me that the young man's objections to the woman's presentation constructed women as objects of practices which were experienced by him as unproblematic; the threat of physical violence is not one which most men experience on a daily basis. By objectifying women through his question, he reinforced male privilege. I needed to find a way of repositioning us—women and men—in such a way that the young man had no options but to face his own social location as problematic.

The stage was set for dramatic performance. Reassuring the young man that indeed he was right, that "other sides" of issues need to be considered whenever possible, I wondered if *he* would perhaps be the one who could tell us about the "other side" of violence against women. My memory of this moment again focuses on the breath: the men's as it escaped their bodies and the women's as it replenished them.

Turning the question away from the women in the class created the self-reflexive space that I believed could truly challenge the men in the class to take up not women's subordination but their own positions of privilege. Given the social realities of violence against women, he was no more able to answer his own question than it might have been possible for the women to do so. At the same time, it remained for him to tell us why he couldn't answer his own question. He found himself speechless. This time the silence that followed reversed the order of privilege to name the social realities we live. The young man's failure to find a salient way of taking up the issue he had raised made it possible for the young woman to continue with her presentation without challenge to her fundamental right to do so.

The incident ended at this point and the class presentation proceeded. Reflecting on my own practice in this instance, I cannot deny that my politics embraced and supported the struggle for women's autonomy and self-determination. Working with women to create the space for our voice is fundamental to this politic. Whether the young man experienced transformation or was simply intimidated into silence was something that required sorting out. I was willing to let him undertake the hard work of doing so for himself. If I had silenced him I could only hope that perhaps the experience would provide him with a deeper understanding of an experience women encounter every day. That the incident was experienced by the women in ways that signalled a moment of possibility for them is captured by a young woman who came over to where I was distractedly picking up my papers after the long three-hour class. She lightened the load of my exhaustion with the announcement that she wanted to be a sociologist and a feminist and would I tell her "how to become it." Both her naivete and mine embarrassed us into shared laughter; but then such fleeting moments of embrace are sometimes all we have, it seems to me, to collect ourselves and move on. Such experiences reveal the feminist classroom as profoundly relevant to women's lives.

Sexual Dynamics in the Feminist Classroom

Finally, the sexual dynamics of mixed-gender classrooms are complex and often contradictory. Particularly for younger women, at times still caught in the glare of sexual exploration and identification, the feminist classroom can feel threatening. The following example is a case in point.

Recently, during the introductory lecture I use as a way of framing the seminar session, I was addressing the educational concerns over the low number of women in mathematics and science programs. On this occasion, trying to concretize the issues for the students, I asked them to indicate, by a show of hands, which of them were preparing to be math and science teachers. A number of students raised their hands. As might be expected, many of those who raised their hands were men. However, a number of women also raised their hands. A "guffawed" and embarrassed laughter rose from the back corner of the room after a young man whispered a comment to a young woman who had raised her hand.

I do not generally make use of or support embarrassment as a pedagogical strategy. In this instance, however, I felt certain that I knew what the laughter was about and wanted to capture the moment as a concrete example of exactly the issues I was raising. I requested that the young man tell us what he had said. He resisted; I insisted. The use of institutional power, I believe, should not always be viewed as counterproductive to our politics. Feminism is a politic that is both historical and contingent on existing social relations. I had no problem justifying the use of my institutional power to create the possibility for privilege to face itself and own its violation publicly. Using power to subjugate is quite different from using power to liberate. The young man complied. He told us that he had whispered to the young woman that perhaps she had had a sex change.

The assumed prerogative to pass such commentary on women's choices of career and life possibilities is not, of course, new to any of us. However, in the feminist classroom such commentary and attendant laughter become overtly political issues that can be taken up as instances of gender politics. I used the incident as an example of the kind of academic environment created for women when such interactions are not treated as problematic. In doing so, I was aware that both the women and the men experienced various degrees of discomfort. Many of the men and some of the women insisted that I was making too much of an innocent joke, while many of the women and none of the men, as far as I could tell, sat quietly with faces flushed. In thinking about how I approach my teaching, I can recall the salient details of this example to understand how gender politics can be transformed into sexual dynamics in the classroom. Not only gender, but sexuality is a deeply present organizing principle in the classroom and one which enters into the dynamics of how we come together as women and men in pursuit of shared meaning.

The production of shared meaning is one of the ways we experience deeply felt moments of psycho-sexual pleasure, whether across or within gender. Yet, in a patriarchic culture, women and men can find the articulation of shared meaning profoundly elusive, and the desire for pleasure in conflict with mutual understanding.

While women have always found support in separate women's communities, education cells, political movements, work, and so on, these sites of solidarity have usually existed outside of the dominant male culture—a culture of which, we cannot forget, women are also an integral part. Social, political, and economic relations are articulated through the personal/collective experience we have of the world. Feminist politics insist on using these experiences as the lens through which to look at the barely perceptible yet tenacious threads that hold the social forms and forces in place. For women who refuse subordination, who refuse to pretend that we don't know, standing against these social forces has not only economic and political consequences but psycho/sexual ones as well. bell hooks (1989) comments:

> Sexism is unique. It is unlike other forms of domination—racism or classism—where the exploited and oppressed do not live in large numbers intimately with their oppressors or develop their primary love relationships (familial and/or romantic) with the individuals who oppress and dominate or share in the privileges attained by domination. . . . [For women] the context of these intimate relationships is also the site of domination and oppression. (p. 130)

This dynamic is seldom, if ever, talked about in the feminist classroom, and yet, it explains the conflicting emotional and analytic responses women have to the content of the course.

Exploring the sexual parameters of the conditions under which women are required to undertake their intellectual work is crucial. Finding examples is not hard; relating them is. It is with difficulty that I cite specific examples, and then only briefly, because of my own complex emotions associated with writing these words and having them stand starkly, darkly on the page to be read and reread; knowing that stories of violation violate at each retelling. These stories are not lightly told nor lightly received; they are often related in the privacy of my office. One woman's books disappeared (an event reminiscent of the one related in Janice Radway's *Reading the Romance,* 1984); another, alerted by the words, "maybe you should be reading this instead," had a copy of a pornographic magazine flung at her as she sat reading her course material; and yet another was told, as a "joke" at a social gathering, that to "celebrate" the completion of the course she would be "rewarded" by being "raped" so she could "get it out of her system" and return to her "old self." The monitoring and banning of what women read is shown in these examples to be closely associated with demands for women to conform to a particular version of male-defined sexuality. While the above may represent especially harsh examples, the antagonistic relationship drawn between women's desire for knowledge and our embodiment as sexually desirable human beings is an issue that lies always just below the surface in the classroom.

For many women, a feminist worldview is deeply incorporated at the level of everyday practice. Yet, we need to be aware that by requiring women to challenge masculine constructs—as I had done in the classroom example cited above—we also require them to break with the dominant phallocentric culture. While as feminist teachers we might believe that such a break may offer the only possibilities for the resolution of this conflict, we must be aware that for many women the concrete possibility of doing so is difficult to contemplate. As

Claire Duchen, quoted in Rowbotham (1989), suggests, "the tailoring of desire to the logic of politics is not always possible or acceptable" (p. 85).

Feminist critique of phallocentric culture is at once fundamentally necessary for and profoundly disruptive of the possibilities for shared meaning across gender, leaving women vulnerable to what Sheila Radford-Hill (1986) has analyzed as the potential "betrayal" and "psychosexual rejection" of women by men (pp. 168–169), attended by more or less severe economic and political consequences. None of this dynamic escapes women's awareness. "The personal is political" is not just a useful organizing concept, it is also a set of material enactments that display and reflect back how the political is personal.

As Susan Griffin (1981) suggests, a woman knows that "over and over again culture tells her that men abandon women who speak too loudly, or who are too *present*" (p. 211). Coupled with the strong cultural message that "her survival in the world depends on her being able to find a man to marry" (p. 211), many young women in the feminist classroom find themselves caught in the double bind of needing to speak and to remain silent at the same time in order to guarantee some measure of survival. While the salience of this politic is more immediately obvious in the case of heterosexual women, woman-identified (Rich, 1986, p. 57) women who do not comply, at least minimally, with acceptable forms of sexual self-presentation do not escape the consequences of marginalization and exclusion. For all women in professional schools specifically, compliance with particular displays of femininity can mean the difference between having or not having a job.

As women and men struggle over establishing and articulating shared meanings, we need to notice the reality that, for many women, such struggles often take place in the context of deeply felt commitments reverberating with emotional psycho/sexual chords and attended by the material conditions of unequal power. While perhaps these relations are lived most deeply not in the classroom itself but in those private spaces lived out between women and men beyond the classroom, for women, course content can be instrumental in raising these relations as questions.

The following is an example of how one woman took up these struggles in her private life. After a particular encounter in the classroom regarding the issue of voice/discourse discussed in the context of who has the right to name whether or not a joke is funny, she wrote me the following note:

> The articles at this point in the course . . . have plunged me into the next phase of my feminist awareness, which is characterized by anger and a pervading sense of injustice. . . . The "feminist" anger that I feel is self-perpetuating. I get angry at the discrimination and stereotyping I run up against so I blame the patriarchal society I live in in particular, and men in general. Then I think about women who feel that feminism is unnecessary or obsolete and I get angry at that subset of women. Then I think about the good guys like Mike and

Cam and I get angry because the patriarchal society biases the way I think about these men, simply because they're members of a particular gender (sex class?). Then I think about men who stereotype and discriminate against women and criticize us for being "overly sensitive" when we get uptight or even just point out or suggest humanistic egalitarian changes that are good and smart and I get REALLY angry because I realize that they're all a bunch of (expletives deleted) [sic]. . . . One of the most difficult aspects of this anger is that I become frustrated and impatient with people who can't see the problems or don't see the urgent need for solutions. (I am writing) a lot during this time because I often can't communicate orally with people who don't at least respect my feminist views.

hooks states that feminist works that focus on strategies women can use to speak to males about male domination and change are not readily available, if they exist at all. Yet women have a deep longing to share feminist consciousness with the men in their lives (the 'good guys'), and together work at transforming their relationships. hooks goes on to say that "concern for this basic struggle should motivate feminist thinkers to talk and write more about how we relate to men and how we change and transform relationships with men characterized by domination" (p. 130).

Yet despite their desire genuinely to share the meanings they have drawn from their experiences, for young women in the feminist classrooms, phallocentric myth-making often collides with the theoretical agenda of the course. Phallocentric myths are those beliefs that continue to marginalize women through the process of naturalizing politically created gender inequalities: "Women are not in positions of decision and policymaking because they don't want to be"; "Everybody has equal opportunity to become school principal. Women choose not to be because they like teaching better"; "If abused and battered women don't leave their partners it is because they have deviant personalities"; "Women who are raped did something wrong"; "Boys are better at math, girls are better at reading"; "Women who do math are not really women"; "Jokes, sexually offensive to women, are funny"; "There are no women in history because they didn't do anything"; "Women like staying home with children"; "Men share equally in housework"; and so on. I have heard some version of all of these statements in the classroom. While the men might express a comfortable indignation at such beliefs, they don't often understand what practices are required of them to change how they live their lives. For example, one man recently told the class that he supports his wife's career by "babysitting" the children while she goes to work. It is precisely this imbalance of power that constructs the women's silence, suppressed behind embarrassed laughter.

The pedagogical implications of such gender relations in the feminist classroom must be taken seriously if we are to understand how and why women students might wish both to appropriate and yet resist feminist theoretical and political positions that aim to uncover the roots of our deeply misogynist culture and give legitimacy to women's desires and dreams of possibility. As feminist teachers we need to look closely at the psycho/sexual context within which we propose the feminist alternative and consider the substance of why women may genuinely wish to turn away from the possibilities it offers.

Women know through experience that the threat to our sexuality is a way of controlling our political activities. In her review of Spender (1982), Pierson (1983) points out that there is a long history to the process of displacing women's legitimate political and intellectual critique and struggles into distorted evaluations of women's sexuality as a form of social control hammered into place by the material conditions of women's lives. The meaning that patriarchy has assigned to the term "lesbian" has resulted in its use as a pejorative term to undermine the serious political work in which women as women have been engaged in resistance to a set of social relations marked by patriarchic domination. The misogyny of such a designation violates all women at all points of the heterosexual/lesbian continuum (Rich, 1986). Clearly "the regulation of speaking and silence" (Walkerdine, 1985) is not just achieved through concrete regulatory practices, but also through the emotional, psychic, and sexual sphere—articulated through the practices of patriarchic myth-making—that combine in our hearts and heads to silence us from within. Given the terms of such social conditions it would be a surprise, indeed, if women did not feel the constraints of contradictory choices and conflicting interests.

The power of patriarchic social controls on women's sexuality does not escape even (or perhaps especially) very young women. For example, within a recent three-week period, two separate groups of elementary and high school students were invited to participate in different events sponsored by the faculty where I teach. The first was a forum on women and education, attended by 150 students, at which the guest speaker, Dale Spender, presented an address entitled "Young Women in Education: What Happens to Girls in Classrooms." Three weeks later, a dramatic presentation by a feminist acting troupe, The Company of Sirens,[3] presented an upbeat production called *The Working People's Picture Show,* dealing with such issues as women in the work force, day care, unionism, and sexual harassment. The question period that followed each event was telling. In each case the young women's concerns were well demonstrated by the almost identically phrased question aimed at the presenters, who were seen as the embodiment of feminist critique: "Are you married and do you have children?" I don't believe this was a theoretical question. For many young women the concern about the compatibility of feminist politics with marriage and family is the concrete realization that making public what our feminist consciousness reveals about women's experiences of patriarchy can result in potential limits on desire. To the extent that any woman who displays autonomy and independent personhood is seen as a threat to male power and therefore subjected to male violence was reaffirmed by the massacre at the Université de Montréal. Such events are not lost on young women.

My response to the sexual dynamics in the classroom is to create a context that offers "space" and "safety" particularly to women students. Men in the feminist classroom often state that the course readings and class discussions feel threatening and that they experience various degrees of discomfort. I would like to understand more about these feelings of threat and discomfort—where do they come from, what do they fear? I am concerned that all students—women and men—have access to the analyses we take up in the class. I am also concerned that all students feel equally validated in doing the hard work toward a transformed consciousness. However, this work is different for women than it is for men. Women need space and safety so that they are free to speak in order to better understand and act against the violations they have experienced in a social/cultural setting that subordinates them in hurtful and violent ways. The consciousness around which men need to do hard work is the pain of their complicity in benefitting from the rewards of this same culture. I support men in doing this hard work. Personally, I have not seen many of them try. Those who have are strong and welcome allies.

The language of "space" and "safety" is not new to discussions of feminist teaching. However, I believe that it is not always clear what practices attend these abstractions. I believe, first, that women don't need to be taught what we already know: fundamentally, that women are exempted from a culture to which our productive and reproductive labor is essential. The power of phallocentrism may undermine our initiative, it may shake the foundations of our self-respect and self-worth, it may even force us into complicity with its violence. But it cannot prevent us from knowing. Nor do women need to be taught the language through which to speak what we know.

Rather, the challenge of feminist teaching is in finding ways to make speakable and legitimate the personal/political *investments* we all make in the meanings we ascribe to our historically contingent experiences. In this context, I raise with students the contradictory reality of women's lives, wherein one's interests, at the level of practice, lie both with the dominant group and against it. Through such discussion emerges the deeply paradoxical nature of the conditions of the subordinate in a hierarchical culture marked by gender, class, and race inequalities. Approaching women's lives from this perspective means that practices previously understood by students, to be a function of choice can be seen as the result of a need to secure some measure of emotional, intellectual, and quite often physical survival (Wolfe, 1986, p. 58).

Pedagogy that is grounded in simple notions of false consciousness that articulates teaching as meditation or, worse, as a charitable act, does not support knowledge invested with the meanings students ascribe to their own experiences. This not only buries the complexity of human choices in an unproblematized notion of self-interest but, further, can only offer validating or supplementary educational options without transforming the conditions under which we learn (Lewis, 1989). By fusing women's emotional and concrete lives through feminist critique, it is possible to make problematic the conditions under which women learn, and perhaps to make a feminist political agenda viable in women's own lives wherein they can transcend the split between personal experience and social form.

Conclusion

What are the possibilities of doing feminist politics/pedagogy in the classroom? In answering this question I want to examine the potential for feminist teaching that does more than address the concerns of the already initiated. For me, the urgency of this issue arises from my own teaching. On one hand, the often chilling stories women students share with me and each other in the context of classroom relations point to their clear understanding of the politics of gender subordination. Within the confines of traditional academic practices, the politics of personal experience are often seen to be irrelevant. In contrast, the feminist classroom can be a deeply emotional experience for many women, offering the opportunity to claim relevance for the lives they live as the source of legitimate knowledge.

On the other hand, I also hear the young woman who speaks to me in anger, who derides me for being the bearer of "bad news," and who wants to believe that our oppression/subordination is something we create in our own heads. Given the context of violence within which students are being asked to embrace a feminist politic, their concerns about their emotional, intellectual, and, quite obviously, physical safety have to be recognized as crucial. For women, overt acts of violence, like the one that occurred at the Université de Montréal, are merely an extension of their daily experiences in the psychological/social/sexual spaces of the academy. Resistance to the emancipatory potential of a liberating politic indicates the extent of women's subordination. Thus, we cannot expect that students will readily appropriate a political stance that is truly counter-hegemonic, unless we also acknowledge the ways in which our feminist practice/politics *creates*, rather than ameliorates, feelings of threat: the threat of abandonment; the threat of having to struggle within unequal power relations; the threat of psychological/social/sexual, as well as economic and political marginality; the threat of retributive violence—threats lived in concrete embodied ways. Is it any wonder that many women desire to dissociate from "those" women whose critique of our social/cultural world seems to focus and condense male violence?

The challenge of feminist teaching lies for me in the specifics of how I approach the classroom. By reflecting on my own teaching, I fuse content and practice, politicizing them both through feminist theory and living them both concretely rather than treating them abstractly. To elaborate: as I reflect on my teaching, it is clear from the detailing of the examples I provide above that feminist teaching practices cannot be separated from the content of the curriculum. Specific political moments arise exactly because of the content of the course. As is suggested by Gayle MacDonald (1989), "the process by which teaching occurs in a feminist classroom is one which is very different from technique/pedagogy used in other settings" (p. 147). I want to extend this idea by suggesting that the "difference" MacDonald identifies in the feminist classroom is that, as students articulate their interests and investments through particular social practices, a dialectic develops between students and the curriculum in such a way that the classroom dynamics created by the topic of discussion reflect the social organization of gender inequality. Indeed, the irony is that feminist critique of social relations reproduces exactly the practices we are critiquing. When these practices are reproduced, so are the attendant violations, marginalizations, struggles, and transformation which again lend themselves to be revisited by the critique of feminist politics.

An interesting case in point is the experience I have had on various occasions when I have presented some version of this argument at academic conferences. On each occasion, in responding to my presentation, some members of the audience tended to reproduce to some extent the practices that I take such great pains to critique in the text. The caretaking practices, the concern that men not feel unfairly marginalized or attacked, the willingness of men in the audience to speak unproblematically on behalf of women, and the dynamics of sexual marginalization have all played a part in the reception of my article-in-progress. My purpose here is not to suggest that every instance of critique of feminist social/cultural analysis is a display of phallocentric power or male privilege. Indeed, as feminist scholars we put our work forward in good faith and both invite and welcome articulate and substantive engagement of it (Ellsworth, 1989). My point is, rather, that responses to feminist critique often take forms that reproduce the gendered practices that I have described in this paper.

The strategies I have employed in the classroom have been directed toward politicizing not only what we take up in the class as course content but also the classroom dynamics that are generated by our topic and subsequent discussion. These practices included: shifting our focus from larger social issues to the dynamics in the classroom so that we might explore the relationship between the two; legitimating the meanings women bring to their experiences by turning challenges to these articulated meanings back on the questioner, thereby requiring the questioner to make different meanings sensible; disrupting the order of hierarchy regarding who can speak on whose behalf; requiring that men in the class own their social location by exploring the parameters of their own privilege rather than the limits on women of their oppression; providing opportunities for self-reflexive critique of unequal power relations; staying attentive to the political context of women's lives—those seemingly unconnected experiences made to seem livable by the tumble of daily life—in order to offer a vision of a future that women might embrace; attending to the ways in which women have been required historically to invest in particular and often contradictory practices in order to secure their own survival; and, finally, treating women's resistance to feminism as an active discourse of struggle derived from a complex set of meanings in which women's practices are invested.

The above suggestions are intended to be neither exhaustive nor prescriptive. Pedagogical moments arise in specific contexts: the social location of the teacher and students; the geographic and historical location of the institution in which they come together; the political climate within which they work; the personalities and personal profiles of the individuals in the classroom; the readings selected for the course; and the academic background of the students all come together in ways that create the specifics of the moment. It is not appropriate to think of what I have presented here as a "model" for feminist teaching. "Models" can only be restrictive and reductive because they cannot predict and thus cannot take into account the complexity of contingent and material realities. My intent, rather, has been to articulate how, at particular moments in my teaching, I made sense of those classroom dynamics that seemed to divide women and men across their inequalities in ways that reaffirmed women's subordination, and how making sense of those moments as politically rich allowed me to develop an interpretative framework for creating a counter-hegemony from my teaching practice. My hope is that through such shared struggles in the classroom women might embrace for themselves the politics of autonomy and self determination rather than reject it as a liability.

Notes

1. This article is dedicated to the fourteen women massacred at the Université de Montréal on December 6, 1989: Genevieve Bergeron, Helene Colgan, Nathalie Croteau, Barbara Diagneault, Anne-Marie Edward, Maud Haveirnick, Barbara Maria Klueznick, Maryse Laganiere, Maryse Leclair, Anne-Marie Lemay, Sonia Pelletier, Michele Richard, Annie St-Arneault, and Annie Turcotte.

2. I thank Barbara McDonald for providing me with a deeper understanding of this reality through the work we share.

3. The Company of Sirens, 176 Robert Street, Toronto, Ontario, Canada, M5S 2K3.

I wish to thank Gayle MacDonald, Barbara McDonald, Elizabeth Ellsworth, and Roberta Lamb for making helpful comments on earlier drafts of this paper.

Works Cited

Belenky, M. F., Clinchy, B. M., Goldberger, N. R., & Tarule, J. M. (1986). *Women's ways of knowing: The development of self, voice and mind.* New York: Basic Books.

Brodribb, S. (1987). Women's studies in Canada [Special issue]. *Resources for Feminist Research.*

Brookes, A-L. (1988). *Feminist pedagogy: A subject in/formation.* Unpublished doctoral dissertation, University of Toronto.

Childers, M. (1984). Women's studies: Sinking and swimming in the mainstream. *Women's Studies International Forum, 7*(3), 161–166.

Corrigan, P. (1987). In/forming schooling. In D. Livingston & contributors, *Critical pedagogy and cultural power* (pp. 17–40). Toronto: Garamond Press.

Daly, M. (1978). *Gyn/ecology: The metaethics of radical feminism.* Boston: Beacon Press.

DuPlessis, R. B. (1985). *Writing beyond the ending: Narrative strategies of twentieth-century women writers.* Bloomington: Indiana University Press.

Ellsworth, E. (1989). Why doesn't this feel empowering? Working through the repressive myths of critical pedagogy. *Harvard Educational Review, 59,* 297–324.

Giroux, H., & Simon, R. (1988). *Critical pedagogy and the politics of popular culture.* Unpublished manuscript.

Griffin, S. (1981). *Pornography and silence: Culture's revenge against nature.* New York: Harper and Row.

hooks, b. (1989). *Talking back: Thinking feminist, thinking Black.* Boston: South End Press.

Jaggar, A. (1983). *Feminist politics and human nature.* Sussex, Eng.: The Harvest Press.

Khayatt, D. M. (1987). *Gender role conformity in women teachers.* Unpublished doctoral dissertation, University of Toronto.

Lather, P. (1988). Feminist perspectives on emancipatory research methodologies. *Women's Studies International Forum, 11,* 569–581.

Lewis, M. (1988a). *Without a word: Sources and themes for a feminist pedagogy.* Unpublished doctoral dissertation, University of Toronto.

Lewis, M. (1988b). The construction of femininity embraced in the work of caring for children: Caught between aspirations and reality. *Journal of Educational Thought, 22*(2A), 259–268.

Lewis, M. (1989). The challenge of feminist pedagogy. *Queen's Quarterly, 96*(1), 117–130.

Lewis, M. (1990a). *Solidarity work and feminist practice.* Paper presented at the annual meeting of the American Educational Research Association, Boston, MA.

Lewis, M. (1990b). *Framing: Women and silence disrupting the hierarchy of discursive practices.* Paper presented at the annual meeting of the American Educational Research Association, Boston, MA.

Lewis, M., & Simon, R. I. (1986). A discourse not intended for her: Learning and teaching within patriarchy. *Harvard Educational Review, 56,* 457–472.

MacDonald, G. (1989). Feminist teaching techniques for the committed but exhausted. *Atlantis, 15*(1), 145–152.

MacKinnon, C. A. (1983). Feminism, Marxism, method and the state: An agenda for theory. In E. Abel & E. Abel (Eds.), *The signs reader: Women, gender and scholarship* (pp. 227–256). Chicago: University of Chicago Press.

MacKinnon, C. (1987). *Feminism unmodified: Discourses of life and law.* Cambridge: Harvard University Press.

Malette, L., & Chalouh, M. (Eds.). (1990). *Polytechnique, 6 Décembre.* Montréal: Les Éditions du remue-ménage.

Martin, B., & Mohanty, C. T. (1986). Feminist politics: What's home got to do with it? In T. de Lauretis (Ed.), *Feminist studies/critical studies* (pp. 191–212). Bloomington: Indiana University Press.

McCormack, T. (1987). Feminism, women's studies and the new academic freedom. In J. Gaskell & A. McLaren (Eds.), *Women and education: A Canadian perspective* (pp. 289–303). Calgary: Detselig Enterprises.

McMahon, M. (1986). *A circuitous quest: Things that haunt me when I write.* Unpublished manuscript.

Pierson, R. R. (1983). Review of women of ideas and what men have done to them. *Resources for Feminist Research, 12*(2), 17–18.

Pierson, R. R. (1987). Two Marys and a Virginia: Historical moments in the development of a feminist perspective on education. In J. Gaskell & A. McLaren (Eds.), *Women and education: A Canadian perspective* (pp. 203–222). Calgary: Detselig Enterprises.

Radford-Hill, S. (1986). Considering feminism as a model for social change. In T. de Lauretis (Ed.), *Feminism studies/critical studies* (pp. 157–172). Bloomington: Indiana University Press.

Radway, J. (1984). *Reading the romance: Women, patriarchy and popular literature.* Chapel Hill: University of North Carolina Press.

Rich, A. (1986). *Blood, bread and poetry.* New York: W. W. Norton.

Rockhill, K. (1987a). The chaos of subjectivity in the ordered halls of academe. *Canadian Women Studies, 8*(4).

Rockhill, K. (1987b). Literacy as threat/desire: Longing to be SOMEBODY. In J. Gaskell & A. McLaren (Eds.), *Women and education: A Canadian perspective* (pp. 315–331). Calgary: Detselig Enterprises.

Rowbotham, S. (1989). To be or not to be: The dilemmas of mothering. *Feminist Review, 31,* 82–93.

Spender, D. (1982). *Women of ideas and what men have done to them.* London: Routledge and Kegan Paul.

Spender, D., & Sarah, E. (Eds.). (1980). *Learning to lose: Sexism and education.* London: The Women's Press.

Walkerdine, V. (1985). On the regulation of speaking and silence: Subjectivity, class and gender in contemporary schooling. In C. Steedman, C. Urwin, & V. Walkerdine (Eds.), *Language, gender and childhood* (pp. 203–241). London: Routledge and Kegan Paul.

Williamson, J. (1981/1982). How does girl number twenty understand ideology? *Screen Education, 40,* 80–87.

Willis, P. (1977). *Learning to labour: How working class kids get working class jobs.* New York: Columbia University Press.

Wolfe, A. (1986). Inauthentic democracy: A critique of public life in modern liberal society. *Studies in Political Economy, 21,* 57–81.

7

Feminists in Action

How to Practice What We Teach

Rae Rosenthal

Editors' Notes: Rosenthal, a composition instructor, argues that a distinctly feminist pedagogy must support classes devoted to feminist issues. Her students, who study the gender of discourses, codevelop the syllabus, choosing the number and type of assignments, course content, classroom rules, and criteria for grading. They also work in groups for peer feedback. They analyze concepts of gender, sex, women, carefully avoiding essentialist views, and take their own gender-typed behavior and writing as subjects for the course. Rosenthal describes how she confronts resistance to feminism from students and faculty, yet insists upon the value of examining gender in writing and teaching.

In the fall of 1989, I taught a composition class which completely bombed. The room was tense, the interchange unpleasant, and not all that surprisingly, the level of student writing did not improve significantly. In the years since then, I have wondered again and again about that class. Was it my decidedly feminist reading list? Was it my increasingly visible pregnancy? Was it the combination? Or was I simply "off" that semester? Gradually, what I have come to realize is that the failure of that course was rooted in my failure to connect, in any meaningful way, theory with practice. I was teaching, or trying to teach, feminist theory in a conventional, dictatorial, hierarchical classroom, and it just doesn't work. Clearly, as Dale Bauer suggests, "it is not enough to try to convince students to adopt feminism using a traditional teaching model of authority" ("Meanings" 8). In fact, I now see attempts to do so as the classic case of the round peg and the square hole. My failure then was that I did not know what I have learned forcibly since: you cannot just put your chairs in a circle and assume you have a feminist classroom.[1]

A composition class committed to feminist issues must be supported by a distinctly feminist pedagogy. Neither can survive without the other. And so in my most recent evolution, I am teaching a composition class which focuses, in terms of content, on feminist issues in rhetoric and which, in its pedagogical approach, is deliberately and openly feminist.

Feminist rhetoricians have, of late, had a great deal to say about writing and the teaching of writing. Indeed, feminist theory and rhetoric have become increasingly interconnected, and logically so—both fields are fundamentally concerned with issues of power and persuasion. During the course of the semester, my classes have read works by Pamela Annas, Joan Bolker, Helene Cixous, Elizabeth Flynn, Olivia Frey, Clara Juncker, and Jane Tompkins, amongst others; these women have in common their interest in rhetoric and feminist theory and their concern with the historical privileging of masculine discourse and the corresponding exclusion and devaluation of feminine modes of rhetoric. And as the class reads and becomes more educated about discourse communities and the effect of gender on these communities, I have noticed that students become more aware of their own language and more skilled in the manipulation of that language. Indeed, by the end of the semester, most students are able to differentiate between masculine and feminine discourse and to alternately adopt that which seems more appropriate to their subject and audience. Having thus become "bilingual," they are, as a result, more sophisticated writers and more knowledgeable about issues of writing.

I suspect that almost any composition issue would work well—postmodern theories of language, collaborative writing, technology and writing, standard versus nonstandard dialects, personal versus academic discourse, or a composite (I have also experimented with the latter two)—but I have found gender and writing to be the most thought provoking and most potentially reformative. Among the many benefits to having students read composition theory, regardless of focus, especially notable has been the resulting examination of their own writing which inevitably follows. By reading essays about writing, students begin to talk and think about writing—their own, their classmates', mine, and that of the authors whom they have been reading. I suspect that this is, in and of itself, a significant step towards improved student writing. But when assigned readings focus on feminist issues in rhetoric, students gain, additionally, insight into the interconnectedness of sex, power, and language and the ways in which those relations affect their own writing and their own lives.

In planning an introduction to this course, I kept in mind my earlier disaster and deliberately set out to establish a clear feminist pedagogy.[2] If we are going to be serious about a feminist classroom, which to my mind means both the acknowledgment and redistribution of power, to whatever extent possible within institutional constraints, then we must find ways to make that work for us and for our students. Surely, as Mary Rose O'Reilley points out, "the worst thing we can do is pretend we don't have power" (146). College professors pretending to be powerless over their students is undoubtedly a most sanctimonious, hypocritical trick, which students invariably sniff out at once. On the other hand, professional efforts to openly give away power are also doomed; you cannot completely overturn the classroom structure when the larger institutional edifice remains looming overhead.[3] And, as many of us remember from our own educations, a dictatorial approach to teaching leads only to student passivity and recitation. Still, teachers are the major shareholders of power in the classroom, and as such, it seems to me that we had better think long and hard about what we intend to do with it. I see no advantage to feigning powerlessness, giving our power away, or clutching it possessively; none of these will further our cause. We must be willing and able to come up with other alternatives, pedagogical practices which incorporate feminist values and feminist power into classroom technique. One possibility is that we candidly identify the source of our power, clarify the way in which that power structure operates, and acknowledge the limitations of that power. And it is, I would argue, the limitations, the areas where our power need not extend, which are most often disguised, but which can, paradoxically, be our greatest strength. In exploring the edges of that power, we can be most creative and energetic, most empowering of our students.

So as often as possible, I seek ways to minimize my own decision making in favor of student choice. On the first day of class, the students and I collectively make various decisions about the syllabus. Students choose the number of assigned essays (within the departmental requirements of six to ten, and no, students do not automatically vote for six); they decide how many of those essays will be research papers (again, assuming that the departmental requirement of one research paper must be fulfilled); and students decide how the grades for these essays will be weighed (evenly, or more heavily towards the end of the semester). Students also decide whether to "count" attendance and class participation in calculating final grades. Other possibilities abound.[4] I suspect, though, that the actual array of decisions matters less than the process itself, which amidst all this talk about empowerment of students, actually does give students some measure of control over their educational experience. If feminists are committed to the redistribution of power, then they must honor that commitment in their classrooms. According to Dana D. Nelson, during a conversation about women and power in which the majority of women were denouncing power as a source of corruption, Dale Spender asserted the contrary: "'I want as much power as I can possibly get. Share it with me mates'" (33). This strikes me as an excellent motto for the feminist classroom, one rooted in the realities of our educational system.

When initially selecting material for this course, I assumed that most, if not all, of my students would come to class with no knowledge of composition theory or of gender studies, so I decided to begin each semester by trying to establish some theoretical foundation. First, I introduce some of the basics of feminist terminology and theory. We briefly review the history of feminism, noting that its origins are as old as patriarchy and that twentieth-century America did not invent the "women's movement," despite all media myths to the contrary. I try to make clear the various feminist agendas, pointing out the range of positions within the ideological framework of feminism. I also hand out a definition sheet, based on Gerda Lerner's excellent glossary, which clarifies various terms useful in the feminist conversation: *gender, sex, feminism, sexism, patriarchy,* and *matriarchy.* (Often students will assert that we live in a matriarchal culture because their mothers control the home and hearth; it is useful for students to consider that in doing so, women are merely fulfilling their culturally determined gender role, which decrees that the home is the only acceptable sphere of female influence.)

Distinguishing between the biological given (sex) and the culturally created (gender) has proven especially useful. Clarifying these two terms eliminates a classroom problem that commonly occurs when discussing feminist issues: in any discussion of gender roles and domestic habits, for instance, at least one student is likely to exclaim, "but I know a male who does the laundry, or cooks dinner, or bathes the children," or "I know a female who does household repairs, fixes the car, or does yard work." Such arguments, I point out, would be meaningful only if gender were identical to sex, if gender could not be altered, if there were an innate, essential female/male being. Through these discussions, students gradually come to realize that because gender is culturally created and culturally determined, inevitably (and fortunately so) there are always exceptions; some of us have been more thoroughly indoctrinated than others. So the existence of a male who does the laundry or a female with her own tool box does not in any way contradict the prevalence of gender-determined stereotypes. And as long as these examples continue to be exceptions rather than the norm, then gender-prescribed roles still have us firmly within their grip. Correspondingly, a male who writes in a feminine mode about feminine topics does not in any way negate the existence of feminine writing, or feminine topics; it merely indicates that this particular individual has had some success in resisting the gender lessons of our culture. Clarification of this issue is especially important in discussions of gender and writing, as it allows students to see that while writers cannot change their sex, they can change the extent to which their writing supports the gender-determined categories upon which our culture has been built. In this way, the seemingly simple task of defining *gender* and *sex* provides the basis for the entire semester, because distinguishing between the two brings to the forefront the most fundamental aspect of feminism—the possibility of change.

Following the definition of terms, we begin our reading of introductory material, starting with discussions of gender and its effect on children, speech, and classroom behavior. We read Gilligan, Lakoff, and Spender (Chodorow, Belenky, and Sadker would do just as well, among others), and following this brief introduction to basic feminist issues, we move directly to feminist rhetoric and Cixous. I like to begin with Cixous because her writing is the most innovative, the most obviously distinct from the prose my students have previously encountered. In selecting other articles, I try to choose those which strike me as most intriguing, most (not least) debatable, and least abstruse. (Other choices have previously included Annas, Booker, readings from Caywood and Overing, Farrell, Flynn, Frey, Juncker, Lamb, Pigott, Tompkins, and Zawacki.) I suggest to students before they begin that they should attempt to read each article in its entirety and that rather than quit when they encounter an especially difficult passage, they should simply mark it and go on. We begin each day with a review of those passages which have proven difficult. And once the entire class feels comfortable with basic comprehension of the material under discussion for that day, we work in groups summarizing the argument and analyzing the strengths and weaknesses of the essay. Besides aiding in student comprehension, this procedure has a number of additional benefits; first, students learn to work and write collaboratively, an important feminist skill; second, they discover multiple possibilities for the construction of an argument, multiplicity being another important feminist value; and finally, and perhaps most usefully, they learn the difference between summarizing and analyzing, all without my having to employ any of the traditional pedagogical techniques such as lecturing, testing, or, worst of all, assigning exercises.

Through our readings, we gradually piece together definitions of masculine and feminine discourse, deciding collectively that masculine writing tends to be (with heavy emphasis on the "tends") argumentative, factual, conclusive, and impersonal, whereas feminine writing tends to be suggestive, intuitive, open-ended, and personal (see Cixous, Farrell, Juncker, Rosenthal, Tompkins). It is important to keep in mind that masculine does not necessarily translate to male, nor feminine to female. The terms "male" and "female" writing are commonly used, and I have used them in the past as well (see the title of my 1990 *Focuses* essay), but it seems to me more and more that such usage encourages precisely the confusion which Lerner seeks to avoid, and leads us directly into the essentialist trap. Male and female denote sex, feminine and masculine denote gender, and as such they can be questioned, (con)tested, and altered.

All of this might sound, still, dangerously "essentialist," a loaded and hotly disputed label. In response to the theoretical charge of essentialism, I try to explore, with the class, this site of feminist contention. We discuss the limitations inherent in theories of difference, the so-called essentialist position, and we consider the danger of stabilizing through the study of gender differences that which is ever unstable and of further restraining that which has long been restrained. On the other hand, though, we must consider, too, the importance of commonality, of maintaining a sense of connection between all women, a connection which the poststructuralist, antiessentialist position seems to threaten in its insistence on indefiniteness. In the dialogue between the cultural/ radical feminists (read *essentialism*) and the poststructural feminists (read *antiessentialism/constructivism*), there has been a good deal of oppositional posturing. What has emerged for many feminists, though, is a desire for what Ritchie terms "a 'both/and' perspective that recognizes the complexity of women's identity" (255). For, as Alcoff suggested early in the debate, "we can't say at one and the same time [despite the protestations of both camps to the contrary] that gender is not natural, biological, universal, ahistorical, or essential and yet still claim that gender is relevant because we are taking gender as a position from which to act politically" (433). We cannot have feminism without some concept, albeit preferably a broad, shifting, inclusive concept, of "woman."

Accordingly, I try to keep in the forefront of the class this idea of "woman" as both different and yet similar, as having certain common experiences within a patriarchal environment, but recognizing at the same time that those experiences can and do vary widely, as a result of race, class, sexual orientation, and culture. In this way, I try to offer a way out of the binary trap of essentialism or constructivism and to offer in its place "a concept of women's identity that is neither fixed, powerless essence nor endlessly dissolving and invisible, but multiple and changing within a social, linguistic, and political context, and that has agency because of its reflective, self-analyzing power" (Ritchie describing de Lauretis 256). Through classroom discussions of these issues, I emphasize over and over again to my students that we are not examining masculine and feminine discourse in order to reinforce restrictive categories of essentialness, but rather in order to explore, expand, and experiment with those categories. (Readers further interested in the complexities of the essentialist debate should see Weedon, Fuss, Alcoff, hooks, Ritchie, and the 1988 special issue of *differences,* especially the influential lead article by Teresa de Lauretis.)

In reading the selected feminist rhetoricians, especially Cixous, Tompkins, and Zawacki, students are exposed, usually for the first time, to a different type of scholarly writing. These essays, they often notice, tend to be less combative, definitive, and formulaic and more anecdotal and questioning than is academic discourse generally. And in the intertextuality and self-referencing of many of these essays, there is a spirit of cooperation, a sense of building upon one another rather than in place of one another. Noticeably absent is the oftentimes embarrassing tone of aggression which frequently characterizes academic writing particularly in the reply sections in the back of our journals.[5]

After having examined for ourselves these discussions of masculine and feminine discourse, we begin to turn to our own writing. In class, we experiment daily with the ideas introduced by the feminist rhetoricians we have been reading. The emphasis, for each activity, is on multiplicity and exploration. After reading Joan Bolker's now famous "Teaching Griselda to Write," we identify the Griseldas in our class, those students of docility whose writing "aims to please all and offend none" (907); together, we try to move consciously towards and then away from that correct but lifeless tone which so often typifies the "good girl" essay. Following Joan Bolker's suggestions for the annihilation of Griselda, we seek to develop our own individualized, personal voices, a process through which we seek the dismantling of restrictive gender roles. In class, we practice by selecting a group topic, which we then explore through both masculine and feminine discourse, thereby simultaneously clarifying and questioning the influence of gender on voice. Following our discussion of Clara Juncker's essay, "Writing (with) Cixous," we experiment with a number of her suggestions, including class without speech (only written communication allowed), dialogue essays where students converse on paper about a topic of mutual interest, and exploratory papers which avoid closure.

For each graded essay, students select their own topic and a mode of discourse (masculine, feminine, or an androgynous blend) which they feel will work well for their topic. I have found that student selection of topics, rather than assigned topics, is crucial to the success of this course, and so paper topics is another pedagogical decision over which I have relinquished control. In addition to the advantages of further power redistribution, I think it is important for students to have the experience of independently searching for a topic, an experience which to my mind constitutes the most difficult aspect of writing, but one which must be surmounted. Students cannot though be sent adrift without the proverbial life jacket, and I have experimented with a number of different "life jacket" techniques. For example, I used to see students individually in my office, asking them to bring to their conference a list of three potential topics, all of which interested them and about which they had some knowledge. Together, we would work through this list, selecting what appeared to be the topic most likely to generate an effective paper. As you can imagine, this was an exhausting task for me. (I slowly was forced to acknowledge that the first student received a good deal more from me than did the last.) This arrangement had the additional negative side effect of separating the group; collaboration, which I see as crucial to a feminist classroom, was lost during the most critical part of the writing process.

Recently, I have found what seems to be a much better system. Each student brings to class three possible topics; students then put their list on the board, and the class as a whole works through each student's list, offering suggestions and opinions as to which topic seems most fruitful. The benefits to this system are many: students get to consider a wide range of topics, students get to participate in and listen to a sustained discussion about the process of topic selection, and each student gets the benefit of a variety of opinions about his or her own topic. Also of great importance is that students gain skill in working, writing, and thinking together. And in addition (and of no less significance), I am far less exhausted because of the burden of the discussion does not lie solely with me, and whatever useful comments I might make are available to the entire group rather than just to the individual student who happens to be sitting in my office first thing in the morning when I am still fresh.[6]

What has proven especially interesting, though, is the almost universal influence of gender on topic selection. I have found that once freed from assignment sheets and prescribed topics, students choose, with little exception, to write on subjects which readily fall into gender-determined categories. They tend to select topics (even the females who cling to typically academic/male voices) which our culture has deemed appropriate for their sex. Male students tend to write about sports, politics, cars, and physical experiences, a hiking trip for example. Female students tend to write about personal relationships, literature, and emotional experiences. The only topics which regularly cross gender boundaries are education, the environment, and music. This pattern, according to Linda H. Peterson, is not unusual; in a study of two composition classes, one at Yale and one at Utah State, Peterson discovered that the "topics that women students choose are almost always 'relational'" and that "In contrast, male writers more frequently choose topics that focus on the self, the self alone, the self as distinct from others" (173). In response to this gender gap, halfway through the semester I set aside a day to discuss gender patterns in student-generated topics, and invariably, the consistency of these patterns surprises students.

In one of my early classes, the students suggested, in light of this—to them—new and surprising information, that we experiment with "cross-dressing," that males write on a typically female topic in a feminine mode and that females try the reverse.[7] I have since used this assignment repeatedly, always with a good deal of success. By forcing themselves to write in the opposite gender mode, students learn a great deal about voice, tone, diction, and about their own writing style. This activity also encourages students to become more self-conscious about their writing and more stylistically innovative. Through the deliberate adoption of masculine discourse, students gain skill in the type of academic writing they will be so often called upon to write in the next few years. They gain, in this way, confidence in their ability to speak the language of the academy. In addition, through the reverse—the deliberate adoption of feminine discourse—students gain a wider perspective, a sense of the alternatives and possibilities beyond that standardized format. Also through this assignment, it is possible to reinforce one of the most basic premises of feminism—the long-standing feminist assertion that the personal is the political and the political is the personal. The historical devaluation of all that is personal, a devaluation which inevitably indicts all that is female because the two are so often conflated, has led to the academic exclusion of the personal in its discourse, its pedagogical practice, and its institutional values. By experimenting with writing in a deliberately feminine/personal mode, students experience, firsthand, the personal as a legitimate intellectual subject.

It becomes important, then, to validate the personal in classroom dialogue, as well. Once a number of female students have been heard from, describing the various ways in which they have experienced their femaleness, it is no longer possible to collapse all women into a single, universal, fixed identity. At the same time, students begin to recognize the common threads of oppression, the inherent political subtext of what has traditionally constituted the female experience. Personal knowledge thus becomes evidence of both the difference and sameness with which the class readings have been concerned. In this way, personal experience becomes acceptable as an appropriate learning tool in the classroom and is seen to work in conjunction with the theoretical material of this course. Once experience gains value as a legitimate means of knowing, students can gain skill in self-education; they can learn to theorize (not generalize) from their own stories. By merging the personal and the public, the overall quality of the learning process is enhanced; indeed, like bell hooks, "fundamentally I believe that combining the analytical and the experiential is a richer way of knowing" (181). The validation of personal experience in the classroom and in academic discourse thus provides yet another means for the further feminization of our educational system.

When students first begin self-selecting their topics, I encourage them to write about subjects with which they feel comfortable, even if those happen to fall into stereotypical gender categories. I have found that this introductory "comfort zone" enables students to begin to experiment and explore. But after perhaps two or three essays, I begin to encourage students to leave their comfort zone—to move beyond gender-determined topics. By having students generate their own topics and by confronting them with the inevitable gender gap in their own choices, they are forced to recognize the way in which they have been unwittingly coopted by the gender restrictions of our culture. It then becomes possible to move beyond cultural stereotypes of gender, to emphasize the feminist goal of choice for all.

Once having selected a topic, but before beginning to write, students meet in prearranged groups of three in order to discuss their topics and to solicit suggestions about various strategical matters: voice, organization, length, and so on. The inevitable questions about length are all handled in the group; in this way, students learn for themselves the way in which the choice of topic predetermines length. As a group, they decide for themselves when an issue has been explored thoroughly and when greater development is needed. Throughout the semester, these groups remain constant. I aim for groups which are balanced in terms of sex, ability, and outspokenness. By having the groups remain constant, I find that students develop a sustained rapport which ultimately enables them to get to work more quickly and to offer suggestions more readily. They also then have the additional benefit of prior knowledge; while working on any given paper, every student in the group has read and commented on all preceding papers. In this portfolio approach to peer-response groups, they have the advantage of the whole picture, as do I.

After having created a presentable working draft, students return to their peer-response groups, each with three copies for distribution. The system is set up so that the author of the draft under discussion has the responsibility to raise questions about his or her own paper; I suggest that students draw attention to the trouble spots in their essay and seek assistance, rather than defensively hide whatever weaknesses the draft may have. This way, peer editors are made to feel helpful rather than critical. I remind the groups repeatedly that comments such as "This is really great; I wouldn't change a thing" are useless and should not be tolerated. Students also know that if insurmountable problems arise within a group, changes can be made, but usually they work out their own differences. Student groups chart their own progress by regularly filling out evaluation forms which ask each student to comment on the effectiveness of the group and the value of his or her own contribution. Through this process, students become practiced and skilled at collaborative writing, and as a result, they produce better writing. They also gain, along the way, an appreciation of collaborative activity. And if collectivity and cooperation are, as I believe, central to all feminist activity, then students have begun to participate in and appreciate one of the most basic feminist principles.[8]

While overseeing these groups in class, I have often noticed peer editors pointing out those essays which were written exclusively in either the masculine or feminine mode, and in most instances, the editors have then been able to articulate the disadvantages resulting from that exclusivity of discourse. And a number of female students have been surprised to discover that they had been writing entirely in a masculine mode. Their academic indoctrination had been so complete, so thorough, that they had no individualized and/or feminized voice of their own; in their efforts to enter the academy, they had been writing flat, correct, and distinctly masculine prose—or in Joan Bolker's words, they had a Griselda complex, one which prevented them from recognizing alternative modes of discourse. Most often, too, these were the students who had been insisting that feminist issues are no longer relevant and that our culture is now thoroughly egalitarian. These students have now learned what many of us have had to face long ago: that patriarchy thrives upon invisibility and that the most oppressed are often the least aware of their own oppression.

In terms of student writing, by about midterm I generally begin to see evidence of change. Of course, this is the point in the semester when we usually begin to see change; our students' writing becomes sharper, stronger, and more correct. But with this course, other changes tend to occur as well. With a peculiar combination of hesitancy and determination, students begin to experiment; first, they usually select topics from the opposite gender mode and, then more daringly, they try to write in the opposite gender mode. For some, their first experiments are notably unsuccessful. The males who try to write about personal issues, who try to put something of themselves on paper, often sound, as the females quickly point out, like a Hallmark card. The females, on the other hand, often have difficulties of a different nature. Every semester, several remain trapped in a world of personal anecdotes, experience without context, and they find it uncomfortable to enter the formal world of academic discourse; others have so long been imitating masculine prose that self-expression feels foreign to them. Slowly though, most students begin to profit from their experiments, and with each essay, the results are more impressive. They steadily become more adept at identifying masculine and feminine prose and, in turn, at willfully creating masculine and feminine prose. They learn to switch, from one to the other, in a rather sophisticated display of "bilingualism." Most importantly though, they begin to think, talk, and wonder about writing.

Without fail, though, each semester, there are resistors: the students who sit, arms crossed, faces scowled, and eyes narrowed. They feel cheated because they did not get the class which they expected. In contemplating these students, I am reminded of a colleague of mine who commented, when he heard what goes on in my composition class, "It's as though the student signed up for composition and found himself in Football 101." I have always appreciated that comment, as it brought back to me with great clarity how many times I found myself in a "liberal" arts class which might more honestly have been titled "Football 101." In response to both my students and my colleague, I contend, along with Dale Bauer, that in these complaints, "I hear a suggestion . . . that feminism is not a discipline, that gender issues are based on perspectives unsuitable for the labor of the intellectual" ("The 'F' Word" 386). Such a suggestion stems from the historical devaluing of all that is feminine, and as such, should be resisted mightily, both within the classroom and out.

Despite what some of my students and colleagues might think, my goal within the classroom is not to convert each student; I aim rather to educate each student about writing, about discourse, about power, and about the distribution of that power. And I want them to see most vividly the connections between language and power and power and sex. I want them to understand too, the goals of feminism, whether they agree with those goals or not. Some might argue (as does Maxine Hairston) that I have no business teaching this class as a feminist—it's only a composition class. But no one ever told my college professors, or some of my colleagues for that matter, that they have no business teaching their courses, regardless of subject matter, as white male supremacists. I cannot teach this class, or any other, as anything but a feminist because that's what I am. I can no more leave it in the hall than I can my femaleness or my Jewishness. I am a package deal, as are we all. And we have only two choices: open acknowledgment of what we are, or pretense. The choice to me seems obvious, especially as the latter doesn't work.

I am still left, though, with those cross-armed, squinty-eyed students, and the troubling question of how best to "handle" them, as we too often say. I am reminded, peculiarly, of *Dallas,* a TV show which I still consider to be among the most revealing of all twentieth-century artifacts. In one memorable scene, when JR found himself in need of additional funds but unable to attain the assistance of either friends or family, Sue Ellen cleverly inquired, "Well if your friends won't help you, why not try your enemies?" Such thinking I have taken to be my motto for encounters with classroom resistance. Student opposition can be wonderfully useful if we can only learn to think of these students as a source of dialogue and contrast, rather than as the enemy.

Jane Tompkins, in her "current rules of thumb," suggests that we "Talk to the class about the class" ("Pedagogy" 659). I have found this to be exceptionally good advice (it seems so obvious, but then perhaps that's why it's so successful), and I incorporate such discussions into each daily class plan. The success of these conversations depends, though, upon the presence of real dialogue which encourages, even invites, all expressions, both those of support and of resistance. In order to create such an environment, students must become accustomed to hear themselves speak, which is why I plan for the first day of each semester an activity in which everyone participates; after having spoken once, students more readily speak again. I make it clear, too, from the beginning that as a writing workshop, the success of the group as a whole depends upon the willingness of all individuals to contribute. Students must also regularly hear ideas being challenged by both student and teacher. If we value only consensus, that is what we will hear, but if we truly value dialogue, then we must not only acknowledge, but listen and respond to all comments. I also state early on two overarching classroom rules: all comments are welcome; no rudeness is tolerated. Once an atmosphere of candidness and civility has been established, resistance to feminist content or pedagogy can be usefully explored. If we profess to be feminists, we must act accordingly, and as openness and dialogue are fundamental values of all feminist movement, they must be fundamental to our classrooms.

Interestingly, though, I have found that few, if any, students ever resist feminist pedagogy. Shared decision making, collaboration, and validation of the personal do not often find resistance in my classes. Feminist content and theory, on the other hand, often lead to student discomfort and dismay, and understandably so. Most of what our students have been led to view as natural and permanent is being openly redefined by the feminist classroom as socially constructed and transmutable. If I am going to engage in pedagogical approaches which I know will lead to student defamiliarization, then it is my responsibility to create an opportunity for the expression and exploration of the new location in which they find themselves. I try to encourage student questioning of such changes, and in turn, I feel free to question students about their resistance. In the end, we often still do not agree, but for the most part, we have gained enormous respect for and knowledge of one another, and, I suspect, some self-knowledge as well. Without resistance in such a class, much of this would be lost.

Another means of engaging with student resistance is to schedule midsemester teaching evaluations. Most colleges and universities now require that evaluation forms be completed at the end of the semester, but by then the course is over. I now have students complete course evaluations during the middle of the semester as well. It might be feared that such timing would not promote honesty, but I have found that if evaluations are presented as a vehicle for making suggestions, and if it is made clear that such suggestions are genuinely desired, then students are as honest at midsemester as they are during finals. These evaluation forms then provide a wonderful occasion for discussion of feminist pedagogy. But in order for this conversation to be inclusive, a sincere attempt must be made to solicit the opinions of the resistors. They need to be heard, and their dissatisfaction examined. I try, as Dale Bauer suggests, to work "from the notion that the classroom is a place to explore resistances and identifications, a place also to explore the ambiguous and often ambivalent space of values and ethics" ("The 'F' Word" 387). In such an environment, dialogue includes all voices, all participants, regardless of location.

One complaint commonly heard about the feminist classroom—why are politics being brought into this _____ (read *English, History, Philosophy,* etc.) class?—deserves special attention. This line of questioning assumes that all other classrooms have no political agenda, and that the feminist classroom has violated the principle (I would say myth) of academic neutrality and objectivity. Students making such arguments have been led, mistakenly, to believe that any class in which there is no overt mention of politics therefore has no politics. They fail to see the way in which silence reinforces the status quo. They fail to see the way in which, for example, a literature course which reads only canonical writers and focuses on the history of traditional literary movements inherently endorse a conservative agenda. Because the politics of such a course are rarely articulated, and because such courses reflect the politics of the culture at large, a factor which contributes to their seeming innocuousness, students generally fail to question the agenda of such a course. They do not see that the traditional classroom is no more neutral or objective than the feminist class about which they are currently complaining. This is an important lesson for students, though, because if they are going to benefit from their educational experiences, then they must be given the means by which to read those experiences. They must become aware of the inevitability of a political agenda, and when that agenda has not been articulated clearly, as it should be, then they must be able to discern it for what it is. So I especially welcome questioning of my approach, as it allows me to introduce the concept of education as politics. And if they don't like the politics of my class, I remind them that at least they know what those politics are. I point out, too, that the classroom has been set up in such a way that students are not only allowed but encouraged to discuss, question, and resist the politics of the course.

In order to assist students in the assessment of classroom climate and politics, I provide a checklist which I suggest that they apply to all classes, mine included. The questions on the checklist include: Whose view of the world is being offered as truth in this class? Who are the generators of knowledge and what populations are being studied? Is this class chilly or comfortable for women, students of color, students of differing religions, sexual orientation, and other historically marginalized groups? Whose interests are being served by how the course is taught?[9] With this tool in hand, students can begin to interpret their own educational experiences, to recognize the inevitability of political orientation, and to appreciate the advantages of a direct pedagogical approach, one which makes clear from the very beginning the answers to the questions above.

At the end of the semester, two compelling questions remain: how do we define good teaching, and how do we define good writing? In answer to the latter, some students argue for the inherent superiority of either the masculine or feminine mode. A number of other students argue for androgyny; they feel that the best essays include personal input as well as an ability to generalize beyond the particular, that good writing should be factual and intuitive, expressive and argumentative. But at some point, this reasoning breaks down. Writing cannot be both conclusive and open-ended, combative and noncombative; choices must be made. As for myself, I find that after years of teaching writing, I am no longer able to offer a standard definition of good writing; more and more it seems to me that while there might be a number of ways to write poorly, there might be an even greater number of ways to write well. Defining good writing is, after all, much like defining good literature, a task which we have all learned is far more problematic than it once seemed. My new aim for my students then is a multiplicity of voices; I would like for them to be able to consciously select and shift their mode of discourse, moving freely from masculine to feminine and back again. Such command of their writing would surely lead the way to excellence.

As to the question of good teaching, the answer is equally complicated. Feminists need to find a way to incorporate both content and practice; the two cannot responsibly be separated. To do either without the other is to diminish our cause altogether, and leads, further, to the specter of legitimate student disillusion with a theory which fails to practice what it preaches. Ritchie argues, I think wisely, that "[s]uch a separation subverts one of the most important contributions of feminism: the model of a discipline that constantly connects intellectual activity—the study of literature, language, and ideas—to the history and experience of people's lives" (271). By avoiding that separation, by taking the risk of active feminist pedagogy, one furthers the possibility of change, which is, after all, the foremost purpose of all feminist movement.[10]

Through this new course, a great deal has been gained. I have found a new and invigorating approach to teaching composition. My students have found that by reading about writing, they in turn can become better writers. And by examining the influence of gender on writing and teaching, they also have become educated about the ways in which our culture is gender determined and the ways in which they have been brought into that culture. It is then their choice whether they acquiesce or resist, but at least they know that there is a choice to be made.

Notes

1. Mary Rose O'Reilley makes a similar point in her thought-provoking confessional "Exterminate . . . the Brutes," where she states, quite rightfully, "you can't just put your chairs in a circle and forget about the human condition" (146).

2. Joy S. Ritchie reports that in a women's literature class taught by her colleague, Barbara DiBernard, DiBernard began the semester by assigning an article on feminist teaching which she had written. Ritchie explains that "Barbara believed that sharing her philosophy of teaching from the outset of the class was consistent with her desire to help them see 'teaching as a political act'" (252). This strikes me as an excellent idea, one with which I would like to experiment.

3. Jerry Farber tells an apt tale of his officemate, Jackie, who "walked into Intro to Lit and said, 'OK, people, it's your class. What do you want to do with it?' But, of course, they didn't want to do anything with it. They didn't even want to be there. It was a GE class, for God's sake. Was she kidding?" (135).

4. I once had a graduate professor who compiled the reading list for the course on the first day of class. The course was Comparative Fiction, and he distributed a list of approximately one hundred novels from which we could choose, and the twelve earning the most votes were then the texts for the semester.

5. I have often thought that one of the most interesting aspects of Jane Tompkins's widely discussed essay, "Pedagogy of the Distressed," was the aftermath—the number of sharp, bitter, aggressive attacks made in reply. The antagonistic spirit of the ensuing conversation was exactly what Tompkins has been trying, in that essay and in "Me and My Shadow" and "Fighting Words: Unlearning to Write the Critical Essay," to expose.

6. Unfortunately, women all too often respond to cultural training which encourages female selflessness. We tend to put our own needs last and assume that, somehow, what is not good for us must be good for those around us. More and more, I have begun to take into the classroom the motto which I have adopted at home: "The best mother (teacher) is a happy mother (teacher)." If I overextend myself, I cannot possibly meet the needs of my children or my students, so I am not really doing them any favor.

7. Coincidentally, Linda Peterson offers basically the same suggestion; she says, "For insight and originality, try 'cross-dressing'—that is, use the writerly strategy of viewing experience through the eyes of someone of the opposite sex or from a different racial or ethnic background" (178).

8. Another unexpected side benefit to these groups is the frequency with which they spill over into nonclass time; I am told that students within a group often call one another for advice and support during the writing process. (At the beginning of every semester, I distribute a sheet which has each student's name, address, and phone number.) This type of intellectual connection is particularly important at a commuter school, like mine, where a sense of community can be difficult to build, and I suspect that non-constant peer-editing groups are less likely to have the same result.

9. The idea for this checklist came from Richard Bucher, a colleague at Baltimore City Community College.

10. In imitation of bell hooks, I deliberately refer not to "the" feminist movement but to feminist movement, a term preferable in its inclusivity: hooks says, "I drop the definite article rather than speaking of 'the' feminist movement. When we do not have a definite article, we are saying that feminist movement can be located in multiple places, in multiple languages and experiences" ("Conversation" 68).

Works Cited

Alcoff, Linda. "Cultural Feminism Versus Post-Structuralism: The Identity Crisis in Feminist Theory." *Signs: A Journal of Women in Culture and Society* 13 (1988): 405–36.

Annas, Pamela J. "Style as Politics: A Feminist Approach to the Teaching of Writing." *College English* 47 (1985): 360–71.

Bauer, Dale M. "The Meanings and Metaphors of Student Resistance." Conference on College Composition and Communication. Cincinnati, March 1992.

———. "The Other 'F' Word: The Feminist in the Classroom." *College English* 52 (1990): 385–96.

Belenky, Mary Field, Blythe McVicker Clinchy, Nancy Rule Goldberger, and Jill Mattuck Tarule. *Women's Ways of Knowing: The Development of Self, Voice, and Mind.* New York: Basic, 1986.

Bolker, Joan. "Teaching Griselda to Write." *College English* 40 (1979): 906–908.

Caywood, Cynthia L., and Lillian R. Overing, eds. *Teaching Writing: Pedagogy, Gender and Equity.* Albany: State U of New York P, 1987.

Chodorow, Nancy. *The Reproduction of Mothering: Psychoanalysis and the Sociology of Gender.* Berkeley and Los Angeles: U of California P, 1978.

Cixous, Helene. "The Laugh of the Medusa." Trans. Keith Cohen and Paula Cohen. *The Signs Reader: Women, Gender, and Scholarship.* Ed. Elizabeth Abel. Chicago: U of Chicago P, 1982. 279–97.

de Lauretis, Teresa. "The Essence of the Triangle or, Taking the Risk of Essentialism Seriously: Feminist Theory in Italy, the U.S., and Britain." *differences* 1 (1988): 3–37.

Farber, Jerry. "Learning How to Teach: A Progress Report." *College English* 52 (1990): 135–41.

Farrell, Thomas J. "The Female and Male Modes of Rhetoric." *College English* 40 (1979): 909–21.

Flynn, Elizabeth A. "Composing as a Woman." *College Composition and Communication* 39 (1988): 423–35.

———. "Composing 'Composing as a Woman': A Perspective on Research." *College Composition and Communication* 41 (1990): 83–89.

Frey, Olivia. "Beyond Literary Darwinism: Women's Voices and Critical Discourse." *College English* 52 (1990): 507–26.

Fuss, Diana. *Essentially Speaking: Feminism, Nature, and Difference.* New York: Routledge, 1989.

Gilligan, Carol. *In a Different Voice: Psychological Theory and Women's Development.* Cambridge: Harvard UP, 1982.

Hairston, Maxine. "Diversity, Ideology, and Teaching Writing." *College Composition and Communication* 43 (1992): 179–93.

hooks, bell. "A Conversation about Race and Class." *Conflicts in Feminism.* Ed. Marianne Hirsch and Evelyn Fox Keller. New York: Routledge, 1990. 60–81.

———. "Essentialism and Experience." *American Literary History* 3 (1991): 172–83.

Juncker, Clara. "Writing (with) Cixous." *College English* 50 (1988): 424–36.

Lakoff, Robin. *Language and Woman's Place.* New York: Harper, 1973.

Lamb, Catherine E. "Beyond Argument in Feminist Composition." *College Composition and Communication* 42 (1991): 11–24.

Lerner, Gerda. *The Creation of Patriarchy.* New York: Oxford UP, 1986.

Nelson, Dana D. "Being a Woman Academic, or, The Importance of 'Me Mates.'" *Concerns* 22.3 (1992): 32–37.

O'Reilley, Mary Rose. "'Exterminate . . . the Brutes'—And Other Things That Go Wrong in Student-Centered Teaching." *College English* 51 (1989): 142–46.

Peterson, Linda L. "Gender and the Autobiographical Essay: Research Perspectives, Pedagogical Practices." *College Composition and Communication* 42 (1991): 170–83.

Pigott, Margaret B. "Sexist Roadblocks in Inventing, Focusing, and Writing." *College English* 40 (1979): 922–27.

Ritchie, Joy S. "Confronting the 'Essential' Problem: Reconnecting Feminist Theory and Pedagogy." *Journal of Advanced Composition* 10 (1990): 249–73.

Rosenthal, Rae. "Male and Female Discourse: A Bilingual Approach to English 101." *Focuses* 3 (1990): 99–113.

Sadker, Myra, and David Sadker. "Confronting Sexism in the College Classroom." *Gender in the Classroom: Power and Pedagogy.* Ed. Susan L. Gabriel and Isaiah Smithson. Chicago: U of Illinois P, 1990. 176–87.

Spender, Dale. "Disappearing Tricks." *Learning to Lose: Sexism and Education.* Ed. Dale Spender and Elizabeth Sarah. London: The Women's P, 1980. 165–73.

———. "Talking in Class." *Learning to Lose: Sexism and Education.* Ed. Dale Spender and Elizabeth Sarah. London: The Women's P, 1980. 148–54.

Tompkins, Jane. "Fighting Words: Unlearning to Write the Critical Essay." *Georgia Review* 42 (1988): 585–90.

———. "Me and My Shadow." *New Literary History* 19 (1987): 169–78.

———. "Pedagogy of the Distressed." *College English* 52 (1990): 653–60.

Weedon, Chris. *Feminist Practice and Poststructuralist Theory.* Oxford: Basil Blackwell, 1987.

Zawacki, Terry Myers. "Recomposing as a Woman—An Essay in Different Voices." *College Composition and Communication* 43 (1992): 32–38.

8

Keeping Our Activist Selves Alive in the Classroom
Feminist Pedagogy and Political Activism

Jennifer Scanlon

Editors' Notes: Scanlon makes political activism a part of her Introduction to Women's Studies course by requiring her students to connect the course to their experiences outside the classroom. Students learn to see themselves as agents of change while doing "Outside Activity" reports and taking responsibility for teaching the last quarter of the semester. This essay is packed with vivid details of group projects and assignments.

Feminist instructors, intent on keeping the "feminist" part of our descriptive titles alive, attempt to foster in students a desire for both personal and social change. We stress that women's studies is the academic branch of the feminist movement; in fact, this is what keeps many of us in the academy and allows us to remain hopeful in our institutions. We are, in this sense, visionaries. However, if what students learn in our classes does not reach outside the classroom door or stretch beyond the end of the semester, our work bears the label "instruction" far more than it does "feminist."[1] The feminist academy cannot, as Minnich argues, be a retreat; we must encourage activism in our classrooms in order to keep feminist culture alive.[2]

There are good reasons why our messages often fall flat at the end of the semester. Students return to more traditional classes in which their experience may not be validated. As a result they may feel that their active participation in the educational process is limited only to classes in which sexism, racism, homophobia, or class oppression are expressly written into the syllabus. They do not clearly see how the voice they had discovered and/or cultivated in a women's studies course can carry over to their other classroom experiences. The "chilly climate" that still pervades academia appears to be far too foreboding for many of our students, well trained as they are to receive rather than to claim an education, to challenge.[3]

As faculty, though, and as feminists, we hope that students' voices will carry over to their other classes. We also hope students will use their new knowledge to challenge their friends on campus and work toward the continued creation of a more just society. Without being able to "check in," though, on how real life compares with various feminist visions, as they can in a women's studies class, and with the overwhelming amount of contradictory information coming from the media, the fiction they read, and the somewhat independent yet highly structured nature of their social life on college campuses, it should be no surprise that much of what we encourage gets lost quickly in students' real-life experiences. How is a student to demand serious communication with her peers when alcohol permeates virtually every social situation? How is a young heterosexual woman to demand safer sex practices when she is considered a slut if she even carries condoms in her purse?

Providing students with information alone is not sufficient. By the end of the semester in my introductory women's studies classes, students have adequate and compelling information about the importance of communication, the need for safer sex practices, the realities of women's lives, and the need for social change. Unless I provide them with tools as well as this information, however, and unless I encourage them to use what they learn, my work has to some degree been in vain.

Current feminist pedagogy provides some solutions to this problem by encouraging us to go beyond providing information to empower students so that they see themselves not only as victims of injustice but as people capable of creating change in society. In this way, we can pass our activism on to the students who want and need it. We can continue to forge the connection between women's studies in the classroom and the feminist movement outside the academy.

I have thought a great deal about what I want students to carry with them when they leave my classes. I cannot force them to become advocates for change. I cannot, for example, require that a student confront homophobia in the residence halls on campus. Students must decide if and when they are ready to take what they have learned to the world outside the classroom. For some, the process of using what I teach may occur many years later when they learn firsthand the realities of job discrimination, the humiliation of sexual harassment, or the rewards of economic independence. Others will remain sexist, homophobic, and/or racist; I cannot hope to reach everyone. A number of students, however, appear ready to take on challenges right away, with their peers, within their families, or in their college work. The challenges they seek can be met by actually engaging with housemates about controversial topics, choosing topics for research papers in other classes that challenge existing gender stereotypes, or confronting their own racism by acknowledging it and finding ways to move beyond it. The possibilities for action are endless, but an articulation on my part of the risks and rewards is often necessary for those challenges to occur outside the relatively safe confines of the women's studies classroom.

I am clear from the first day of class that I do have clear political opinions, that I want to see social change occur, that I am not "objective." However hopeful I might be that some students will agree with me politically, I do not try to legislate their politics. In fact, the politics of a feminist classroom purposefully allows for much disagreement, and I pride myself in the fact that students feel free to express their own opinions in my classes, however they may differ from my own. Nevertheless, I can and do offer students the opportunity to put their developing ideas in action.

The purpose of this article is to offer concrete suggestions, in the way of assignments, on how to keep our activist selves alive in the classroom by promoting activism in our students. Feminist educators can modify our classroom practices and assignments in the hopes of collectively, with our students, articulating a new vision and then actively challenging the patriarchal social structure. As Giroux and Simon argue, "to propose a pedagogy is to construct a political vision" (1989, p. 222). One aspect of my vision is that at least several students each semester will choose to confront issues of racism, sexism, heterosexism, and class oppression well after the semester ends. The following classroom assignments provide interested students the opportunity to take a political step and agitate for social change.

Outside Activity Paper No. 1

In my Introduction to Women's Studies classes, students must complete five two-page outside activity papers. Possible outside activities include participating in any event on campus that is relevant to the issues of our class, visiting an organization in the community that deals with women's issues, or attending our weekly Women's Studies Forum and writing about what occurs there. The papers, half summary, half critique, are graded on the effectiveness of the summary, the thoughtfulness of the critique, and the quality of the writing.

In keeping with the goal of encouraging feminist action, I recently revised one of these activity paper assignments. Previously, students could, for one of the five papers, read and critique an article in a magazine, journal, or newspaper. I found that without any more specific directions, however, most students would read and critique an article from a mainstream publication. I quickly grew tired of reading about feminism from the perspective of *Time, Cosmopolitan,* or *USA Today.* Students who read and critique articles from these sources are learning something, but they are not learning about the feminist culture, already strong, that exists.

The revised assignment states that if students choose to critique an article, it must be from a feminist publication. Most students are completely unfamiliar with feminist publications; in fact, many are surprised that they even exist and even more surprised that our library subscribes to several.

There are several reasons why I now believe this assignment is so successful and a far cry from the original. First, students are being exposed to information produced by and for rather than about feminists. They read, often for the first time, what feminists are writing in the world of journalism. Second, this initial exposure may inspire them to broaden the sources they consult for other academic papers. Third, students delve into an entire publication about women's issues rather than an isolated article or, in the case of mainstream women's magazines, a small piece of a larger agenda that denies active change. Students who pick up an issue of *Ms.*, for example, see far more than the one article they critique. They notice the lack of advertisements, other compelling articles, feminist comics, and as much information about women as agents of change as there is about women as victims of male dominance.

Students note that reading these journals validates what we do in the classroom; this provides an assurance that feminism is what I say it is: a movement, rather than embittered words of a few women in the academy. Student responses to this assignment are very positive, and I am convinced that fostering student participation in the broad and diverse written feminist culture is a necessary first step toward carrying a political vision outside the classroom.[4]

The one caution I have is that students may respond to the wider variety of articles they read in ethnocentric ways. I am looking for ways to do more in my classes to challenge the ethnocentrism that allows students to read an article about the shortage of marriageable men in the United States uncritically and an article about love marriages versus arranged marriages in Japan with disgust. I do talk about the need for us to be anthropologists in our own culture, but I feel that I—and they—can work harder in this area.

Outside Activity Paper No. 2

Students often tell me that they see me as someone who can use all of these wonderful feminist ideas; I teach others and can, therefore, actually be a feminist. Too often they see themselves as people detached from feminist work or action, even when they desire personal and social change. "It's easy for you," one young woman argued, "but what can I possibly do with all of this? I'm going to be a marketing specialist, not a women's studies professor." To respond to these concerns, I added a new outside activity paper option, an action paper, for as Hayes argues, "the educational process is not considered complete unless learners take concrete steps to apply what is learned toward change" (1989, p. 63).

For this assignment, students devise a way to actively challenge racism, homophobia, or sexism and their paper is their report on the experience. I make it clear that students do not have to attain their desired goal to complete the paper; they write both of their successes and their failures.[5] To write this activity paper students must see themselves as people capable of engendering change. We discuss risk taking and the experience of unmatched expectations, but I encourage them to discover what they can do with their new knowledge.

Many students have chosen to complete this assignment this semester, and they learned far more than I had anticipated. One student discussed homophobia with a friend. They talked for hours, but the student was not able to break down the barrier she initially encountered. When she wrote about the experience, the student reported that she learned two things: how difficult it is to change someone else's opinion and how important it is that she "know her stuff." She also learned that because someone is oppressed in one way, there is no guarantee that she/he will be sensitive about the oppression of others: her Latino friend saw no connection between the discrimination he faced and that faced by lesbians and gay men.

A second student discussed date rape with a male friend. She told him of a situation she knew about on our campus which she identified as date rape. She described the incident and asked him if it was rape. He replied that it was not rape, for the young woman willingly kissed the young man and accompanied him to his room. The discussion that followed was both intense and productive. In the end her friend acknowledged that it was rape. This student learned that women really do have to watch out for their friends and acquaintances who have not learned that "no" means "no."

A third student talked with her parents about AIDS education. Her father, a teacher, and her mother, a nurse, work with young people and will—if they have not already—encounter AIDS cases; however, the young woman and her parents differed radically in their opinions. The student argued that education about safer sex is necessary in the high schools; her parents believed this would encourage promiscuity. In the end, they did not agree on many of the issues related to AIDS, but the parents told their daughter they appreciate that she is thinking and forming opinions about important social issues. They encouraged her to be involved and not to, as they too often see, remain an apathetic outsider.

Several things I had hoped for were accomplished through these papers, but the rewards in the end of allowing students to take risks and be activists were greater than I had anticipated. Students learned about themselves, about others, and about the feminist process. The students discussed here and the others who took on this assignment had the opportunity to try out their developing feminist voices outside of the classroom. They took risks by confronting those they are close to about great differences in opinions. They learned how difficult it is to change someone else's opinions and how important it is to be clear in one's own thinking. They clarified their own ideas and/or gained another perspective to compare with their own. They were, in short, learning to be activists, and most reported that while others did not necessarily agree with their ideas, everyone involved enjoyed the intellectual and emotional challenges posed. The students reported favorably on this assignment, which can clearly help them see what feminism has to do with their own lives.

Group Project: "What Can I Do?"

Students divide into groups of four to complete a group project on any of nine topics, including gender socialization, media images of women, and international issues. Students run the class for the last quarter of the semester, as two groups a day present their material to the class. This is, in and of itself, a way of practicing feminist pedagogy in the classroom, as students decide how to break down a topic, how to present material to the class, and how to work together as a group. They have done very creative things, from talk shows to videos they produce to role plays that involve the audience.

This year I added a new topic to the list: "What can I do?" This group performs on the last day of the group projects and informs the class about what kinds of things people can do to keep feminism alive beyond the end of our class. During the first semester with this option, one group of students focused on activities available for students who want to become involved. The first member of the group discussed volunteer opportunities with women-centered organizations in the community. The second highlighted volunteer opportunities on our campus. The third presented information about the feminist journals and newspapers she had learned about. Finally, the fourth participant discussed and provided a handout listing various women musicians/women's music performers and women writers. The group members were dynamic, excited about their discoveries, and eager to share with their peers.

This assignment is perfect for those people in the classroom who identify as feminists from the start. They often feel the frustration of not taking what they learn outside class, and this assignment provides them the opportunity to be activists in the classroom as well as outside. It is a wonderful catalyst, too, for those who may not have initially embraced any feminist label but who are opening up to new possibilities in their lives as a result of what they have learned in the class.

Other groups in my introductory classes have worked on "What can I do?" and the excitement has been evident among these students as well. One student went to the national pro-choice rally in Washington, D.C. She made an hour-long videotape which she edited for her presentation, and in addition to showing it to our class she showed it to interested student groups on campus. The argument she made to her classmates was that if she, a parent of three young children, can be an activist, so can they. A second student came to speak with me shortly after the beginning of the semester. A political science major and a junior, she learned more about women's political history in several women's history lectures in my class than she had in her years of political science courses. Her advisor, in fact, had advised her against taking a women's studies class. When the day arrived for choosing topics, her hand shot up for "What can I do?" Her presentation was about what kinds of opportunities are available for women in politics, and she outlined lobbying, internship, and graduate school opportunities.

Final Examination

Kathleen Weiler argues that feminist theory is weak "when it fails to address forms of oppression other than gender oppression" (1988, p. 59). By the end of the semester, most students in my introductory women's studies classes are acquainted with and understand the nature of the various oppressions and privileges we live with. What is often more difficult in my teaching, though, is to help students see the connections between various oppressions and privileges. Many want to place the oppressions in some kind of hierarchy list: racism is the worst, and then sexism, etc. Others don't argue that one is more oppressive than another; instead, they want to think of them as completely separate entities.

I believe, however, that the most successful activists outside my classroom will be those who understand that in fighting one oppression they must at least be opposed to the rest. They are the ones who will make connections, build alliances, forge coalitions, find strength in related struggles. The final examination I use is my attempt to allow and in fact encourage students to make the necessary connections between various issues and to imagine how, in the immediate or near future, things might be different.

The final examination that follows here is an adaptation of an idea designed by Margaret Andersen (1986, p. 15). Wanting to reach both the intellectual and the emotional sides of her students, Andersen gave students a take-home essay about four fictional characters taking an introductory women's studies class. The characters get together at the end of the semester and discuss what they learned in their class. The job of the real students is to write, in dialogue, diary format, or in any other form they choose, just what the students say. In Andersen's exam, the fictional characters are varied and do not conform to stereotypes, but they do demonstrate in their brief biographies the diversity of women's lives.

Andersen's enthusiasm over the results of this exam prompted me to try it with my own classes. Her statement that the essays were "the best I've ever received" (p. 15) was enough encouragement for me to try it once, and I have used it for three semesters since then. Andersen offered the exam to others, and I offer my version in that same spirit of collaboration and as a replication of her excellent results.

What follows is a sample of my final exam. I follow the format Andersen proposed, but rather than ask the students to write a general discussion, I have asked them to have their characters discuss Roseanne Hoefel's oppression and hierarchy sheet (see Table 1), which lists the many oppressions and privileges we discussed throughout the semester (1992, p. 49). The sheet outlines which people are valued in our society, which are devalued, in terms of body, sexuality/gender, class, and race. There are many other approaches one could take, including having students focus on one theme, providing them with a comic strip to discuss, or providing them with the lyrics to a song. The characters in my exam change from semester to semester, depending upon the composition of my classes and on the issues we focus on. This semester I added the first male character at the suggestion of several male students.

Sample Exam

Four students, Pamela, Lee, Sharon, and David, have been enrolled in an Introduction to Women's Studies class. Throughout the semester, they have listened to each other in class, but they have never talked much outside class. Following the last class session, they go out for something to eat and drink. Each of them has the following handout, which the professor asked them to discuss. They talk about how they interpret this sheet in the context of what they have learned in women's studies.

> Your assignment is to write a description or transcript of what they talk about. Here are brief profiles of the four students.
>
> Lee, an Asian-American woman, is a returning adult student from Plattsburgh whose three children are grown. From an early age, Lee did well in school but received little encouragement. When she became pregnant in high school, Lee dropped out of school. Lee later married and had two more children. When her husband died at an early age, Lee collected a little bit of Social Security and found a job as a secretary. Lee recently discovered an experimental program for women to collect Social Security benefits while they attend college. Lee has not chosen a major, but she enrolled in a women's studies class because she felt she might hear something about women like herself.
>
> Sharon is a young (19) black woman from Albany. She is the first in her family to attend college. Sharon is doing fairly well in her accounting major but is having a difficult time personally. She is discovering and coming to terms with her lesbian identity. This is tremendously exciting for Sharon but terrifying as well, as she is afraid to tell her roommate and her new friends. Sharon is taking Introduction to Women's Studies because she thinks she may hear the word "lesbian" spoken out loud.
>
> Pamela is a young (21) white woman from a small town, and she is working toward her degree in nursing. Last summer Pamela read an article about eating disorders. She recognized that she has an eating disorder: bulimia. Pamela feels she cannot tell anyone about it, but she enrolled in Introduction to Women's Studies to learn more about why she feels so trapped by her body.
>
> David is a third semester international business student from New York City. He comes from a large, traditional family. David's women friends in the dorm charged him with sexism and urged him to take a women's studies class. Many of David's beliefs have been challenged this semester, and he's now questioning his own ideas as well as the ideas of the course.
>
> Directions: write approximately eight pages (typed) about/on what these four students have to say about the handout. Answers may be in the form of a conversation, a short story, a play, a diary, letters, or whatever you come up with.
>
> You must make SPECIFIC reference to information from class lectures, discussions, readings, group presentations. This is an important part of the

Table 1.
Hierarchies & Oppression chart

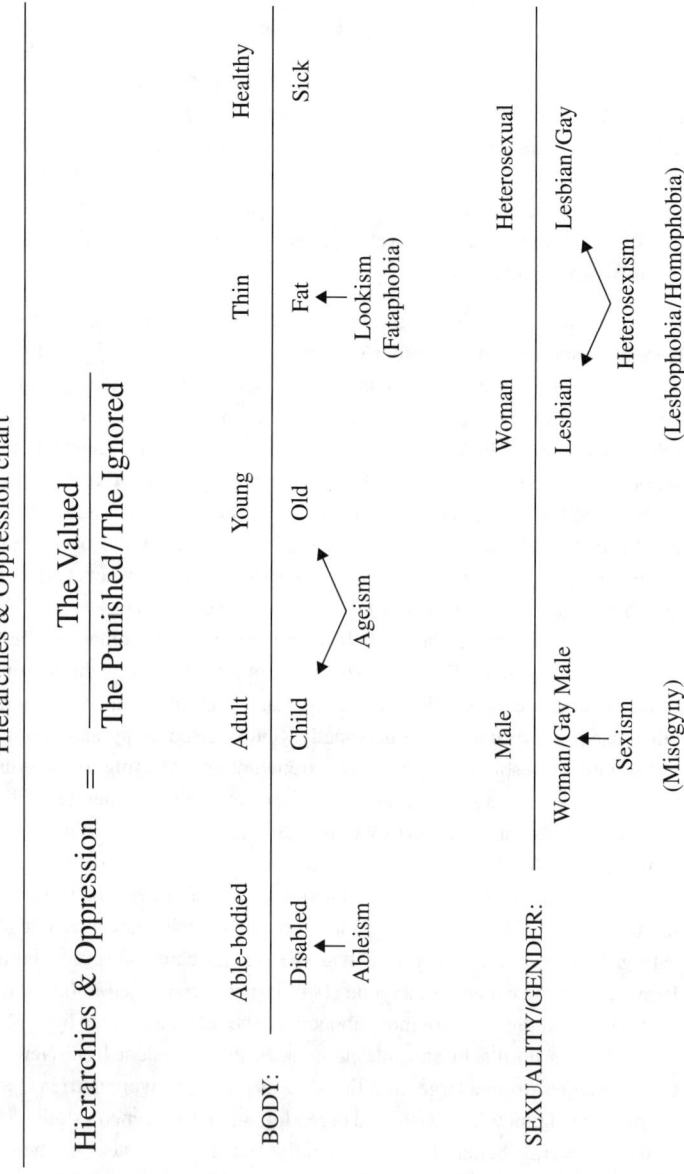

CLASS:	Rich	Boss	Educated (Schooled)	City	Intelligent
	Poor ←	Worker	Uneducated (Self-educated)	Rural	Dumb
	Classism →				

RACE:	White	Christian	At Least Second Generation & White & Australians, North Americans or Western Europeans	Humans
	Black	Jewish	Africans, Asians, Central-South Americans, Eastern Europeans, Mediterraneans, Middle Eastern, Soviets	Plants/Animals
	Of Color Asian, Latina North American	← Anti-semitism	← Colonialism (Xenophobia)	← Speciesism
	↙↘ Racism			

Chart by Caroljean Coventree reproduced in Roseanne Hoefel's "Confronting Exclusionary Ideologies in the Classroom," in *Transformations: The New Jersey Project Journal*, Vol. 2, No. 2 (Fall 1992), 36–49. (Chart on p. 49) paper, one which provides me with a basis for grading. You may examine any of the hierarchies/oppressions on the sheet, but since you must limit yourself, focus on the issues that are most significant to you.

The Results

Like Andersen, I found that students did tremendously creative things with this exam. In terms of the setting, they placed the characters at various restaurants in town and lavishly described what they ate and drank. They provided varied formats for the exam, from diary entries to letters home to poetry. The narrator of one paper was a fly on the wall of a local restaurant, who found the conversation if not the food of this group particularly interesting. My students also varied the time, from a distinguished visiting alumni speaking to the campus 15 years later to a presidential candidate's later recollections about her formative women's studies class. Another exam described how a group of students in the 21st century discover a time capsule containing this dialogue; they found it very confusing, as these forms of oppression no longer existed. Students have responded well to the exam and, as they bring these characters alive, everything they have learned during the semester comes alive as well.

There are several reasons I believe this exam fulfills the goal of my activist agenda. First, it views diversity as a source of strength and as a potentially powerful organizing theme.[6] I add new concerns of women each semester; eating disorders and men confronting sexism are two of my additions this past semester. Second, it allows students to step outside themselves for a change. They are not asked to do so, however, before they are ready. Were they asked, for example, to role play these women's lives at the beginning or even the middle of the semester, we probably would have observed stereotyping in action. By this point the students, armed as they are with a semester's worth of readings and much-raised consciousnesses, are prepared to step outside themselves without stepping all over others.

Another benefit of this exam is, as Andersen argues, that students "express their feelings about the topics without losing intellectual understanding" (1986 p. 15). They work through, in their own minds and hearts, how feminist theory can combine with personal solutions to problems. My goal is to promote activism that is grounded in everyday reality rather than in theory alone. This exam encourages that kind of balance. It also allows for the idea of women expressing themselves to each other; there are women with very different voices here—and other women to listen to them. We will see what changes with the addition of a male character. As is the case in class, the male presence may change the nature of the exam considerably.

One of the unanticipated benefits of the exam for me is that students have not made everything work out perfectly for the characters in their fiction. In most cases, the poor woman remains poor—but fighting—and the woman with the eating disorder is often hospitalized at the end of the story. Other papers have had the characters engaged in heated but constructive arguments. What students envision, rather than simple solutions, is an emphasis on the need for services for women and the need for continued and strong demands for social change.

Positive things come out of this exam. For one, students generally enjoy it. The best exams, of course, are the ones which truly integrate theory and emotional response. Not all students are capable of doing that well, but most sincerely take the challenge and all try, especially since the grading is based on their ability to integrate material from readings, lectures, films, group projects, and discussions.

Hayes argues that feminist pedagogy rests on the assumption that "educational benefits cannot be fully realized unless learners apply new knowledge to make changes in their own lives and in society" (1989, 58). I believe this is true, and that the women's studies classroom is a place where this engaged learning can be promoted and nurtured. Students are taught for so many years to be passive learners, passive citizens, and, for most our students, passive women. Feminist educators are taking on a lot when we hope to empower students both personally and politically, but it can be done. And, if we like to think of our work as political work, we must forge the connections between the classroom and the larger community.

Notes

1. For discussions of the connection between feminist pedagogy and social change, see Elisabeth Hayes, "Insights from Women's Experiences for Teaching and Learning," in *Effective Teaching Styles,* ed. Elisabeth Hayes (San Francisco, CA: Jossey-Bass, 1989), 58; Carolyn Shrewsbury, "What is Feminist Pedagogy?" in *Women's Studies in the South,* ed. Rhoda Barge Johnson (Dubuque, IA: Kendall/Hunt, 1991), 4; Kathleen Weiler, *Women Teaching for Change: Gender, Class and Power* (South Hadley, MA: Bergin and Garvey, 1988), 113; Miren Uriarte, "Contributing to a Dialogue: Approaches to Teaching About Race and Culture to Human Service Students and Workers," *Women's Studies Quarterly,* 14, No. 1/2 (Spring/Summer 1986), 33–35; Nancy Schniedewind, "Feminist Values: Guidelines for Teaching Methodology in Women's Studies," in *Learning Our Way: Essays in Feminist Education,* eds. Charlotte Bunch and Sandra Pollock (Trumansburg, NY: Crossing Press, 1983), 270; Christine Sleeter, Introduction to *Empowerment Through Multicultural Education,* ed. Christine Sleeter (Albany: SUNY Press, 1991), 6.

2. Elizabeth Kamarck Minnich, "Friends and Critics: The Feminist Academy," in *Learning Our Way: Essays in Feminist Education,* 324. On the importance of building feminist culture, see Mary Bricker-Jenkins and Nancy Hooyman, "Feminist Pedagogy in Education for Social Change," *Feminist Teacher,* 2, No. 2 (1987), 36–42.

3. On the chilly climate in higher education, see R. M. Hall, and B. R. Sandler, "The Classroom Climate: A Chilly One for Women?" (Washington, D.C.: Project on the

Status and Education of Women, 1982). On claiming an education, see Adrienne Rich, "Women and Honor," in *Lies, Secrets and Silence* (New York City: W. W. Norton, 1977), 231.

    4. On the need to build an alternative culture with our students, see Bricker-Jenkins and Hooyman, 39.

    5. On the need to discuss the risks, the potential successes, and the potential failures of such work with students, see Uriarte, 35.

    6. Bricker-Jenkins and Hooyman argue that we can use diversity as both a source of strength and as an organizing tool in teaching human service practitioners, Bricker-Jenkins and Hooyman, 38.

Works Cited

Andersen, Margaret. (1986) "Giving Life to Student Exams." *Women's Studies Quarterly* 16(3): 14–15.

Giroux, Henry A. and Roger I. Simon (1989) "Schooling, Popular Culture, and a Pedagogy of Possibility." *Popular Culture, Schooling, and Everyday Life.* Eds. Henry A. Giroux and Roger I. Simon. New York: Bergin and Garvey.

Hayes, Elizabeth. (1989) "Insights from Women's Experiences for Teaching and Learning." *Effective Teaching Styles.* Ed. Elizabeth Hayes. San Francisco: Jossey-Bass. 58.

Hoefel, Roseanne. (Fall 1992) "Confronting Exclusionary Ideologies in the Classroom: Transforming Toward Inclusion and Diversity." *Transformation* 2(2): 49.

Weiler, Kathleen. (1988) *Women Teaching for Change: Gender, Class and Power.* South Hadley, MA: Bergin and Garvey.

9

Empathy Education

Teaching About Women and Poverty in the Introductory Women's Studies Classroom

Jennifer Scanlon

Editors' Notes: Scanlon describes a workshop for her students that raised the profile of female poverty and questioned the demonization of welfare mothers and the racist attitudes held by some students. Scanlon's students worked in groups to compose a monthly budget for families living in poverty, discovering firsthand the essential need for much-maligned social services. Scanlon acknowledges both the possibilities for women's studies students and the limitations of this open workshop's effect on students.

Many traditional-aged college students, growing up as they did during the Reagan-Bush years, solidly identify with an individualist ethos, a renewed creed of the American Dream. Often accustomed to and sometimes eager for discussions of gender and race, they become uncomfortable when class issues are raised. Whether middle or working class, they are reluctant to acknowledge the demographic, political, or economic factors in the United States that may make their future work lives unstable financially. Working-class students usually are certain that they will achieve a class status higher than their parents'; middle-class students seem equally certain of attaining at least the same status as their parents. And a college degree, they believe, will largely eradicate any sexism or racism in employment opportunity, wages, or advancement.

Women's Studies faculty attempting to teach about the realities of women and poverty in the U.S. try to challenge these myths, as well as the notion that the poor suffer from a lack of character rather than a lack of money. After several unsuccessful attempts at breaking through the stereotypes and having students recognize the realities of poor women's lives, I designed a group workshop for the classroom. This article outlines what I hope to teach about class in an introductory level Women's Studies course, presents the workshop, and discusses some of the results. I have found that the workshop succeeds in providing what might be called "empathy education" and could be used by other Women's Studies faculty.

The setting for this workshop is a four-year public college, part of the state university system of New York. Many of the students are first-generation college students. A large percentage rely heavily on state-supported education, not being able to afford the expense of a private college. In a course like "Introduction to Women's Studies," many of the students are in their first year, but there often is a balance between them and more advanced students. With the great demand for Women's Studies classes, some students must wait several semesters before gaining admission to the introductory course. As our program has gained a reputation for excellence in teaching across the campus, we have also gained greater diversity in student enrollment. As a result, the student composition of the classes in many ways mirrors the composition of the student body as a whole. Most of the students are white and many are members of sororities or fraternities. The one way our students do not mirror the general student population is in terms of gender: about one quarter of the students in our introductory courses, on the whole, are male.

Through this introductory course, the Women's Studies Program reaches approximately two hundred students each year. Our goals for the course include encouraging an understanding of issues relating to race, class, and sexuality in addition to gender. In keeping with the goals of our General Education program and the goals of feminist pedagogy generally, the course contains many opportunities for active learning: group activities, the use of music and films, group presentations, and a great deal of in-class discussion. This exercise is one of many that engage the students in finding answers to, or at least further questions about, social issues.

In the post-election environment of 1995, with the State University of New York (SUNY) under assault, it is in some ways strange that students should fail to respond to issues about class identity and class struggle. Busloads of our students descended on Albany to speak their minds about budget cuts. Many others participated in teach-ins and collegewide discussions of the potential impact of our new governor's proposed cuts for SUNY. At the same time, though, students remain uneasy about considering the long-term consequences of political decisions based on class. It might appear bewildering to many faculty members that events directly affecting students should prove to be impediments to rather than opportunities for questioning and learning.

In defense of the students, steeped as they are in contemporary media and political rhetoric about the poor, they have good reasons for keeping to their misconceptions about social class. In the twelve-year assault of the Reagan-Bush years and, unfortunately, in the rhetoric of the Clinton administration thus far, poor people are blamed for their problems. The current mood in the U.S., with an emphasis on "welfare reform" but little discussion of needy people, encourages students to believe that poor people lack not money but morality, not jobs but souls.[1] Although the students are often blind to the supports they receive as participants in a heavily subsidized state-supported higher education system, then, they are acutely aware of the ways in which the poor secure taxpayer-supported services.

After discovering repeatedly that students responded to my discussions of class issues and of poverty by introducing racist and sexist examples of welfare mothers and Cadillacs, someone they know who cheats the system in order to have a television set and a VCR, or poverty as a "lifestyle," I realized I needed an approach that would get beyond the stereotypes and at the personal side of poverty. I had to do two things: first, as Ardeth Deay and Judith Stitzel argue, I had to get beyond my own feelings of frustration with the conservative environment and my students' conservative attitudes (Deay and Stitzel 29); next, I had to change my approach: if what I was doing in the classroom was not working, I had to try something else.

Feminist pedagogy, fortunately, provided me with several strategies. I am not an expert on the statistics about women and poverty. Since, in any case, statistics just seem to elicit from students examples of apparently well-off poor people, I looked for an approach that would actually teach empathy rather than numbers, understanding rather than abstraction. I searched for a way to provide "connected learning" (Hayes 57) by forgetting about my own lack of expertise in social stratification or economic theory and concentrating instead on my ability to engage students in a process that provides the tools for critical reflection (Hayes 55). From my experience, in-class workshops, where students work in groups and then present their findings, promote that kind of engagement. I decided to approach the problem using what Weiler calls the three major themes of feminist pedagogy: to make no claims of objectivity, but instead place women firmly at the center of analysis; to emphasize the lived experience of women; and to have as a goal social change (Weiler 58–59).

The format I now use in teaching about women and poverty evolved both from my reading on feminist pedagogy and from my classroom experience. First, I introduce students to key concepts, arguing that the concepts are not objective, probably differing significantly from what the students have heard in or out of the classroom about poverty in the United States. I then introduce them to the workshop, hopefully forcing the students to get outside themselves for a bit and enter the lives of others in order to feel their struggles. We end the class by making a collective attempt to identify new social policies that could meet the needs of poor women and facilitate positive social change.

Introduction to Women's Lives in Poverty: Just the Facts

To provide a bit of context for the group activity, I provide some statistics, as well as my argument, about women and poverty in the United States. I ask whether or not poverty has a gender, a race, an age. I provide a few statistics to help complicate the students' analysis. A single parent of two children who works for the minimum wage earns $2300 a year below the federal poverty line. There are 13 million people on AFDC, but only four million are adults, and ninety percent of those are women. The average salary needed to keep a family of four out of poverty is $7.00 an hour. Nearly one of two Black children live below the poverty line (Astor 5). I try then to get them to talk about some of the reasons why people of color and white women and children are over-represented in the statistics. Together, we identify some of the issues, including child care, part-time work, and low wages. Inevitably, though, some of the stereotypes arise, so I provide only a few statistics and then divide them in groups, giving each member of the class a copy of the following worksheet.

The Group Activity Worksheet

Your group will discuss the life of one of these women and/or children. Give your characters names and other identifying characteristics (age, ethnicity, race, sexual orientation, etc.). Make them as real in your minds as you can. Then take out a calculator and construct a monthly budget for the family. Include all possible expenses, making a separate list for expenses the family has but cannot meet. Talk about how the economic situation affects each individual involved. Prepare to introduce your woman and/or children to the class; when you do, make any relevant connections between your characters' situation and the issues we discussed at the beginning of class.

1. Single Parent with Two Children

This woman has a high school education and is employed as a receptionist at a local want ad newspaper. She earns $6.00 an hour but receives no medical or dental benefits. Her ex-husband is supposed to pay child support but has moved out of state and pays her one or two times a year, if that. Develop a budget for her and her children. Describe a typical day for this mother. What does she do if one of her children is ill? What does she do during school vacations?

2. Single Mother Receiving AFDC and Food Stamps

This single mother has two children under six. She did not complete high school. Like many other women, she left her partner because he was violent. Her AFDC allotment is $334 a month with $182 a month in food stamps. Where will she live? How is she perceived by the society around her? Describe a typical day in this woman's life, and discuss how and when she might move towards self-sufficiency. Identify social supports that could help her in such a transition.

3. Child of Single Parent

This junior high school child lives with her/his mother and younger sister. The mother earns minimum wage at a manufacturing job, a job which provides no health or dental insurance. The child is not old enough to work but lacks many of the extras other kids have in school. Create a monthly budget for the family, including rent, food, utilities, etc.; then figure out what money is left over for the child. Consider things like school trips, video games, haircuts, movies, sports activities, etc.

4. Married Couple with Two Children

This couple has been married for six years, living month to month primarily but saving about $3000 along the way. The man lost his job nine months ago and has been unable to find another. His unemployment benefits are about to run out. The woman works part-time at a department store, but she receives no benefits. Right now, with the wife working, they are not entitled to receive any social service support. In addition, the automobile they have paid off is worth $5500, and in order to receive benefits your car must be worth less than $4800. If they spend all their money and go on welfare, they will receive $516 a month for a two bedroom apartment, including all utilities. What steps should they take?[2]

My Role in the Group Activity

I move around the room, talking briefly with each group as the students work. My objective during this time period is to put hitches in their solutions. For example, if they decide one of the children is a baby, thinking they will cut food costs, I bring up the issue of diapers, pediatrician visits, clothes that fit for short periods of time. If they talk about women doubling up or moving in with family members to save money, I let them know that the woman will most likely lose her benefits as a result, since the income of all people living together will be counted for food stamps, even if they do not share food (Clarke 44). If they argue that the woman receiving AFDC can get a part-time job, I let them know that in order to keep any benefits she must, in twenty-nine states, earn less than 60 percent of the federal poverty level (Amott 123). If they argue that a single parent can sue her ex-husband for regular child support, I ask them if she is entitled to take time off from work, if there is room in her budget for court fees, if she has money for child care so she can go to court. I purposefully look for what they leave out and I disturb their accounting as I walk around the room. This frustrates them in what I consider positive ways: they see that as tightly as they may construct their budgets, things come up that they had not considered.

Group Introductions of Characters, Situations, and Budgets

When the groups report back, some are smug about their ability to have their characters live within their means. Most, however, are quick to point out just how difficult the women's and children's lives must be. When two separate groups have the same characters, they advise each other about how they calculated expenses or complain about how they could not handle the child care, transportation, medical care. They introduce strategies the poor women might use, and as a group we discuss the good and bad points of those strategies. The discussion is light years away from the blaming the victim approach they take at first. Most of the students now identify with their characters; they want them to make it. Suddenly, social service supports are necessary and humane, rather than supplementary and debilitating. Not all the students take this exercise seriously; some defensively find no connections between themselves and these imaginary characters, but most take up the challenge and make the connections. "She can't even go to the movies," one student woefully remarked, while another pointed out that a receptionist has to look nice but earns too little money to buy the clothing and cosmetics necessary to pull it off.

The Public Policy Agenda

The last part of the workshop, after the characters have been introduced and discussed, is to make a list, collectively, of what kinds of public policy and social change would help these women and children. Now on-site day care, raising the minimum wage, health insurance, affordable and accessible public transportation, job sharing, job training, and other issues make some sense—and come from the students, not just the professor. We talk about the ways in which middle-class women are encouraged to stay at home and take care of their children, but poor women are not. We talk about the work and value of mothering, in contrast to the social validation of work that pays, no matter how inconsequential or even detrimental it is for the society. I introduce a quote by Pat Gowens, founder of the Welfare Warriors, who argues, "There is no recognition of mothering as work. Raising children is invisible in this society" (Astor 4). We discuss, perhaps briefly, sex segregation in employment and the need for pay equity programs; sexual harassment on the job; and proposals for securing child support through the IRS or other agencies. What might otherwise be an almost meaningless list on the board has now become a list of solutions for the people these students have in their heads. The problems as well as the solutions become both meaningful and urgent.

Evaluation

Although I consider the exercise effective, I see several weaknesses. These students have been trained to see poverty as something that affects people outside the American Dream. They see themselves as people living inside the American Dream. One day's exercise cannot overturn years of conditioning. Also, traditional-aged students, partly because of their youth, are unlikely to feel vulnerability—or at least admit vulnerability. This exercise, like many I use, benefits by the participation of nontraditional students, who often can attest to the accuracy of some of the life stories we discuss.

I have learned, in doing this exercise with students and in discussing issues of social class, that I have to tread carefully over the issue of their futures. Although I wish for them a more comprehensive understanding of poverty, I do not wish to discourage them from pursuing their studies or fighting to improve their lives. I recognize the need for anger and the power of anger for propelling social change; I also recognize the debilitating effect of resignation and depression. My long-term goal is to get students to engage with issues of class for a sustained period of time without fostering in them a listless and apathetic approach to great social problems.

Another difficulty arises when the students' racism emerges. On several occasions students remark that these women do represent the "deserving poor," but they know that many others abuse the system. They bring up women living like "queens," a common reference to African-American women on welfare. The real women they have discussed get lost behind the more familiar stereotypes. I address this by asking them about the ways in which race might influence a woman's visit to a social service agency or to a job interview. Poor African-American women, of course, do not have the luxury of choosing to deal with one identity at a time; they are poor, African-American, and female simultaneously. I ask students to think about why it is that they have a race-based image in their minds when they think of welfare, when in fact the majority of welfare recipients in the U.S. are white. I ask them about the high percentage of welfare recipients in our area, almost all of whom are white. I have found that the best approach to the stereotypes is to get them out in the open and then examine them. Students seem better equipped to do this after conducting this in-class exercise than before it.

Conclusion

The characters and situations for this worksheet could be as varied as the faculty who invent them or the students whose individual life experiences they might or might not reflect. I offer these only as a starting point and a pedagogical approach for others. This exercise provides students with an opportunity to actively think about the contradictions between messages they receive in the media and messages they hear in a Women's Studies classroom. It provides one more piece of evidence encouraging students to see that multiple readings of societal issues are possible. My greatest fear is not that these particular examples are not the best; my greatest fear is that faculty, because of student apathy or even hostility, will shy away from addressing in their classrooms the same class issues that the feminist movement has yet to address adequately outside the classroom. Diana Pearce writes that our task is "not about finding out how poor women are different or how they need to be changed, but to recognize the universal and embedded nature of women's poverty in the gender, racial, and class inequalities that characterize American society today" (Pearce 94). Feminist faculty can accomplish this by educating for empathy as well as for knowledge. This workshop is one way to approach that task with respect both for the students, through engaging feminist pedagogy, and for the subjects, poor women and children, who must form more than simply a footnote in the work that goes on in the Women's Studies classroom.

Notes

1. The literature on welfare mothers, orphanages, and the poor who cheat the system proliferates. For background reading to help provide reality checks for students completing this exercise, see Wahneema Lubiano, "Black Ladies, Welfare Queens, and State Minstrels: Ideological Warfare by Narrative Means," in *Race-Ing Justice, En-Gendering Power,* ed. Toni Morrison (New York: Penguin 1992), 323–363; Renu Nahata, "Persistent Welfare Stereotypes," in *Issues in Feminism,* ed. Sheila Ruth (Mountain View, CA: Mayfield Publishing Company, 1995), 347–349; and Gina Tessier, "Whose Welfare?" *Ms.* 4.2 (Sept./Oct. 1994): 90–92.

2. The automobile figure of $4800 has not been adjusted since the 1970s. That and other current figures are supplied by Clarke, p. 43.

Works Cited

Amott, Teresa. *Caught in the Crisis: Women and the American Economy Today.* New York: Monthly Review Press, 1993.

Astor, Kathy K. "Punishing Women Who Break the Rules of Patriarchy." *New Directions for Women.* 22.1 (January–February 1993): 3–5.

Clarke, Kevin. "Hunger in America Is Increasing." *Poverty: Opposing Viewpoints.* Ed. Katie de Koster. San Diego, CA: Greenhaven Press, 1994. 37–45.

Deay, Ardeth and Judith Stitzel. "Reshaping the Introductory Women's Studies Course: Dealing Upfront with Anger, Resistance, and Reality." *Feminist Teacher* 6.1 (Spring 1991): 29–33.

Hayes, Elisabeth, ed. *Effective Teaching Styles.* San Francisco, CA: Jossey-Bass, 1989.

Pearce, Diana M. "Something Old, Something New: Women's Poverty in the 1990s." *American Women in the Nineties: Today's Critical Issues.* Ed. Sherri Matteo. Boston: Northeastern UP, 1993. 79–97.

Weiler, Kathleen. *Women Teaching for Change: Gender, Class and Power.* South Hadley, MA: Bergin & Garvey, 1988.

10

Human Labor and Literature
A Pedagogy from a Working-Class Perspective

Janet Zandy

Editors' Notes: Noting the absence of workers, class-based issues, and the subject of human labor in literature, Zandy discusses pedagogical strategies for increasing their visibility. In her Literature and Technology course, Zandy has students examine economic inequities, recognize worker identity, and connect technology to oppression through various novels, films, and photographs. With the many possible materials she suggests, her critical approach provides students with alternative views of work and class.

What place does human labor have in the study of literature? What is the relationship between the flourishing of critical theory inside the academy and the decline of economic justice outside the academy? What pedagogical strategies offer some resistance to the expropriation of intellectual and cultural labor to proprietary interests? Or, how does one put one's head in the mouth of the lion, and cause the lion some irritation?[1]

For nearly a decade I have been experimenting in my writing and literature classes with the concept of work and workers' perspectives as subject and as strategy for study. My approach is not career training; actually, it is a form of career resistance. I am interested in fostering within the liberal arts a point of reference about what constitutes good work for human beings. I want to raise questions about the way work is defined, shaped, and controlled. I want to explore the relationship between work and leisure, to question the assumed dichotomy between the terms "work" and "leisure." I desire an investigation of worker artistry and worker spirituality, or to put it another way, the artistry and spirituality of good work. In short, I want to establish a beachhead of resistance to the usurpation and control of ordinary people's working lives by corporate

America.[2] And, I propose to do this in literature and writing classes with students whose primary concerns and driving interests are in getting a good job.

Human labor as a subject in American educational practice is generally neglected, and as a perspective or theme in literary study is labeled either "proletarian" and/or dismissed. Literary anthologies claiming to present "the human experience" include innocence and experience, life and death, and other predictable universals, but they exclude work.[3] Workers are invisible—particularly in academic culture.

A small example: In a major American city, an academic conference is held. In the lobby of the hotel a professor of English makes small talk with me. He asks, "What is your field?" I answer, "American working-class literature." After a significant pause, he replies: "Oh, I didn't know there was a working class anymore." I suggest that there still is a working class as I glance around the hotel lobby to see people clearing tables, carrying food, cleaning ashtrays, washing windows, setting up chairs, etc. The lobby hummed with human activity, but individual workers blurred into the deep background of academic humanism.

Seeing is central to my purposes here. In *In Visible Light: Photography and the American Writer: 1840–1940,* Carol Schloss (1987) describes our culture's "unequal distribution of visibility" as a "disturbing pattern of American experience, a pattern in which Rousseau's ideal of the state as a transparent community of mutually visible citizens and motives is rarely achieved," hence preventing "any truly reciprocal interaction in the world from becoming a reality" (266–67). This essay proposes a pedagogical practice that explores possibilities for reciprocal visibility. My intent is to use the commonality of work as a place from which I can practice a pedagogy that takes into account particularity and partiality without sacrificing consensus about what constitutes a just society.

Standpoint

As a first generation college student, a scholarship girl, I had to choose between "getting an education" and my working-class identity. I learned that the language of home was not the language of school, that family history and stories were far removed from what was officially labeled as historical or literary. I was taught to repress and devalue my working-class identity and believe in aesthetic perfectionism. This condition of doubleness, of equivocality, of bifurcation, of competing and multiple identities is an old story, hardly unique or particularly acute to me.[4] It is a much less submerged story now because we have theoretical tools to name that condition, and with them, the power of language to democratize educational practice.[5] But, I get ahead of myself.

Too often theoretical language either alienates those most inclined toward democratic pedagogy or languishes in a state of theoretical narcissism—the theoretician dazzled by the shiny brilliance of the tool.[6] I propose that we use theory as a map to trace those locations where different epistemologies intersect. These intersections, occurring outside and at the borders of the academy, are sites where outsiders can become visible to each other (and are not just points of linguistic pleasure). We can begin to reconstruct sites of reciprocal visibility by focusing on work and class identity.

I'm aware of how easy it is to betray working-class lived experiences. I do not wear my working-class identity as a trendy badge for academic conferences. Rather, I choose to keep that identity, particularly the realities of economic struggle, unsafe and dead-end jobs, and the memories of collective celebration and commitment. These memories serve to center me in opposition to academic elitism and enable me to see how the world of work is not separate from literary study.

In oral and written narratives, speeches, letters, essays, poems, and songs, we find evidence of how ordinary people pooled their resources in a common struggle against an economic system that prefers profits to people. Muted, fenced away from academic discourse, these stories are an inheritance of risk taking and mutuality. They offer a clarity about bosses and workers, a way of fusing worker consciousness with consciousness about race, gender, and ethnicity. But these central narratives are not public. They are hidden from working people themselves, obscured by narratives of minuscule possibility—stories of winning, stardom, and lucky breaks. Playing Lotto has replaced an earlier generation's belief in sainthood—a way to make it big. Class consciousness is thwarted by spurious narratives. What might happen if narratives of common struggle weren't blocked? What might happen if patterns of oppression were visible to working people, to students and teachers?

I am not interested in human labor as "theme" in literature; rather, I want to penetrate texts with a system of thought that concerns itself with work and the dignity of human labor. The historicity of work can be a tool to cut through those pedagogical practices that pen in rather than liberate consciousness. The theologian Dorothee Soelle (1984) offers this perspective on work and social relatedness:

> All workers act within a particular society and culture. All have inherited tools, technology, knowledge from past generations of workers. . . .
>
> To develop a historical sense of what work has been, to know what our grandparents did and the path they took to their achievements, is the aim of an educational process that puts self-understanding and human worth before capital. Yet this approach to work is almost unheard of in a nation like the United States, which evaluates labor primarily in terms of productivity. . . . Work is communal not only in the space of a given community but also in time, as the shared memory of what we have received from the past that accompanies us into the future. (94–95)

I make this distinction between work and class in my methodology: I use work in its broadest definition (including paid and unpaid labor, domestic and caretaking work) as an inclusive matrix. Work is common territory where differences of gender, race, and ethnicity can be visible and where questions of what constitutes good work can be raised. I use class, that is, human relations based on economic differences, to illuminate relationality, in particular, life at the border of difference, a site of disruptive fissures.[7] This dis/located position is a good place from which to question obedience, particularly accommodations to power that thwart self-knowledge. It is also an appropriate position from which to examine central and marginal stories.

In *Landscape for a Good Woman,* the British writer Carolyn Kay Steedman (1987) creates an autobiography about the tangled working-class lives of her mother and herself, and offers this insight:

> the processes of working-class autobiography, of people's history and of the working-class novel, cannot show a proper and valid culture existing in its own right, underneath the official forms, waiting for revelation. Accounts of working-class life are told by tension and ambiguity, out on the borderlands. The story—my mother's story, a hundred thousand others—cannot be absorbed into the central one: it is both its disruption and its essential counterpoint: this is the drama of *class.* (22)

This way of seeing, its relationality, is inherent to practicing a pedagogy of possibilities and liberation. What follows is a contextualization of this approach in relation to my students in an upstate New York technical institute and to the peculiar and particular historic moment of living in the United States in the 1990s.

Reagan's Kids

In December 1988, a bomb exploded on Pan Am Flight 103 over Lockerbie, Scotland. Two hundred and seventy people were killed, including a number of upstate New York students. In response to this event, one of my students wrote this in her journal: "[F]rom 31,000 feet they had no chance to save themselves. Thirty-eight students, thirty-eight fewer people competing for jobs."

How is knowledge so constituted for this American student that she might read the explosion of a packed airplane in terms of job competition? She does not speak for everyone, but she is not necessarily in the minority, either. Having read hundreds of journals, essays, and fragments of student thought, I am inclined to believe that this person voiced what others tend to think but not say aloud.

I call them "Reagan's Kids"; they are representatives of the generation who grew to adulthood under the reign of this ideological Mr. Magoo, a cheerful gent who has no consciousness of his own destructive legacy. I don't assume that my generation is inherently any better; only, at the moment, the 1960s generation is getting better press, now that it has been rendered harmless.[8] But, Reagan's Kids have had to face a different set of historical circumstances and more rigid economic opportunities. Even governmental statistics indicate the shift of wealth, the decline in real wages, and the narrowing of economic choices. It is also an era in which accountability and mutuality, like savings and loan institutions, have been deregulated. Life is a game based on an ethos of scarcity, and the rules say that, if someone else loses, I may win.

So fearful of falling out of the middle class (Ehrenreich 1990),[9] these students don't have time for what John Willinsky (in a study [1990] of British nineteenth-century working-class literacy) calls "economically disengaged" knowledge, that is, knowledge without discernible market value.[10] Having had part- or full-time jobs since they were fifteen or sixteen, they are accustomed to earning and consuming, not contemplating. In harness, waiting to race down a narrow career track, functioning within a tight quarter system, dazzled by lucrative cooperative employment opportunities, these students don't have the leisure time or the inclination to question their goals, to ask about the ideological implications of the managerial positions they seek, or to wonder what is missing from degree programs shaped to corporate demands. Reality has been flattened for them in the homogenization of malls, news "shows," and popular culture. Small wonder that they are often emotionally flat; small wonder they resist knowledge, display symptoms of what James Moffett calls "agnosis," a fear of knowing.[11]

Mostly, these students want to find their place, to fit in. I want them to see that the world they are striving to fit into is much more complex, unstable, fragmented and endangered than their disembodied coursework might indicate. Or as Gwendolyn Brooks put it in a 1990 commencement address at Trinity College: "I shudder when I consider the possibility that squads of young people are struggling to fit in . . . Look at the craziness. Look at the fear. See the sickness. Into this you want to fit?"

I want to suggest that we recognize students' real fears about employment and use work as an epistemological position in the teaching of literature and writing. In *A Feminist Ethic of Risk,* Harvard theologian Sharon Welch (1990) describes responsible action as "the creation of a matrix in which further actions are possible, the creation of the conditions of possibility for desired changes" (20). I turn to human labor for such a matrix, a position where my aspiring engineers, hotel managers, and package designers can begin to see patterns of control and economic inequalities. There is nothing new about looking at work from an owner's or corporate perspective; indeed, that is presented in most academic institutions as normative, not perspectival. I want students to recognize worker consciousness and identity, to develop new subjectivities, ways of discerning, through the juxtaposition of texts, their own replication of, or resistance to, oppression. I am not advocating economic determinism, that work is the central or only perspective, but rather that it is a site of intersection and mutual visibility of competing concerns and constituencies, where differences of race, gender, ethnicity, geography, and culture might be seen.

Pedagogy, Theory, and Curriculum

It is the rare student who has overt awareness of the "domestication" of his or her consciousness. When queried whether or not they are "free," most students react with ambiguity. They acknowledge the dogma of freedom, but, somehow, they don't *feel* it. It is that fissure of doubt between the rhetoric of freedom and the experience of control that I wish to begin my conversation with students over literary texts. That fissure of doubt is also an appropriate intersection for theory, politics, and pedagogy—a place to ask if theory is aiding a liberatory practice.[12]

A pedagogy that insists on the visibility of human labor is also self-conscious about its theoretical girding. Jim Merod, in *The Political Responsibility of the Critic* (1987), draws the connection between "the world of everyday labor and that other world of intellectual exercise which seeks an essentially theoretical clarity" (1). In noticing the curious omission within critical practice of a "vocabulary for the world of human labor" (4), Merod draws attention to criticism as intellectual labor, as a kind of work, that can either reinforce or disrupt the status quo.[13]

There are no theoretical safe places. Theory, like technology, is situated within structures of power. The fragmentation of postmodern existence partially explains why workers in a hotel lobby may be invisible to humanities professors, and bombed planes might become job opportunities, but—as critical praxis—postmodernism offers little resistance to the further rendering of the fabric of human relationality. Linda Hutcheon argues, in *The Politics of Postmodernism* (1989), that it is not enough to "de-doxify" systems of meaning (153); there must also be a "move into political agency" (157).

It seems to me that any theory that holds relevance for the twenty-first century must move beyond an ethos of critique and an ethos of despair. We need theoretical hybrids that contain paradigms for reassembling as well as disassembling. We need to be less anxious about origins, philosophical parentage, and labels, and feel at home in the blurring of political, scientific, and literary theoretical boundaries. Interactive political models that go beyond monism (single-cause theories) and pluralism (celebration of diversity) offer the potential for coalition building (without erasing differences) by emphasizing intersecting rather than competing oppressions.[14] Human labor and literature, imagined as a site of interaction, allow for the recognition of difference without necessarily producing greater fragmentation.

An imaginative, startling, indeed, blasphemous paradigm for affinity rather than identity politics is Donna Haraway's (1985) reappropriation of the cyborg myth, "A Manifesto for Cyborgs." Haraway illuminates the conditions of human labor and the formation of culture by offering what she calls a "slightly perverse shift of perspective": "[a] cyborg myth . . . about transgressed boundaries, potent fusions, and dangerous possibilities. . . ." Instead of a cyborg as "a grid of control on the planet," Haraway imagines "a cyborg world [which] might be about social and bodily realities in which people are not afraid of their joint kinship with animals and machines, not afraid of permanently partial identities and contradictory standpoints" (585).

Such an imagined cyborg world might very well unsettle technological hegemony and offer a revolutionary and democratic interplay between the liberal arts and the sciences. But in the meantime, I must acknowledge my students' genuine concerns about their economic futures, and, at the same time, warn them that trading education for job training will not deliver them into the promised land of secure employment—not to mention what restrictions it may impose on their development as human beings. It seems to me that my task in teaching literature at this historical juncture is to practice a pedagogy of visibility and resistance that would offer opportunities for students to deconstruct false promises of easy fits, and simultaneously to construct alternate realities of mutuality and accountability, to move from self-serving individualism to relationality and toward community. The pedagogy I wish to practice builds on a vision that takes in the concrete (the worker, the necessary, the sturdy underpinnings), acknowledges the specificity of race and gender, of paid and unpaid work, *and* evokes the visionary, the possibilities of alternative, economically just realities.

The motto for the college where I teach is "to make a living and to live a life."[15] Dazzled by the technology of solar cars, imaging science, and state-of-the-art computers, it is understandable why many students give the living-a-life part of the motto short shrift. A study of work that is not driven by the requisites of job training offers an opportunity to examine the tensions between life and work and the possibilities for fusion. I have used work as a thematic base for composition courses and have focused on work in literature and not just works *of* literature. I want to elaborate here on how worker consciousness can shape a course that has appeal for technocratic students—"Literature and Technology."

An appropriate course to question the balance of life and work, "Literature and Technology" offers a borderland where competing interests and subjugated knowledges can intersect. I avoid the stance of the humanist opposed to technology; it is unauthentic and beside the point. I ask, instead, for an investigation of the impact of technology on what it means to be a human being. I wish to push beyond the dated "Man Versus Machine" dualism and move from the nebulous effects of technology to a more specific interrogation of deskilling, dehumanization, and the technologizing of humanity as slaves, birthing machines, or cyborgs. There are certain questions that always need to permeate the texture of the course: Who has the control? Where is the power? Who is subject? Who is object? Since technology and literary texts are both embedded in historical relations, I begin with readings that raise central questions about literary response to technological change. I surround five or six central texts with historical essays, news articles, journal excerpts, slides, videos, music, enough specific supplementary material to establish a context, a sense of relationality rather than textual isolation. Like photomontage, this literary montage approach offers a kind of aperture to a larger world and the possibility of dialogue with that world. I begin with Hawthorne's "Ethan Brand," Melville's "The Paradise of Bachelors and The Tartarus of Maids" and Leo Marx's *The Machine in the Garden* (1964). These provide a symbolic and literary landscape for raising questions of dislocation and showing the intertextual effect of reading about rich lawyers in juxtaposition with "girl" paper-mill workers. These readings also signal a central concern of the course—whether humans become subjects or objects, agents or victims. The terminology of subjectivity is useful, and students will keep track of those moments in the course when technology or labor transforms a human being into an "it." The garden and the machine juxtaposition in Leo Marx's famous essay exposes a powerful conundrum in American consciousness: a longing for a pastoral, greener America and an adoration for gadgets, for the control that machines promise.[16]

The Education of Henry Adams would be an appropriate next text, but I choose instead *The Lowell Offering: Writings by New England Mill Women, 1840–1845* (Eisler 1980) because I wish to emphasize class and gender in relation to work. This is a good place for students to see female workers as subjects who, although ambivalent about the noise and tedium of factory life, about lives lived "half in sunlight—half in shade" (77), are also proud of their literacy, culture, and passion for knowledge.

Next, to witness the degradation of work and the use of immigrant labor in relation to industrialization, we study Thomas Bell's moving novel *Out of This Furnace* (1976 [1941]). This fictionalized account of three generations of Slovakian steelworkers shows that for the working class, the boundary between work and home is very blurred, as women do laundry and keep boarders because "the job" does not pay men living wages. Often this novel evokes family memories for students: "[I]t compelled me to think of . . . how my grandfather and father [would] go to work very early in the morning and come back tired and hungry. I took this workday experience for granted. . . . This novel opened my mind to exactly how technology dictated life." In a victim-blaming culture, the sources of oppression can be invisible. Bell's novel offered this clarity for another student: "The reason for this inability to move out of these poor conditions is the mills themselves and the management of these mills . . . This is a very disturbing novel."

I contextualize Bell's novel with Lewis Hine's (1977) photographs of Slovakian immigrants as they land in Ellis Island and as they are "Americanized" as steelworkers in Homestead and Pittsburgh. I include technical explanations of Bessemer furnaces, with facts on American immigration policies in relation to industrial growth, and news articles about the displaced steelworkers of the 1980s. I have invited the contemporary photographer Margaret Evans to show slides of her photographs that document what she calls the "deconstruction" of the American steel industry.

I use Charlie Chaplin's wonderful and prophetic *Modern Times* as a transition to a study of the engineer, technology, and literature. This is an appropriate preamble to the satire and irony of Kurt Vonnegut's *Player Piano*. Originally published in 1952, *Player Piano*'s prescient and funny depiction of displaced workers is uncomfortably close to today's newspaper stories. A favorite selection, students enjoy Vonnegut's satire of the corporate world even as they trudge into class perspiring in their job-interview suits.

For a theoretical understanding of what Vonnegut and Chaplin are up to, I draw from Frederick Taylor's *The Principles of Scientific Management,* Karl Marx on "Alienated Labor," C. Wright Mills's "The Idea of Craftmanship," and David Noble's *America by Design* (1987). Cecelia Tichi's *Shifting Gears: Technology, Literature, Culture in Modernist America* (1987) offers excellent visual documentation as well as acute cultural analysis. Tichi's analysis of the interpenetration of technology and poetry establishes a context for an analysis of technology as subject (Whitman's "To a Locomotive in Winter") and technology as form, what Tichi describes as "the machine-age poetics" of William Carlos Williams (230). This is also a good point at which to introduce working-class women's poetry, particularly Susan Eisenberg's tradeswoman poems (*It's a Good Thing I'm Not Macho;* 1984) and Sue Doro's railroad poetry (*Heart, Home & Hard Hats;* 1986) and selected women's coal-mining songs (*They'll Never Keep Us Down;* 1984).

I ask students to make an intellectual and imaginative leap in the final third of the course during their study of Margaret Atwood's *The Handmaid's Tale* (1987) and Octavia Butler's *Kindred* (1979). Because there are no Bessemer furnaces to light the way, these narratives elicit a more complex understanding of how social relationships are not only impregnated by technology, but are metamorphosed into technology. Atwood's dystopia about the usurption and control of women's bodies, particularly their reproductive capacity, provides a chilling parallel story to *The Lowell Offering,* the corporate "utopia" of 1840. Atwood's "aunts" and Lowell's housemothers are controlling mediators, all serving the "guardians" or corporate owners.

The Handmaid's Tale is a problematic text for many male students. In his paper, Alan writes: "I suspect there is something I didn't get out of his novel. I was extremely impressed with the writing quality and depth . . . but I was left wondering what is Atwood's agenda or mission."[17]

I conclude with a science fiction novel, *Kindred,* written by the African American writer Octavia Butler, and excerpts from Haraway's "A Manifesto for Cyborgs" as a way to examine the curious parallels between slaves and cyborgs. In *Kindred,* time travel, a science fiction cliché, is redefined in the context of slavery—the ultimate exploitation of workers—dehumanization, control, and resistance. Another student said that the "message or warning" in *The Handmaid's Tale* escaped him until he read *Kindred:* "Now . . . I can see that a society existed over 150 years ago with striking similarities to Margaret

Atwood's creation. The plantation owners acting much like the Commanders, using their female slave reproductive resources for their own gain." Students had little difficulty with the concept of "technology of slavery," and they were willing to question their assumptions about progress when they realized that improved technology (for example, the cotton gin) actually increased the market for slaves.

I like to conclude by reading from Genesis and Exodus. I remind them that Biblical scholars agree that the Exodus story probably predates the expulsion from the Garden narrative—and that labor should not be studied apart from liberation.

There are many other possibilities for configurations of texts in a "Literature and Technology" course. I may use Marge Piercy's *Woman on the Edge of Time* (1976) or Christa Wolf's *Accident* (1989) the next time I teach this course. Texts that incorporate technology are plentiful; finding material that reveals technology as a force affecting class differences or race and gender oppression is not so easy.

Students choose final projects from a range of topics on technology and culture. I coax them to go beyond technological cheerleading, to problematize and question. Still, I've received a number of praise songs to the automobile from mechanical engineers and paeans to the brave new world of "highways of data" from computer scientists. Others, though, have been more critical and inventive: a paper on artificial intelligence using novels by Robert A. Heinlein and Arthur C. Clarke to argue that "artificial intelligence is by no means an equivalent to the human thought process"; another suggesting that fractals by themselves are not art, but that they can be shaped by artists to create unique images; a good paper on *Walden* that criticized Thoreau's "self-praise" and looked at the possibility of escaping into the woods in the 1990s; another explaining the themes of isolation and dehumanization in the work of sculptor George Segal and the wrapping technique he invented; a witty paper entitled "Star Trek: The Final Paper," in which the author used interviews to examine the appeal of both series (first and second generation) to children and college students; an interesting photo essay on the now defunct, behemoth grain elevators along the Erie Canal in Buffalo, New York; and a brave, feminist analysis of reproductive technology by a student majoring in biomedical technology.

I think that students are excited by the intellectual approach of this course. Dan writes: "I appreciate and like this class because of the multiperspectives I get out of it. Some perspectives are of the past; others are what it could be like in the future. This class has made me sit back and reflect on how technology has shaped my life."

There are complaints about the reading being "too depressing." I agree and sympathize; we all want to divert our eyes, our awareness. Our students have been encouraged to gloss over the unpleasantness of American history with smiley buttons; they are literally *trained* to end every verbal exchange with "have a nice day"; they yearn for closure, for getting on with it without ever identifying "with" or "it." How, then, to see that a little depression is necessary in the struggle for justice?

Who controls work is a question that needs to be raised in literary as well as economic contexts. Whether students find artistry or degradation in their work lives may very well depend on their knowledge of the history and literature of workers. American work literature reveals the underside of American history. If we wish good work for our students, we have to see and teach its complexity. It is not a prepackaged lifestyle; it is not careerism. We need to reclaim it as a primary human concern. We need strategies of resistance to the usurpation and control of work by the military and the corporation.[18] We need to offer our students alternatives to the roles of servant or boss, slave or pharaoh. We need possibilities for good work for ourselves, as well.[19]

Notes

1. Consider Ralph Ellison's allusion to the Book of Daniel in "Battle Royal," the first chapter in *The Invisible Man,* and the need for models on how "to struggle in the camp of the enemy" in practicing a pedagogy of resistance.

2. See Barbara Ann Scott's *Crisis Management in American Higher Education* (1983), especially chapter 8, "The Transformation of the Curriculum," for ways in which universities become handmaidens to corporate interests.

3. One example among many is the anthology entitled *Literature: The Human Experience* (5th ed.), edited by Richard Abcarian and Marvin Klotz (1992). A notable exception is Nicholas K. Bromwell's (1990) article "'The Bloody Hand' of Labor: Work, Class, and Gender in Three Stories by Hawthorne."

4. Many theorists and intellectuals have focused on double consciousness and border perspectives, particularly W. E. B. Du Bois, *The Souls of Black Folks;* Gloria Anzaldúa, *Bordlerlands = La Frontera* (1987); and bell hooks, *Feminist Theory: From Margin to Center* (1984). In *The Practice of Everyday Life,* Michel de Certeau (1984) sees "marginality" as "no longer limited to minority groups" (xvii). See also Trinh T. Minh-ha, *Woman, Native, Other: Writing Postcoloniality and Feminism* (1989), and Barbara Harlow, *Resistance Literature* (1987), for important theoretical analyses of marginality and culture; see also, Nancy Harstock, *Money, Sex, and Power: Toward a Feminist Materialism* (1983).

5. I felt the rupture in an atomistic way; I had no language or community that could explain or affirm it. One generational difference between the experiences of working-class college students in 1991 as compared with my experience as a college freshman in 1963 is an access to a language that names the experience of rupture—a discourse about otherness, difference, marginality, which provides a way of intellectualizing the distance between school and home. The discourse owes much to the presence of women's studies, ethnic studies, African American studies, and other nontraditional disciplines, but it cannot guarantee, a priori, a genuine challenge to oppressive power structures.

6. Stephen Watt (1992) sees "academic narcissism" as the central problem of the "linguistic left" (A40).

7. Class in America is a knot waiting to be unraveled. Benjamin DeMott (1990) offers this definition: "[C]lass is . . . the inherited accumulation of property and competencies, beliefs, tastes, and manners that determine . . . our socioeconomic lot and our share of civic power" (10).

8. Since "Desert Shield," the 1960s nostalgia has been relegated to fashion and music—both domesticated and depoliticized.

9. See Barbara Ehrenreich, *Fear of Falling* (1990). What percentage of my students are *actually* middle class is difficult to discern (student clothing style is a poor indication); surely, most would identify themselves as middle class.

10. "A Literacy More Urgent than Literature: 1800–1850" appears in an expanded version of John Willinsky, *The Triumph of Literature/The Fate of Literacy* (1991). This paper was presented at the second MLA conference on literacy (September 1990), one of the few academic conferences where there was occasion for interaction among theorists, union representatives, schoolteachers, and workplace literacy teachers.

11. Quoted in the introduction to Lunsford, Moglen, and Slevin (1990, 5).

12. Barbara Christian's "The Race for Theory" (1987; rpt. in Hansen and Philipson 1990) is an important, self-conscious critique of the role of the literary theorist and the interests served by theory.

13. Merod (1987) provides a worthy interrogation of the insularity of academic criticism in the United States. Merod is concerned about the reification of criticism, about the place of critical theory in the world, and about the co-opting and commodification of theory. See also, Cain (1984) and Said (1982).

Why not push Merod's point a bit further and ask under what labor conditions is theory written? What are the models for the structuring of academic work? The strategy of highlighting work as a subject within literary texts not only speaks to the concerns of technocratic students, but also illuminates the hierarchical working conditions within the academy. Consider the privileged conditions of the few and the oppressive situations of the many, and the continuing use of a reserve of adjunct faculty.

14. See "complementary holism" as defined in Albert et al. (1986). For political models for difference and community, see Alperin (1990); Lorde (1984); Reagon (1983); and Bunch (1987).

15. Rochester Institute of Technology originated in 1829 as an Athenaeum and Mechanics Institute. See Gordon (1982).

16. Consider the welcome-home ceremonies for the troops (often portrayed in the media like heroes from WWII movies) returning from "Desert Storm" and the technological pleasures of surgical strikes during the Persian Gulf War.

17. Apropos of Atwood's color-coded division of women's work in *The Handmaid's Tale,* a Penfield, New York high school received a $25,000 grant to conduct a program called "True Colors." The program assigns students to color-coded categories according to their personalities: "Orange students are adventurous, witty, charming . . . blue students are harmonious, enthusiastic, sympathetic, gold students are responsible, loyal, dependable . . . etc." According to the designer, Don Lowry ("[Lowry]" 1991) of California: "[T]he color-coding is meant to help teachers match their teaching to dif-

ferent learning styles and to help students appreciate diversity and improve their self-esteem" (10E).

18. The question of shaping curricula and managing institutions to suit requirements of the military-industrial complex has surfaced at Rochester Institute of Technology over revelations that President Richard Rose was employed by the CIA while on sabbatical during the Persian Gulf War. See "[Richard Rose]" (1991a; 1991b).

19. I want to thank my colleague Joseph Nassar and my student Andrea Marcussen for their comments on this essay, and my "Literature and Technology" students for permission to quote from their writing.

Works Cited

Abcarian, Richard, and Marvin Klotz, eds. 1992. *Literature: The Human Experience.* 5th ed. New York: St. Martin's.

Adams, Henry. 1980 [1918; 1906]; *The Education of Henry Adams.* Franklin Center, PA: Franklin Library.

Albert, Michael, et al., eds. 1986. *Liberating Theory.* Boston: South End Press.

Alperin, Davida J. 1990. "Social Diversity and the Necessity for Alliances: A Developing Feminist Perspective." In *Bridges of Power: Women's Multicultural Alliances,* edited by Lisa Albrecht and Rose M. Brewer. Philadelphia: New Society Publishers.

Anzaldúa, Gloria. 1987. *Borderlands = La Frontera: The New Mestiza.* San Francisco: Spinsters/Aunt Lute.

Atwood, Margaret. 1987. *The Handmaid's Tale.* New York: Fawcett.

Bell, Thomas. 1976 [1941]. *Out of This Furnace.* Pittsburgh: University of Pittsburgh Press.

Bromwell, Nicholas K. 1990. "'The Bloody Hand' of Labor: Work, Class, and Gender in Three Stories by Hawthorne." *American Quarterly* 42 (December): 542–64.

Bunch, Charlotte. 1987. *Passionate Politics.* New York: St. Martin's.

Butler, Octavia E. 1979. *Kindred.* Boston: Beacon.

Cain, William E. 1984. *The Crisis in Criticism: Theory, Literature, and Reform in English Studies.* Baltimore: Johns Hopkins University Press.

Chaplin, Charles, (dir). 1936. *Modern Times.* 89 min. Entertainment, Inc.

Chittenden, Patricia, and Malcolm Kiniry, gen. eds. 1986. *Making Connections Across the Curriculum: Readings for Analysis.* New York: St. Martin's.

Christian, Barbara. 1987. "The Race for Theory." *Cultural Critique* 6 (Spring): 51–63. Rpt. in Hansen and Philipson, 568–69.

de Certeau, Michel. 1984. *The Practice of Everyday Life.* Translated by Steven Rendell. Berkeley: University of California Press.

DeMott, Benjamin. 1990. *The Imperial Middle: Why Americans Can't Think Straight about Class.* New York: William Morrow.

Doro, Sue. 1986. *Heart, Home & Hard Hats.* Minneapolis: Midwest Villages & Voices.

Du Bois, W. E. B. 1969 [1903]. *The Souls of Black Folks.* New York: Signet.

Ehrenreich, Barbara. 1990. *Fear of Falling: The Inner Life of the Middle Class.* New York: Pantheon.

Eisenberg, Susan. 1984. *It's a Good Thing I'm Not Macho.* Boston: Whetstone.

Eisler, Benita. 1980. *The Lowell Offering: Writings by New England Mill Women (1840–1845).* New York: Harper & Row.

Ellison, Ralph. 1972 [1952]. *The Invisible Man.* New York: Vintage.

Gordon, Dane R. 1982. *Rochester Institute of Technology: Industrial Development and Educational Innovation in an American City.* New York: Edward Mellen.

Hansen, Karen V., and Ilene J. Philipson, eds. 1990. *Women, Class, and the Feminist Imagination: A Socialist-Feminist Reader.* Philadelphia: Temple University Press.

Haraway, Donna. 1985. "A Manifesto for Cyborgs: Science, Technology, and Socialist Feminism in the Last Quarter." *Socialist Review,* no. 80 (March/April): 65–107. Rpt. in Hansen and Philipson, 580–617.

Harlow, Barbara. 1987. *Resistance Literature.* New York: Methuen.

Hartsock, Nancy C. M. 1983. *Money, Sex and Power: Toward a Feminist Historical Materialism.* New York: Longman.

Hawthorne, Nathaniel. 1937. *The Complete Novels and Selected Tales of Nathaniel Hawthorne.* Edited by Norman Holmes Pearson. New York: Modern Library.

[Hine, Lewis.] 1977. *America and Lewis Hine: Photographs 1904–1940.* Millerton, NY: Aperture.

hooks, bell. 1984. *Feminist Theory: From Margin to Center.* Boston: South End Press.

Hutcheon, Linda. 1989. *The Politics of Postmodernism.* London: Routledge.

Lorde, Audre. 1984. "Age, Race, Class, and Sex: Women Redefining Difference." In *Sister Outsider: Essays and Speeches.* Trumansburg, NY: Crossing Press.

"[Lowry, Don.]" 1991. News feature. The Rochester *Democrat and Chronicle,* 8 May, 10E.

Lunsford, Andrea A., Helene Moglen, and James Slevin, eds. 1990. *The Right to Literacy.* New York: Modern Language Association of America.

Marx, Karl. 1986 [1844]. "Alienated Labor." In Chittenden and Kiniry, 289–93.

Marx, Leo. 1964. *The Machine in the Garden: Technology and the Pastoral Ideal in America.* New York: Oxford University Press.

Melville, Herman. 1968. *Herman Melville: Selected Tales and Poems.* Edited by Richard Chase. New York: Holt, Rinehart and Winston.

Merod, Jim. 1987. *The Political Responsibility of the Critic.* Ithaca: Cornell University Press.

Mills, C. Wright. 1986 [1951]. "The Idea of Craftsmanship." In Chittenden and Kiniry, 301–4.

Minh-ha, Trinh T. 1989. *Women, Native, Other: Writing Postcoloniality and Feminism.* Bloomington: Indiana University Press.

Noble, David F. 1986. *America by Design: Science, Technology, and the Rise of Corporate Capitalism.* New York: Oxford University Press.

Piercy, Marge. 1976. *Woman on the Edge of Time.* New York: Knopf.

Reagon, Bernice. 1983. "Coalition Politics: Turning the Century." In *Home Girls: A Black Feminist Anthology,* edited by Barbara Smith. New York: Kitchen Table/Women of Color Press.

"[Richard Rose]." 1991a. News feature. The Rochester *Democrat and Chronicle,* 4 June: editorial; 6 June: 10A–11A; 13 June: 15A.

———. 1991b. News feature. *The Chronicle of Higher Education,* 5 June: A2.

Said, Edward. 1982. "Opponents, Audiences, Constituencies, and Community." *Critical Inquiry* 9 (September): 1–26.

Scott, Barbara Ann. 1983. *Crisis Management in American Higher Education.* New York: Praeger.

Shloss, Carol. 1987. *In Visible Light: Photography and the American Writer 1840–1940.* New York: Oxford University Press.

Soelle, Dorothee A., with Shirley A. Cloyes. 1984. *To Work and To Love: A Theology of Creation.* Philadelphia: Fortress Press.

Steedman, Carolyn Kay. 1987. *Landscape for a Good Woman: A Story of Two Lives.* New Brunswick, NJ: Rutgers University Press.

Taylor, Frederick Winslow. 1967 [1911]. *The Principles of Scientific Management.* New York: Norton. See also Chittenden and Kiniry, 296–300.

They'll Never Keep Us Down: Women's Coal Mining Songs. 1984. Rounder Records 4012.

Tichi, Cecelia. 1987. *Shifting Gears: Technology, Literature, Culture in Modernist America.* Chapel Hill: University of North Carolina Press.

Vonnegut, Kurt. 1952. *Player Piano.* New York: Avon.

Watt, Stephen. 1992. "Academic Leftists Are Something of a Fraud." *The Chronicle of Higher Education,* 29 April: A40.

Welch, Sharon D. 1990. *A Feminist Ethic of Risk.* Philadelphia: Fortress Press.

Willinsky, John. 1991 [1990]. "A Literacy More Urgent than Literature: 1800–1850." In *The Triumph of Literature/The Fate of Literacy: English in the Secondary School Curriculum.* New York: Teachers College Press.

Wolf, Christa. 1989. *Accident: A Day's News.* Translated by Heike Schwarzbauer and Rick Takvorian. New York: Farrar, Straus & Giroux.

11

The Inclusion/Exclusion Issue

Including Students in Choosing Texts

Christine Sutphin

Editors' Notes: We return to the women's studies classroom with this essay by Christine Sutphin, who reports on her experiments allowing students to choose reading selections for her Women in Literature course. By increasing student authority and responsibility, Sutphin invites students to consider the political implications of designing a syllabus, as they grapple with issues of diversity and representation.

Which writers and which works to teach in any given course have always been at issue for college and university literature teachers, but only fairly recently have we become aware that our inclusions and exclusions have political implications. Trying to put our political awareness into practice, many of us have challenged and revised the canon, but continue to question whether we are, or should be, establishing alternative canons. We have also come to realize that our teaching *style* is political, and many of us have made attempts to adopt a less authoritarian role. We have tried to move toward the model of interactive or problem-posing teaching recommended by Paulo Freire and others, to (as Freire puts it) "liberate" our students rather than "domesticate" them. But it is often difficult to move away from old models, even in courses that have an explicitly political purpose.

I realized how powerful the old models were when I started designing a Women in Literature course to be offered in the spring of 1990. In order to explore both commonality and difference, I had chosen ethnically diverse texts which could all be read as re-visions (to use Adrienne Rich's term) of heroic and mythological traditions. After making some difficult choices, I worked on the schedule and was confronted with a gap of about two weeks. Who else should I include? Who else would reveal the pattern further or challenge it? Who would perhaps go beyond the pattern to reveal some other issue we needed to see? And then the really important question, which was also an answer, surfaced: Why couldn't the students decide?

I had certainly never intended to "domesticate" students, a particularly telling metaphor considering that the majority of the students in this class would be women. But the fact that I had not included them in the process of choosing made me realize how closely I had been bound by old models even when I thought I was committed to the interactive classroom. In my classes, students participate in presentations, discussions, and workshops and are encouraged to come up with their own ideas for papers. But I had never asked them to be responsible for choosing what we read, just as none of my teachers had ever asked that I take on that responsibility.[1]

Open Question

I have now taught the class twice, and everyone has said what a valuable experience choosing texts was and that it should continue to be part of the course. Several students have said they would like to see this method incorporated into other courses. Whether or not it would work in all contexts is still very much an open question to me. In Women in Literature, I didn't have to struggle with the traditional idea of "coverage," an idea that, while many perceive it as problematic, still governs "survey" courses. Students choosing texts would certainly be appropriate for special topics courses in a wide variety of disciplines.

The first few weeks of class we read material I assign, while the students meet in groups to decide what work each group would like the class to read. I put several anthologies on reserve in the library to help them get started in their search, but they do not have to choose selections from the anthologies. The texts students assign have to be fairly short, for example a few poems or one or two short stories, since book-length works would have to be ordered six weeks before the first day of class. Students and I have talked about how interesting it would be if the course could be organized eight weeks ahead of time, so that we could choose and order books together. So far no one has figured out how to make this early organizing happen efficiently. Other than length, there are no constraints on what student groups may choose. They are not confined to any of the ideas I have raised, although they are encouraged to look for connections. Their responsibility is to assign the reading in advance, put copies on reserve, and lead class discussion on their chosen work. They are asked to make a case in writing for including the work they have chosen and to examine the assumptions and values that led to their choices.

My original intentions were to increase student authority, responsibility, and freedom, and allow them to experience the political implications of choice, rather than merely being told that such implications exist. I hoped students would learn from experience that difficult choices must be made, and that inclusion and exclusion decisions are not "natural." I wanted this experience to demystify the process of choosing texts. The following discussion describes how and to what extent these goals were met, and how problems could be ameliorated.

The two classes were different experiences. The first class was large, noisy, and expressed much disagreement about feminism, the construction of reality, the extent to which individuals can make choices, and the relative power of women and men. Two of the most heated discussions centered on whether we should devote much time to talking about men and on Adrienne Rich's "Compulsory Heterosexuality." Feelings ran high, and the class sometimes veered away from the texts to discuss personal experiences.

The second class was small, gentle, and accomodated each other's views. This time, I asked the students about their own backgrounds. One student was Native American; insights based on his cultural perspective were welcomed by his classmates. Another student told us about her religious background (Christian Scientist), but the rest of the women did not seem to know much about their own ethnicity. Homophobia seemed barely to exist in this group, although the accepting response to lesbianism might be attributed to the works we read, Jeanette Winterson's *Oranges Are Not the Only Fruit* and poems by Judy Grahn, which could be read as less radical than Rich's essay.

Eloquent Response

I have described these groups in some detail to illustrate that, even with extremely different dynamics, the experience of choosing texts was highly regarded by all. No one had a bad word to say about the *idea,* although there were suggestions for improving the process. The main difference in the group selections and responses had to do with the issue of ethnicity. Because the experience of ethnicity issues was different for each group, I have chosen to summarize their responses separately. First I would like to summarize the positive comments participants made in the first group. The most detailed and eloquent response, which represents many of the comments made by others, said:

> Yes, choosing texts is important for several reasons. One, it allows students to actively take responsibility for their own learning, a process that many students deny themselves. Second, it allows for greater diversity in perspective, and fosters the belief that students are capable and knowledgable people. Third, it shifts the focus/emphasis from teacher to student, and promotes the idea that one can learn from others besides those designated "teachers." All those ideas promote something that is incredibly important, which is that of inter-relatedness, both to each other, and to other points of view. In addition, students choosing texts creates an atmosphere that is quite different from most male literature classes. Valuing and allowing student involvement is a radical idea, and a very valid one. What I learned is that I would like to see more of this done in more classrooms.

Other students said the experience was "empowering," that it gave them the "chance to express opinions" that they would not have expressed in a large group. One student said the process gave her "more sense of the class as a whole" because of the connections we found/created between the various works. Another student mentioned the responsibility students took on and how they had to consider their audience. She said we "had to consider the class' needs, abilities and interests, plus consider the significance of the choices and their relevance to our study." More than one student asserted that the process made them feel more "a part of the class," while one said that students "became instruments in their own learning," and another said one of the most important results was "learning to think for yourself." One student stated: "Presenting a reading, instead of responding to reading someone else has chosen, is different. Presenting a group reading takes team work, organization, and communication. It requires a different approach and different preparation." Many students cited the chance to hear different points of view and read a variety of texts as advantages.

Exclusion

Although views and texts in this first group *were* diverse, the frequent mention of diversity struck me as ironic because all the texts chosen were by white women, mostly Americans. I was surprised by the absence of women of color because we had begun the course with *Incidents in the Life of a Slave Girl* and moved on to contemporary Native American poetry (Green). The students seemed to appreciate these texts, and I certainly tried to make clear that the exclusion of writers of color was a political issue. It disturbed me that no one had, apparently, heard me.

Responses to my question about the lack of minority writers were mixed. Especially disturbing was one student's response: "I don't think it matters if some group or issues were not discussed." Perhaps even more disturbing was the response of a student who said, "I thought too much emphasis was put on whether the authors were black, white or lesbian. The reading groups didn't stress the race issues as the assigned texts, and for that I was glad." This last student missed the whole issue of the erasure of difference, so eloquently expressed by Audre Lorde, that we had discussed in the beginning week of class.

Some students, however, were troubled by the absence of women of color, and offered rather similar explanations for it. One student mentioned the reluctance students might feel to move out of their "comfort zones," while another student said: "People choose from what they know, and what they feel most comfortable doing." Still another student thought that writers of color "need to be sought out consciously. We are not familiar with names, etc. Maybe unwilling to *risk* a new author." It occurred to me later that this class had raised many complex and even painful issues for students. Most of them had been challenged by new ideas, and perhaps that was why they sought a "comfort zone" when it came to choosing writers. The only foreign student in the class, from Japan, said she was interested in minority writers, particularly black Americans, but the other members of her group were not.

The student who talked about risking a new author went on to say, "it can be difficult to know where to go to find something fresh. Many readings seemed to be known by some people. It's easy to represent a white, upper-middle class perspective that skews the vision of 'women's' issues." The difficulty with "where to go" to find minority writers struck me as odd since there were plenty of anthologies on reserve that included them or were specifically devoted to them. But as I read the responses I realized that many students had the idea that if a work was in an anthology, that meant it was well known. I would have to work to dispell this notion next time.

With regards to the process, several students asked for more direction. They wanted the groups to get organized early, and, instead of my letting them create their own groups, wanted them assigned. Many also suggested that the "minority issue" could be solved if I assigned them a race and time period, for example, nineteenth century black American.

Loose Control

Some of the groups had to deal with the frustration of group members who did not take their responsibilities seriously and did not show up for meetings outside of class (and sometimes in class). One student asked: "Well, how can you make people come? My group was dedicated and had no trouble meeting and sharing ideas and responsibilities, but I'm sure some groups had troubles. It feels like we lose control of the structure of the class, but I think it may be because we're just not used to that degree of loose control and that we can get used to it and function under it." Some students suggested that having an individual written justification for choosing the texts might prompt more people to participate.

"Loose control" articulates one of the things I had tried to accomplish with this process. I took some of the suggestions. The second time I taught the class, I talked about the group process much earlier and got everyone organized in pairs (because of the small class size) the second week of class. I decided not to assign them a particular time period or ethnic group, and I explained why I wanted them to have as much choice as possible. I explained with much emphasis the politics of inclusion and exclusion, and why I was concerned about the absence of writers of color in the first class. I also made a pitch for the anthologies.

I realize that emphasizing the issues surrounding the absence of writers of color, lesbians, or any other group may seem incompatible with giving students "as much choice as possible." It may seem that I had a hidden agenda that I wanted them to follow: include marginal groups within the category "woman writer." My point here, however, is that students should be encouraged to think about *why* they are choosing particular writers and not others, especially if patterns of exclusion are evident. During the presentations in the first group, no one was criticized for their choices; we took all the choices seriously and never suggested that some might be more "politically correct" than others. My goal here is not to dictate what students choose, but to put them in a position to raise questions of race, class, and sexual orientation.

Personal Biases

In the second group, students did a better job confronting those questions. One or two of the justifications were too general and made me think that I should be more specific about this writing assignment. But the responses to the revised question on diversity were generally encouraging. One student wrote that she had had to "recognize some of my personal biases." Another said, "I probably wouldn't have chosen a few of the writings, but that's really the whole point, to broaden my horizons." This student went on to say, "I don't think I have a *firm* grasp of the political implications beyond that stereotyping writers, whether they be women, men, lesbians, blacks, etc., is very limiting to an audience's perceptions." One student felt that she did not have a clear understanding of the political implications unless "someone points it out to me," yet she also said, "I learned a lot about many different women and their cultures and why they behave the way they do. It helped me understand their beliefs and ideas." Another student said, "I really didn't expect any course at this university to include such a variety of reading materials. The viewpoints of different cultures seemed to open doorways to other cultures and points of view."

It is difficult to convince students that everyone is ethnic. One student wrote that she got more out of the "ethnic" novels than out of the lesbian work, and was going to search out more "ethnic" stories. We didn't discuss ethnic issues in Grahn's and Winterson's work because our attention was focused on lesbian identities and class. I think, however, that this group had a better understanding of the distinction between those problematic words "ethnic" and "minority" than the previous group did, as well as a better grasp of the difficulties of inclusion, exclusion, and tokenism.

What, then, to make of all these reading and discussion experiences and responses? They certainly tell me that these students approve of the principle of choosing texts and that the involved ones love choosing reading and discussion material for the class. It also tells me that students are unused to this kind of "loose control," and that certain kinds of help should be available. In addition to the anthologies on reserve (and an explanation that these are, at least in part, *alternative* anthologies), I will probably make out some specific guidelines for the short justification essay. Perhaps I will come up with some questions on inclusion and exclusion, making clear that the group should create other questions as well. I haven't yet made up my mind whether I should ask for individual justification essays; I can see advantages both ways.

After teaching the course twice, my sense is that students readily grasp the political implications of hearing their own voices in the classroom. But the political implications of diversity among the writers they include or exclude are not so easily apparent to them. My experience indicates that teachers using this approach will have to work carefully with students to make clearer how their own choices determine which writers' voices are heard in the classroom conversation.

Notes

1. A search of ERIC and MLA Bibliography over the last few years turned up nothing on students choosing texts. It was even impossible to find really appropriate descriptors.

Works Cited

Freire, Paulo. 1970. *The Pedagogy of the Oppressed.* Translated by Myra Bergman Ramos. New York: Herder and Herder.

Grahn, Judy. 1978. *The Work of a Common Woman.* Trumansburg, N.Y.: Crossing Press.

Green, Rayna, ed. 1984. *That's What She Said: Contemporary Poetry and Fiction by Native American Women.* Bloomington: Indiana UP.

Jacobs, Harriet A. 1861. *Incidents in the Life of a Slave Girl.* Cambridge: Harvard UP.

Lorde, Audre. 1984. "The Master's Tools Will Never Dismantle the Master's House" in *Sister Outsider.* Trumansburg, N.Y.: Crossing Press.

Rich, Adrienne. 1986. "Compulsory Heterosexuality and Lesbian Existence" in *Blood, Bread, and Poetry, Selected Prose, 1966–1985.* New York: Norton.

———. 1979. "When We Dead Awaken: Writing as Re-Vision" in *On Lies, Secrets, and Silence.* New York: Norton.

Winterson, Jeanette. 1985. *Oranges Are Not the Only Fruit.* New York: Atlantic Monthly Press.

12

Queer Statistics

Using Lesbigay Word-Problem Content in Teaching Statistics

John Kellermeier

Editors' Notes: Kellermeier shares his innovative method of incorporating "lesbigay" issues on the quizzes and exams of his statistics courses and provides many representative examples. At first, students revealed homophobic attitudes. But, as you will see, students' attitudes changed when he increased the amount of "lesbigay" content on the exams. Kellermeier shows how Freirean problem posing can be taken to a course as abstract as statistics, answering the question of whether "hard" subjects can be taught critically and dialogically.

Over the past several years I have been working with curriculum-inclusion issues as they apply to teaching statistics. I have done this by using the content of word problems as a vehicle for including issues of race, class, gender, and sexual orientation in an introductory statistics course (Kellermeier, "Using," "Writing"). In teaching a particular statistics concept, it does not matter whether we use as an example the percentage of red balls in an urn or the percentage of lesbians and gay men in a group of people. By using the latter as an example, we can bring the issue of sexual orientation into the statistics classroom. This is precisely what I have done, using issues of race, class, gender, and sexual orientation in many of the word problems I have used in teaching statistics.

As part of this work on the inclusion of diversity, I have regularly asked students to comment on the word problems as part of my course evaluation. The response from students has, for the most part, been positive (see Kellermeier "Using," "Writing"). They see the issues discussed in the word problems as the important issues of their times. Many comment that the word problems make the course more interesting and in turn make them more willing to learn the statistics.

Yet students often see this inclusion as more substantial than it actually is. Approximately 10 to 15% of students comment that the majority of the problems are about "women's issues" or about gays, lesbians, and bisexuals. In fact, a content analysis of all the word problems I use in a semester shows that only about one-sixth concern gender issues and fewer than 1% actually mention sexual orientation. Typically, some students see the inclusion of even a small number of lesbigay issues as excessive. In particular, one or two students out of every class will comment that the few words problems using issues of gays, lesbians, and bisexuals are "just too much."

As a result, I decided to investigate what students' reactions would be if indeed there were a large number of word problems dealing with "queer" statistics. The word problems given as examples and exercises in the text (a manuscript written by myself) include a very small number of lesbigay issues. The text, however, cannot easily be changed for one semester. Where I do have more immediate control of word-problem content is on quizzes and tests. For two semesters of teaching an introductory statistics course I vastly increased the number of word problems on quizzes and tests that dealt with lesbigay issues. In the spring 1993 semester there were, in total, 39 word problems on quizzes and tests, 29 of which featured lesbigay content (74%). In the summer 1993 semester there were 40 word problems on quizzes and tests, of which 37 featured lesbigay content (93%). I should note that my students spend more time with quiz and test questions, and in a less stressful setting, than is typical in a statistics class. Quizzes are given as take-home assignments on which students are encouraged to work collaboratively. Tests are given in class but without a time limit. Additionally, students spend time reworking missed test questions for extra credit.

In what follows I will give examples of the word problems used in this course and an analysis of student evaluations. The word problems fall into three categories: (1) using lesbigay populations as a background, (2) using facts about lesbigay populations, and (3) using realistic data about lesbigay populations.

Using Lesbigay Populations as a Background

These word problems take typical statistics content and use lesbians, gays, and bisexuals as background.

- An assignment for a gay studies course is to choose two of the following books about which to read and write a report:
  Another Mother Tongue: Gay Words, Gay Worlds by Judy Grahn,
  The Pink Triangle: The Nazi War Against Homosexuals by Richard Plant,
  Gay Spirit: Myth and Meaning edited by Mark Thompson,
  In the Life: A Black Gay Anthology edited by Joseph Beam,
  Living the Spirit: A Gay American Indian Anthology edited by Will Roscoe.

Suppose a student in this course decides to pick the books randomly. Consider the following events:
A: Both books chosen are edited collections.
B: At least one book chosen is about people of color.
a. What type of sampling is used in this situation?
b. List the samples in the sample space.
c. List the samples in each of the events A and B.
d. What are the probabilities of each of the events A and B?

- A researcher on electronic communications sampled seven digests from the lesbian/gay/bisexual e-mail list GAYNET. She counted the number of postings contained in each digest. Her results were as follows: 9 3 6 1 9 10 8. Find the following:
  a. the sample mean
  b. the median
  c. the range
  d. the sample variance
  e. the sample standard deviation

- The lesbian and bisexual student organization at a women's college is holding a 50-50 raffle as a fund raiser. They will sell 100 raffle tickets at $1 each, keep $50 for the organization and return $50 to the winner of the raffle. Suppose you buy one ticket. Let x be the amount of money you win. (Remember that if you lose, your "winnings" are then negative.)
  a. What is the probability distribution of x?
  b. What is the expected value of x?
  c. What is the variance of x?

- The membership of a social and political group for bisexuals is 65% women. Of the women, 55% are currently in a relationship with a woman, while of the men, 45% are currently in a relationship with a man. What proportion of this bisexual group is currently in a relationship with a person of the same sex?

- The monthly sales totals at a bookstore for gay men, lesbians and bisexuals for 40 months (sorted in ascending order) are as follows:
  $27,700 $29,100 $30,900 $32,200 $33,000 $34,500
  $28,500 $29,100 $31,000 $32,300 $33,100 $34,600
  $28,700 $29,500 $31,000 $32,400 $33,400 $35,700
  $28,700 $30,400 $31,100 $32,500 $33,700 $35,900
  $28,900 $30,700 $32,200 $32,500 $34,100 $37,000
  a. Draw a line graph for these data.
  b. Organize these data in a table and draw a histogram.

- John and David kept records of their food costs for a sample of nine days when they were on vacation. Their mean cost was $30.75 with a standard deviation of $7.65. Gertrude and Alice did the same for a sample of 8 vacation days. Their mean cost was $32.89 with a standard deviation of $5.95

- a. Is there sufficient evidence to conclude that these two couples spend different average amounts of money on food per day while on vacation? Use significance level 0.10.
- b. Find a 99% confidence interval for the difference in the average amount of money these two couples spend on food per day while on vacation.

- A producer of lesbian and women's music concerts knows that the concerts she produces have an average attendance of about 380 people with a standard deviation of 45 people. If she produces a total of 32 concerts over several years, what is the probability that the total attendance will exceed 12,800 people? (Note: The total attendance will exceed 12,800 people when the average attendance exceeds 400 people.)

- A test of AIDS facts is given to incoming volunteers for a gay, lesbian, and bisexual youth hotline. The average score on a test is 89. A sample of 10 new volunteers are first given a one-hour presentation on AIDS. Their scores on the test then yield a mean of 94 with a standard deviation of 5.4. Do these data provide sufficient evidence to conclude that all volunteers will have a higher average on the test after the one-hour presentation? Use significance level 0.01.

- A lesbian publishing company wishes to estimate the average cost of the books they print. A sample of 63 books gives a mean of $9.97 with a standard deviation of $3.83. Find a 99% confidence interval for the average price of the books this company prints.

- A reporter wishes to estimate the average age of the people marching in a gay pride march. How many people would this reporter have to sample in order to estimate the average age to within two years at confidence level 90% if the ages range from 15 to 70 years?

Using Facts About Lesbigay Populations

These word problems use statistical information about lesbians, gays, and bisexuals as a basis for the statistical content of the word problems. The information for the first five problems was taken from a report by Vermonters for Lesbian and Gay Rights published in the Vermont newspaper *Out in the Mountains* (June 1987).

- In a survey, readers of a periodical for lesbians, gay men and bisexuals were asked their level of education. Their answers are summarized in the following table:

Level of Education	*Percentage*
High School Graduate	8%
Some College and Two-Year Degree	16%
College Graduate	45%
Master's and PhD	31%

Assume these percentages are accurate for all the readership of this periodical.
   a. What percent of the readership has a four-year college degree or higher?
   b. What percent of the readership does not have a postgraduate degree (master's or PhD)?
   c. What percent of the readership does not have at least a high school diploma?

- A recent study shows that 80% of people who identify as lesbian, bisexual, or gay have experienced some kind of harassment or violence because of their sexual orientation. Suppose a reporter samples 22 bisexuals, gays, and lesbians at a gay pride march.
   a. How many of those sampled would you expect to have experienced some such harassment or violence?
   b. What is the probability that at least 15 of them would have experienced some such harassment or violence?
   c. What is the probability that at least five of them had never experienced some such harassment or violence?

- It is estimated that 20% of lesbian, gay, and bisexual people have experienced housing discrimination because of their sexual orientation; that is, they have been denied rental or purchase of a house or apartment or have been evicted. Suppose a lesbigay group consists of 14 people.
   a. How many of these people would you expect to have experienced housing discrimination?
   b. What is the probability that no more than one has experienced housing discrimination?

- Research shows that 36% of lesbigay people have been threatened with physical violence because of their sexual orientation. If 150 lesbigay people are surveyed, what is the probability that at least 40 of them have been threatened with physical violence?

- A pollster reports that 44% of lesbigay people have been discriminated against in employment owing to their sexual orientation. Suppose a reporter surveys 90 lesbigay people. What is the probability that at least 35 of them would have experienced employment discrimination?

The next two problems use information from a news article out of *New York Times* (Schmalz).

- A recent poll showed that about 80% of Americans feel that bisexual, lesbian, and gay people should have equal rights in job opportunity. In your community a lesbigay equal-employment-rights bill is being considered by the city council. Suppose the twenty people on the city council can be viewed as a random sample of all Americans.
   a. How many council members do you expect would support lesbigay equal-employment rights?

b. What is the probability that at least 15 of the council members support lesbigay equal employment rights?
c. What is the probability that more than four of the council members are against lesbigay equal-employment rights?

- Polls show that 44% of Americans believe that homosexual is something people choose to be. Suppose a reporter surveys 90 Americans. What is the probability that fewer than 35 of them would believe homosexuality is chosen?

The last two problems use information from the Internet E-mail list GAYNET (Richardson; Cheney).

- A poll in early 1993 showed that 91% of people who identify as gay, bisexual, or lesbian agreed with the statement "President Clinton cares about people like me." Also, 62% of people who don't identify as gay, bisexual, or lesbian agreed with the same statement. If people who identify as gay, lesbian, or bisexual constitute 10% of the population, what proportion of people agree with the statement "President Clinton cares about people like me"?
- A community mental-health-agency report suggests that gay and lesbian teenagers are four times as likely to attempt suicide as heterosexual teenagers. The report says that 36% of lesbian and gay teenagers attempt suicide while only 9% of heterosexual teenagers attempt suicide.
  a. Out of a sample of 100 heterosexual teenagers, what is the approximate probability that at least 30 will have attempted suicide?
  b. Out of a sample of 100 lesbian and gay teenagers, what is the approximate probability that at least 30 will have attempted suicide?

Using Realistic Data About Lesbigay Populations

In these word problems statistical information about lesbians, gays, and bisexuals is uncovered by the process of doing the problem. The data used in these problems are not real data taken from research but are realistic in the sense that they were simulated using real statistics as a basis. For example, the first two problems use data taken from the Vermonters for Lesbian and Gay Rights (VLGR) report.

- Gay men, bisexuals, and lesbians who experience violence because of their sexual orientation sometimes face a further problem if they choose to report the incident to the police, namely, that the police themselves may be discouraging in the pursuit of the matter. To study this, 50 lesbigay people who had reported such violence to police were asked whether the attitudes of the police had been encouraging, discouraging, or neutral.

| Neutral | Discouraging | Discouraging | Discouraging |
| Neutral | Discouraging | Encouraging | Neutral |

Neutral	Neutral	Discouraging	Encouraging
Encouraging	Discouraging	Neutral	Discouraging
Neutral	Encouraging	Neutral	Neutral
Neutral	Discouraging	Neutral	Encouraging
Neutral	Discouraging	Discouraging	Neutral
Neutral	Encouraging	Encouraging	Neutral
Neutral	Discouraging	Discouraging	Discouraging
Discouraging	Neutral	Discouraging	Neutral
Neutral	Discouraging	Neutral	Discouraging
Neutral	Neutral	Neutral	Discouraging
Encouraging	Neutral		

Organize these data in a table and draw a bar graph.

- In a sample of 133 lesbians, gay men, and bisexuals, 59 reported they had encountered some type of employment discrimination and 105 said they had experienced some kind of harassment or violence because of their sexual orientation.
  a. Determine a 95% confidence interval for the percentage of lesbians, gay men, and bisexuals who encountered employment discrimination.
  b. Determine a 95% confidence interval for the proportion of lesbians, bisexuals, and gay men who experience harassment or violence.

The VLGR report stated that of lesbian, gay, or bisexual people reporting violence to police, 17% found the police encouraging, 35% found the police discouraging, and 48% found the police neutral. In order to simulate data, I assumed a sample size of 50. With this sample size, there would be 8.5 encouraging, 17.5 discouraging, and 24 neutral police officers. These numbers are rounded off so that in the data given, there are 8 encouraging, 18 discouraging, and 24 neutral officers. The second problem came from report statements that 44% of those surveyed experienced employment discrimination and 80% experienced harassment or violence. Assuming a sample size of 133, this would mean numbers of 59 and 105 respectively.

The next problem uses the fact that of those who believe homosexuality cannot be changed, 57% also consider homosexuality an acceptable lifestyle (Schmalz).

- A gay rights activist thinks that if Americans believe homosexuality is not chosen, the majority of them will then consider homosexuality an acceptable lifestyle. To test this, he asks a sample of Americans whether they believe homosexuality is chosen and whether they consider it an acceptable lifestyle. Out of 178 who believe homosexuality is not chosen, 101 say they consider it an acceptable lifestyle. Can we conclude at the .05 level of significance that the gay activist's belief is true?

This next problem uses information posted on the Internet e-mail list GLB-NEWS (Morin). This posting cites information from polls taken by the

National Opinion Research Center at the University of Chicago in 1977 and in 1991. In 1977 67% of those polled believed sex between consenting adults of the same sex was "always wrong." In 1991, 71% said the same.

- In a 1977 poll of 1225 Americans, 821 said sex between consenting adults of the same sex was "always wrong." In a 1991 poll of 1642 Americans, 1166 said sex between consenting adults of the same sex was "always wrong."
  a. Do these data provide sufficient evidence to conclude that the attitudes of Americans on this issue have changed between 1977 and 1991? Use significance level 0.01.
  b. Find a 95% confidence interval for the difference between the proportions of Americans who believed that sex between consenting adults of the same sex was "always wrong" in 1977 and in 1991.

The data for this last problem were taken from a posting on the Internet e-mail list GAYNET (Herbert). This posting stated that "between 1980 and 1990 women constituted 23% of those discharged [from the armed services] for homosexuality. Also, women constitute about 11–12% of the military."

- It is known that 11% of US military personnel is female. In a sample of 240 people discharged from the military for homosexuality, 65 were female. Does this provide sufficient evidence to conclude that the proportion of females among those discharged for homosexuality is greater than the proportion of females in the military? Use a significance level of 0.01.

The school at which I teach is a four-year state college in the State University of New York system. The student body is primarily white. Only two students in each of the two statistics classes in which lesbigay word problems were used were students of color. The statistics course is taught in the mathematics department. It is the course that most students take to fulfill the general-education requirement in mathematics skills. Consequently, it is taken by a wide variety of majors, in particular those majors who do not require a mainstream calculus course. The gender breakdown in this course is usually about 50% females and 50% males.

In neither of the two semesters during which I used large numbers of lesbigay-content word problems did I announce to students that this content would be used. Nor did either class ask any questions about the information presented in the word problems concerning lesbigay issues. In the first class I had no discussions about these issues with the students. In the second class, taught in the summer, the length of the class period required a five- to ten-minute break each day. During this break, on a few occasions I had conversations with students about the topics of the quizzes. However, these conversations were never carried into the entire class.

At the end of the semester, the students were asked as part of the course evaluations to respond to the following: "Please comment on the word problems you did as part of this course. Specifically, what do you remember of what the problems were about? What do you think of the word problem content?" As is usual with student evaluations, the students were told that I would not have access to these evaluations until after I had submitted grades for the semester.

The students in the statistics course taught during the spring semester of 1993 consisted of traditional college-age students nearly all of whom were in their first and second year. There were 29 women and four men. This ratio was considerably different from the usual 50-50 ratio and seemed to be due to random enrollment patterns. Out of the 33 students, 30 submitted evaluations and 24 of those mentioned the lesbigay content. In my own judgment of these comments, 15 were positive, three negative, and six ambivalent. This last group consisted of comments such as the following:

> The problems would become a little more enjoyable if you didn't always put in lesbian and homosexual terms in it. I don't mean that it was bad, but some variety would be nice.

> The content of the problems is a touchy topic with some people and in a way I do see why every question had to be about "it" but I did not have a problem with them.

The most positive comments spoke of an additional learning benefit from the lesbigay word problem content. Such comments included the following:

> I think the word problem content was good material because I became more informed to this issue and I understand it more. It has a very positive effect on me.

> Knowing that these statistics are approximately correct, I feel that their content brought added value to the course.

The second statistics course was during a five-week summer-school session. The students in this course were older than those I had during the spring semester, with half being 24 or older. There were no first-year students and only one-third were sophomores. Exactly half of the 20 students were female. Eighteen students in all submitted evaluations with 16 commenting on the lesbigay content. Of these, nine were positive, three were negative, and two were ambivalent. There did seem to be an undercurrent of discontent from certain students, a discontent expressed mostly to other students. In speaking of this, one student wrote:

> I think it's scary how upset people in class have gotten over the use of non-sexist, non-heterosexist questions in the course—it's a pretty sad (but unfortunately not surprising) statement about our society. I am always glad to see efforts made that try to equalize the imbalance that exist in education.

However, the majority of the class was positive about the lesbigay word-problem content. Again, there were comments that indicated the positive effect these problems had on students. Two students wrote:

It took me a while to get used to reading material about gays and lesbigays. But now I don't think of the content as being out of the ordinary because of reading it so often.

If anything, being exposed to those problems day after day I got a feeling that this is not the faceless community we see in the media but a living part of this society.

Overall, I felt that the use of lesbigay word problem content in these two courses was successful. First, the majority of the students in both classes reacted favorably to the content of the word problems. For at least some of the students, these word problems heightened their awareness of lesbians, gays, and bisexuals and the homophobia they face.

Second, these problems will help those students who are out, who are coming out now, or who will come out in the future by providing a positive reflection of themselves, one they may not often find in other classes.

Third, I, for my part, developed an appreciation of the use of a thematic approach to word problems. My next venture will thus be to choose a theme and then to combine thematic word problems with a discussion of that theme. Unfortunately, the need to cover the required statistical content in three credit hours makes this plan difficult to execute. I have designed an introductory statistics course, Statistics in Social Context, that adds one credit hour to the usual three to allow time for the discussion of the issues raised in the word problems.

In the end it seems that the best way to deal with students' complaints that lesbigay materials is "just too much" is to integrate more of it into our courses. Once lesbigay issues are repeated often enough, they become commonplace. Then, as these issues become commonplace in the classroom, students may be better prepared to accept, support, and appreciate gays, lesbians, and bisexuals out of the classroom as well.

Works Cited

Cheney, Jerry. "Gay Youth Suicide Facts." GAYNET (MAJORDOMO at QUEER-NET.ORG) 20 Nov. 1992.

Herbert, Melissa. "Women in the Military." GAYNET (MAJORDOMO at QUEER-NET.ORG) 12 Apr. 1993.

Kellermeier, J. "Using Word Problems to Incorporate Women's Studies Issues into an Elementary Statistics Course," *Feminist Teacher* (1994).

———. "Writing Word Problems That Reflect Cultural Diversity," *Transformations* 3.2 (1992): 24–30.

Morin, Richard. "American Attitudes Toward Gays Remain Steady." GLB-NEWS (LISTSERV at BRONVM) 21 Feb. 1993.

Richardson, Sarah. "A Survey." GAYNET (MAJORDOMO at QUEERNET.ORG) 3 May 1993.

Schmalz, Jeffrey. "Poll Finds an Even Split on Homosexuality's Cause." *New York Times*. 5 Mar. 1993: A14.

Vermonters for Lesbian and Gay Rights. "VLGR Discrimination and Violence Results." *Out in the Mountains* June 1987: 7.

13

Disability Studies

Expanding the Parameters of Diversity

Simi Linton, Susan Mello, and John O'Neill

Editors' Notes: We conclude this volume with a new vision of the curriculum. The authors powerfully challenge the traditional curriculum with six ways to integrate "disability studies" into a wide range of courses. They provide an overview of the field, its scholarship, and describe modules that are organized around particular studies, such as metaphor, social arrangements, nineteenth- and twentieth-century belief systems, social construction, the medicalization and pathologizing of difference, and the sciences' constructions of disability. From their experience bringing disability studies to Hunter College, CUNY, these authors are also able to warn readers of the obstacles to transforming the curriculum with this new field.

Disability Studies: An Overview

The social, political, and cultural analyses embodied in disability studies form a prism through which one can gain a broader understanding of society and human experience, and the significance of human variation. As Longmore (1992, personal communication) points out, disability studies deepens the "historical comprehension of a broad range of subjects, for instance the history of values and beliefs regarding human nature, gender, and sexuality; American notions of individualism and equality, and the social and legal definition of what constitutes a minority group."

A disability studies perspective adds a critical dimension to thinking about issues such as autonomy, competence, wholeness, independence/dependence, health, physical appearance, aesthetics, community, and notions of progress and perfection. These issues pervade every aspect of the civic and pedagogic culture. They appear as themes in literature, as variables in social and biological science, as dimensions of historical analysis, and as criteria for social policy and practice. Scholarship in this field addresses such fundamental ideas as who is considered a burden and who is a resource, who is expendable and who is esteemed, who should engage in the activities that might lead to reproduction and who should not, and, if reproduction is not the aim, who can engage in erotic pleasures and who should not. Looking at these issues from a disability studies perspective puts into relief patterns of behaviors and policy that have significant consequences for disabled people.

Within most academic curricula, the meaning according to disability is that it is a personal medical condition, rather than a social issue; an individual plight, rather than a political one. This state of affairs is remarkably similar to the traditional representations of women, described by Carol Tavris (1992) in *The Mismeasure of Woman*. Her book describes the way traditional research has often measured women against some idealized male norm and attempts to explain behavioral differences in terms of perceived biological or psychological differences, rather than differences in power and circumstance. Thomson (1990), in discussing the position of people with disabilities in society, reminds us of the power differential between non-disabled and disabled people, reinforced because "the dominant group defines itself as normative" (p. 238).

Disability studies challenges the idea that the social and economic status and assigned roles of people with disabilities are inevitable outcomes of their condition, an idea similar to the argument that women's roles and status are biologically determined. But disability studies goes beyond cataloguing discrimination and arguing for social change. It challenges the adequacy of the content and structure of the current curriculum. As with women's studies, disability studies redresses omitted histories, ideas, or bodies of literature and also analyzes the construction of the category "disability," the impact of that construction on society, and on the content and structure of knowledge—fundamental epistemological issues.

Unfortunately, both the structure and the content of the traditional curriculum are problematic with respect to disability. The current structure of the curriculum not only isolates the topic of disability in applied fields, but further segregates it in specialized applied fields (e.g., special education, rehabilitation medicine, counseling and psychology, physical therapy). The academy's role in supporting these specialized areas of study is to graduate majors to staff the kinds of civic institutions that provide remediation and treatment services to people with disabilities. Although there is a need for intervention and treatment, and a need for curricula to prepare professionals in these fields, this approach does not provide a liberal arts education.

The specialized applied fields conceptualize disability as a problem that resides in the individual requiring remediation, treatment, or intervention to amend or compensate for what is perceived as wrong, missing, or dysfunctional. This way of viewing disability is sometimes referred to as the deficit model or medical model. The liberal arts curriculum either represents people with disabilities as deviant or abnormal or, more often, ignores the topic.

Incorporated into the liberal arts curriculum, disability studies has the potential to organize and critique representations of disability, expose ways that disability has been constructed as label and category, and reveal the consequences of those actions for the lived experience of people with disabilities. We have organized information below into modules that can fit in a range of courses and can serve as an introduction to disability studies. We hope, of course, that you go beyond the "add and stir" method of curriculum transformation and continue to mine the information in this issue for ideas that can have a more transformative effect on your work.

Examples of the Scholarship

Disability studies captures and organizes works from seemingly disparate areas. It offers insight into the social arrangements constructed around the configuration of the world into disabled and non-disabled, and examines the ideas and beliefs that maintain that bifurcation. Material available comes primarily from the United States, Britain, and Australia, with some recent additions from Africa and Asia. The field both emanates from and supports the disability rights movement, which advocates for civil rights and self-determination based on a minority group model. The field is a form of cultural studies, but one clearly identified with a political movement.

The following material from the field of disability studies is organized into six modules that can be integrated in a wide range of courses. But these offerings only scratch the surface of the wealth of material available and hint at the possibilities of the field to transform curricula.

I: Metaphor

Metaphors endure in a culture because they are evocative and persuasive ways of explaining something and organizing the way we think. Their power and utility are dependent on shared beliefs and assumptions. Women and men with disabilities, and disabilities themselves, are used as metaphors in countless texts. In *Illness as Metaphor,* Susan Sontag (1978) attempts to separate the essential from the nonessential aspects of illness and, by inference, disability. Her purpose is to liberate our thinking from the "punitive or sentimental fantasies concocted about illness" (p. 3). Kriegel (1982), in a discussion of Sontag's work, notes that "disease has become so all-embracing a metaphor that its actual physical consequences have been swallowed up by the welter of moralistic judgments it calls forth" (p. 17).

Disability metaphors abound in fiction. Thomson (1990) faults literary criticism for ignoring the social and political aspects of disability and treating "the representation of disability under the rubric of 'the grotesque'." This "invites treating disability as monstrosity and alien otherness, dehumanizing us, erasing our histories, and appropriating our experiences for aesthetic purposes" (p. 238).

We were struck by an example of this guilt by association in a passage that appears in the front of Elizabeth Kamarck Minnich's excellent book on curriculum transformation, *Transforming Knowledge* (1990). The book presents a framework for understanding the limitations of the traditional curriculum and prescriptions for transformation. Ironically, in an effort to demonstrate the importance of representing women's voices, Minnich chose an opening epigraph that reduces the representation of a man with a disability to a metaphor for inadequacy. The quote is from Anna Julia Cooper's *A Voice from the South,* written over one hundred years ago—in 1892.

> It is not the intelligent woman vs. the ignorant woman nor the white woman vs. the black, the brown, and the red, it is not even the cause of woman vs. man. Nay, 'tis woman's strongest vindication for speaking that the world needs to hear her voice... The world has had to limp along with the wobbling gait and the one-sided hesitancy of a man with one eye. Suddenly the bandage is removed from the other eye and the whole body is filled with light. It sees a circle where before it saw a segment. The darkened eye restored, every member rejoices with it.

This is certainly an evocative quote. Yet, the utility of the passage is dependent on the belief that someone with the use of one eye perceives only a segment of the world, is unsteady, is hesitant, and functions in a body filled with darkness. The parallels drawn between silenced women and disabled man, and then between women given a voice and a man who is "cured" appear to be as meaningful today as they were in 1892. The dilemma now for those who advocate curricular transformation is to find ways to give the one-eyed man a realistic voice. If he remains a metaphor, his experience is defined only by implied comparison to unsteadiness, darkness, limited vision, sadness, ineptness, the absence of light and enlightenment, and any number of other substitutions for the lived experience of women and men with disabilities.

Courses in literature, literary criticism, rhetoric, or philosophy can investigate these metaphors and other devices that seem appealing because they effectively evoke feelings or images that many are thought to share. Not only do such figures of speech further objectify and alienated people with disabilities, they perpetuate stereotypes.

II: Social Arrangements—Their Earliest Beginnings and Current Interpretations

To examine variability in social arrangements of people with disabilities, it is best to start at the beginning. Trinkhaus and Shipman (1993) describe the fossil remains of a Neanderthal male who is believed to have sustained serious injuries which resulted in impaired mobility, partial blindness, and the use of only one arm. He lived for thirty to forty-five years, a long life span. The authors comment that his survival was a result of the "compassion" and "humanity" of the Neanderthals. Stephen Jay Gould (1988) describes an individual from the Upper Paleolithic period whose remains indicate physical disabilities (a form of dwarfism resulting in limited mobility) that would have restricted his participation in the hunting and gathering activities, and the nomadic life of his group. The man was buried in a cave that appeared to be a burial site for people of high status. Gould speculates that his social standing may have afforded him this honor, or that his differences were valued, or that "his deeds or intelligence won respect despite his physical handicaps" (p. 18). The paleontological evidence as well as the contemporary interpretations are valuable reminders of the variation in response to disability.

Scheer and Groce (1988) also review information on prehistoric life and critique the narrow and stereotypical interpretations of the evidence in contemporary literature. They note that in prehistoric societies, people with disabilities existed in greater numbers than current evidence would suggest. They compare interpretations of that data with interpretations of the situation of people with disabilities in contemporary nonindustrialized societies. They refute some commonly held assumptions that "disabled individuals born outside the industrialized world were either killed at birth or died when young" (p. 24). Although these practices did and continue to occur, there is tremendous variation in the practices and in the value systems that determine them. They note how scholars in the United States tend to glorify the modern industrialized nations' treatment of people with disabilities and that tendency shapes interpretations of data. For instance, they quote Birdsell (1972) from a standard textbook on biological anthropology: "Biologically handicapped children are a humanistic concern in our society whereas in simple human populations they died early and were not missed" (p. 384). Scheer and Groce argue for analysis of the social construction of disability within a given society, as well as analysis of the reconstruction that takes place in scholarship as meaning is accorded to data collected about that society.

Nichols also comments on the misinterpretations of traditional societies that exist in contemporary scholarship. His study of traditional African attitudes toward disability is in response to the "observable tendency to reduce African ideas about disability to a few hackneyed scenarios whereby disability is seen either as a result of witchcraft . . . or as a form of divine retribution" (p. 26). He notes that modern industrialized societies tend to dismiss African ideas as "barbaric" or "primitive." Instead, he differentiates between African belief systems based on "*pragmatic spirituality* that reflects knowledge and utility, and *blind superstition* which is in bondage to ignorance" (emphasis added by Nichols) (p. 29), in order to demonstrate the human and humane ideas that inform many African approaches to disability. Courses in history, anthropology, ethics, biology, physical anthropology, African studies, paleontology, or cultural studies might examine any one of these topics from an informed disability perspective. These courses could provide useful perspectives on the ways that researchers' ideas can color the collection and interpretation of data and show how disability is subject to misinterpretation.

III: Nineteenth- and Twentieth-Century Belief Systems

Courses in social history, American or European history, the social foundations of education, or religion might trace variations in beliefs about disability across a particular time period, such as the nineteenth to mid-twentieth century in the United States and Europe. Longmore (1987) discusses beliefs about disability that were dominant prior to the nineteenth century. It was believed that disability was caused by supernatural agency. Often people with disabilities were thought of as possessed by the devil, punished by god for their sins or their parents' sins, or, alternately, blessed by god and possessed of supernatural powers. The practices that emerged from these beliefs ranged from punishment, isolation, infanticide, or ridicule to overprotection and deification. The latter, although preferable in some ways, offered people with disabilities little control or opportunity.

In the nineteenth century, there was a shift from the belief that disability was caused by supernatural agency to a biological explanation that viewed treatment, or some form of rehabilitation, as the only logical response to disability (Longmore 1987). This shift marked the birth of an enormous "care" industry and along with it a variety of institutions and asylums.

The field of education developed its own response to the biological explanation of disability. The birth of special education was based on a humane belief in the right of all children to an education and an optimism about people with disabilities not present in supernatural explanations. Even though special education doesn't rely solely on medical diagnoses, the field by definition forefronts the physical, cognitive, and sensory impairments of individuals. The diagnosis and label become the major defining variable of learners, and pedagogical practice is largely determined by these designations (Linton 1994).

In a variety of courses, this material can be examined as a means to trace the shifts in policies and practices throughout history. Ideas ranging from ancient philosophies to current belief systems can be mined. It would be particularly interesting to examine ideologies popular in America in the nineteenth and early twentieth century, such as Malthusianism, social Darwinism, the science of eugenics, and laissez-faire approaches to government to understand their influence on the accommodation of people with disabilities in the society. These ideas certainly influenced nineteenth-century practices with respect to disability and the vestiges of these ideas persist today.

IV: Social Construction

Faculty in various disciplines try to explain social construction to students. The idea that disability is a construct is particularly difficult to understand and therefore it is a useful and challenging test case. Students in one of the author's classes (Linton's Social and Psychological Aspects of Disability) have made some very useful connections among various forms of social construction when we have discussed some of the following examples of variation in different societies' treatments of groups we currently call "disabled."

Two examples are provided here to demonstrate cultural responses to disability that are likely to differ from most students' own experience. Nichols (1993), in a discussion of various African cultures' beliefs about disability, describes the concept of Ebih, which refers to "aberrations which violate the natural order of things" (p. 32). He notes that "in the past among the Igbo and some other groups infanticide sometimes occurred following the birth of twins" because multiple births are associated with animals. Infants believed to have mental retardation as well as twins were "thrown away" in the bush because they were considered to be animal-like. These are practices that were frequently used in the past, but are no longer actively practiced. The point, though, is that by shifting time and location, twins and infants considered retarded, as well as other infants with physical anomalies, become part of one group, considered undesirable and more animal-like than human.

Disability, specifically deafness, was constructed very differently in Martha's Vineyard, Massachusetts from the eighteenth to mid-twentieth centuries. For over two and half centuries, ending in 1952, there was a higher incidence of hereditary deafness than in the rest of the United States. There were approximately 72 people who lived in Martha's Vineyard in those years who were deaf, approximately one in every 155 people born. Although a very small percentage of the population was deaf, the community was largely bilingual. As one of the surviving hearing members of the community recalls, everyone spoke sign language and the hearing citizens also used spoken English. In Groce's (1985) ethnohistory of Martha's Vineyard, *Everyone Here Spoke Sign Language,* she demonstrates how this community located people with disabilities as insiders, not the "other," by accommodating the customs to insure integration of all people in the community. The people who were deaf participated fully in the economic and social life of the Vineyard. It is likely that they lived more like non-deaf people than deaf people did in any other community in the United States.

These examples show the variability and arbitrariness of the division between disabled and non-disabled people. There is not an absolute and inevitable way of organizing the world. In one case, twins, a group not stigmatized or disenfranchised in most cultures, were systematically eliminated in the same manner as people with significant retardation. In the Martha's Vineyard example, the demarcation that usually exists between hearing and deaf people was erased.

V: The Medicalization and Pathologizing of Difference

The medicalization of disability, the appropriation of the category by the medical profession, has had various consequences for people with disabilities. Medical explanations of disability replaced, to a degree, supernatural explanations that were dominant in Europe and the United States prior to the nineteenth century. The identification of disability as a medical condition has afforded many people with disabilities significant comforts and health. However, along with those benefits there has been a loss of freedom and of rights.

Medical, educational, and social service personnel have wielded enormous power over people with disabilities using the tools of diagnosis, labeling, treatment, and institutionalization. It is often difficult to explain what is wrong with this arrangement. The seemingly benevolent impulses that drive these practices belie the paternalism and control these tools serve. The arrangement privileges the medical definitions of people's lives over the social and political definitions. The solution to the "problem" of disability is seen as residing in the resources and facilities of the medical establishment, rather than in legislative bodies and social institutions. The arrangement buys into the assumption that people with disabilities are more concerned with cures than rights, are more plagued with their condition than with discrimination. It also assumes that all human variations labeled "disabilities" require a medical definition.

Further compounding of the problem occurs when medical labels are used to designate certain characteristics as pathological, or groups as mad or dangerous. Sander Gilman (1985) in *Difference and Pathology: Stereotypes of Sexuality, Race, and Madness* discusses the "conflation of concepts" (p. 71) that occurs when, for instance, women or African-Americans are linked with pathology. The conflation of disability and pathology seems so inevitable that it is hard to disentangle the two. Pathology itself is a huge construct, difficult to strip down to its essential and useful elements. The non-essential elements, the encumbrances, the imposed meanings and inconstant social practices are discussed in Gilman's work and the writing of Thomas Szasz, R. D. Laing, Michel Foucault, Erving Goffman, Margaret Mead, and even Alexander Solzhenitsyn (in *The Gulag Archipelago*). Each analyzes the manner in which pathology has been constructed to serve social ends and the ways that medical and other institutions have gained control over people through labeling and institutionalization. This history is analogous to the way women's autonomy has been constrained "for their own good," and women's efforts to buck authority and demand their rights have been interpreted as medical/psychiatric problems to be controlled.

The higher education curriculum strengthens the control that the rehabilitation/medical industry and the special education system have over disabled people. The curriculum has been designed to prepare service providers and educators. Indeed, the needs of the market support the logic of a curriculum on disability isolated in the applied fields. One of the major struggles that disability studies scholars face is wresting control of the representation of disability from these specialists. Disability studies lies outside these fields and critiques their orientation toward intervention and cure and their reliance on deficit models of disability.

An examination of medical history through the lens of disability studies reveals other ways medicine has had tremendous control over people with disabilities. For instance, in addition to attempts to minimize suffering and maximize functioning, some members of the scientific community have attempted to make the human race more "perfect" by eliminating people with undesirable characteristics from the population. The belief that disability weakens the genetic make-up of the population has fostered overt and covert eugenics practices, including various means of controlling reproductive rights or socially sanctioned practices to eliminate undesirables from the population. The eugenic movement that informed Nazi Germany's practice of genocide of people with disabilities has been reported in Lifton's (1986) *The Nazi Doctors: Medical Killing and the Psychology of Genocide* and in Gallagher's (1989) *By Trust Betrayed: Patients, Physicians and the License to Kill in the Third Reich.* Other writers have compared these practices to more seemingly enlightened practices in England and the United States. Hubbard (1990)—in a chapter titled "Who should inhabit the world?"—compares British and American practices and ideas during a similar period, such as the practice of forced sterilization of those considered unfit for society. Elks (1993) traces the historical acceptance of euthenic practices that, if implemented, would sanction the extermination of people with mental retardation. The use of the "lethal chamber" option was supported by leaders in the field of mental retardation in the United States before it was applied in Nazi Germany. Wolfensberger (1981) discusses the implications of the Nazi policy of extermination and euthanasia for current thinking in the United States about prenatal screening to determine the status of the fetus and the growing acceptance of the practice of selective abortion when disability is predicted. There are obvious differences between Nazi practices and current practices in the United States. The similarities, however, are less obvious and certainly less discussed. Authors who have located disability more centrally in the discourse point out the dangers of accepting a eugenics approach to the use of prenatal diagnosis as a means of controlling the variation of characteristics within the population.

When using these examples in class, it is important to note that raising concerns about the ways prenatal screening and selective abortion are used and promoted is not to support an anti-choice position. When one of the authors, Simi Linton, discusses this topic with graduate students in counseling we focus on the climate in which decisions are made about prenatal screening and abortion, not on the right of a woman to make an informed choice—whatever the outcome. Students often comment on experiences they or friends have had with medical professionals who, they report, pushed them in covert and overt ways to have testing. The students often conclude that a pregnant woman should have the opportunity to learn more about the disability that a child might have, and about the opportunities and resources available for the family and the child. Women need support when they choose not to have testing or choose to proceed with a pregnancy if disability is a possibility. As Hubbard (1990) states in *The Politics of Women's Biology:*

a woman must have the right to terminate a pregnancy whatever her reasons, but she must also feel empowered not to terminate it, confident that the society will do what it can to enable her and her child to live fulfilling lives. To the extent that prenatal interventions implement social prejudices against people with disabilities they do not expand our reproductive rights. They constrict them. (pp. 197–98)

Other measures to limit the population of people with disabilities are part of the history of medical practice. Elks (1993) notes the horrible conditions of custodial institutions, including overcrowding, poor sanitation, and meager food rations. Death from tuberculosis and pulmonary and infectious disease accounted for over sixty-five percent of deaths between 1901 and 1925 in those institutions. This history is rarely discussed in the applied fields, which tend to underscore the humane and benevolent accomplishments of the medical fields.

Medical practices share a peculiar border with such social institutions and rituals as freak shows and carnivals. Fiedler (1978) in *Freaks* and Bogdan (1988) in his book *Freak Show: Presenting Human Oddities for Amusement and Profit* describe how people have been put on public display in circuses and other more sedate institutions, such as museums and medical facilities. A man described as the "Elephant Man" and a woman called the "Hottentot Venus" were displayed in medical and scientific settings, as well as in commercial venues. People have worked in these areas out of economic necessity or because they were under the "care" of medical personnel and had little opportunity to pursue other goals. Either as scientific specimens or amusements displayed for profit, people with disabilities were denied basic rights and freedoms.

Courses in women's studies, history of science, sociology/anthropology of medicine, public policy, ethics, genetics, biology, and philosophy can review this history from a disability studies perspective. Students preparing for careers in medicine or other health related fields should engage in critical examination of the history of their practice. Although ideally that analysis should take place both within the liberal arts undergirding of their education as well as in their training, in reality the internal critique of the applied fields is limited. The presence of disability studies in the liberal arts is the only likely way that students would have access to critical inquiry.

VI: The Sciences' Constructions of Disability

Disability studies scholarship examines the processes by which individuals are marginalized in the society based on physical, cognitive, psychological, or sensory variations. The sciences contribute to the decisions about what is valued and who or what is expendable. These disciplines have created the tools to designate what is normal and acceptable and they have the tools to challenge the power and authority of those designations. Women's studies scholarship has examined critically the mantle of neutrality in which the sciences wrap themselves, and disability studies has done the same. The paradigms and constructs employed in scientific theory as well as the methods of investigation are fertile regions to be explored. Often ideas can function on a subtle level, within an overall structure that gives the appearance of universality and comprehensiveness.

Scholars such as Evelyn Fox Keller have examined such subtle phenomena in writing about the social construction of science. Although such scholars may not have intended to reveal anything about the construction of disability, they have. For instance in her book, *Reflections on Gender and Science* (1985), Keller discusses geneticist Barbara McClintock's perspective on how to conduct scientific research, which is one that, as she describes, "pays special attention to the exceptional case" and entails a respect for individual difference and complexity. Rather than dismiss as aberrant members of a species that stray from the norm, McClintock believes that difference is "evidence not of lawlessness or disorder, but of a larger system of order, one that cannot be reduced to a single law." McClintock's approach offers a way to think about the bifurcations that exist in the social arena based on characteristics labeled disabilities. The approach can inform the discussion on ethical issues related to eliminating difference. For instance, the pursuit of certain notions of perfection are demonstrated in efforts to "repair" the individual with a disability or eliminate people with impairments from the population through the use of prenatal screening and selective abortion.

These are examples that can be included in a range of courses. Readings can be drawn from the "Disability Studies Project Bibliography."

Obstacles to Incorporating Disability Studies in the Curriculum

Despite the efforts of a number of people on campuses across the United States and at institutions in Australia and England, disability studies has not received much attention in the academic community. There are various reasons for this situation. Certainly, the extraordinarily low representation of people with disabilities in academic settings is an important impediment. Whether those individuals would serve as reminders or actively remind the community of the incompleteness of the knowledge we impart to students, their absence lessens the chance for change.

A second obstacle to the incorporation of disability studies in the curriculum is the assumption that disability is already well represented and in its rightful place—in the specialized applied fields. However, as we have noted, a disability studies perspective is not present in the liberal arts or even in the specialized fields.

A third obstacle is the unspoken belief that the university's only responsibility in this area is to provide services for students with disabilities. It is not surprising that the university conceives of its obligation primarily in these terms. The current curriculum supports a helping orientation and the university has adopted the logic of the curriculum. Other agendas, such as curricular reform, affirmative action efforts to ensure representation of people with disabilities on the faculty and in the administration, and the recognition of students with disabilities as members of an underrepresented minority group, are not addressed.

A fourth obstacle has been revealed as groups at various institutions have tried to broaden the definition of diversity. For example, attempts to include lesbian and gay studies or disability studies in curriculum transformation efforts have been welcomed by some, and criticized by others. Ironically, some of the critics are those who are the strongest proponents of diversifying the curriculum. However, their conceptualization of diversity does not include disability. What is even more disturbing is that the criticisms previously heard from proponents of the traditional canon are now being used against the inclusion of disability in curriculum transformation efforts. The following have been said to one or another of the authors in meetings or at conferences on diversifying curricula: "scholarship on disability will 'water down' the diversity requirement"; "its purpose is to increase self-esteem, or capitulate to interest group pressure"; "it's not valid or rigorous scholarship"; "it's parochial, and will further atomize the curriculum."

Were these criticisms framed as questions to be engaged with, the academic community would benefit from the discourse. Why, for instance, is scholarship on disability not considered rigorous, and therefore likely to dilute or compromise the curriculum or diversity initiatives? Has the association of the topic of disability with the applied fields weakened its status and its perceived applicability to other areas of inquiry? Is disability studies considered only for the purpose of raising self-esteem because people with disabilities are perceived as needing a boost? Is disability studies any more, or any less, related to political considerations or identity formation than any other area of inquiry? Are concerns about a parochial, narrow, balkanized curriculum based on the view that the study of disability is about "them" and says nothing about social, political, and cultural processes that the whole society engages in?

These questions about disability studies relate to broader questions about curricular reform efforts in general. For instance, how can we redress problems in the structure as well as the content of the curriculum in reform efforts? How do the structure and status of the disciplines privilege certain points of view and bodies of knowledge? How does the structure of the multicultural curriculum privilege certain points of view and bodies of knowledge? How does the structure of the disciplines constrain our explorations of new epistemologies that can enhance understanding of the social and political situation of people with disabilities and other disenfranchised groups?

Engaging these questions can provide a more open forum to discuss how disability studies can be incorporated in curriculum reform efforts. Whatever the reasons, diversity/multicultural initiatives have formed their own shape and texture and render their own authority. Therefore, the knowledge these initiatives privilege and the knowledge they marginalize warrant consideration, particularly from the perspectives of the margins. The perspective of disabled people and the field of disability studies are conspicuously absent from a broad range of endeavors.

Works Cited

Birdsell, J. D. *Human Evolution: An Introduction to the New Physical Anthropology.* Chicago: Rand McNally, 1972.

Bogdan, R. *Freak Show: Presenting Human Oddities for Amusement and Profit.* Chicago: Chicago UP, 1988.

Elks, M. A. "'The Lethal Chamber': Further Evidence for the Euthanasia Option." *Mental Retardation* 3.4 (1993): 201–207.

Fiedler, L. *Freaks.* New York: Simon & Schuster, 1978.

Gallagher, H. G. *By Trust Betrayed: Patients, Physicians, and the License to Kill in the Third Reich.* New York: Henry Holt, 1989.

Gilman, S. *Difference and Pathology: Stereotypes of Sexuality, Race and Madness.* Ithaca: Cornell UP, 1985.

Gould, S. J. *The Mismeasure of Man.* New York: W. W. Norton, 1981.

Gould, S. J. "Honorable Men and Women." *Natural History* March 1988: 16–20.

Groce, N. *Everyone Here Spoke Sign Language: Hereditary Deafness on Martha's Vineyard.* Cambridge: Harvard UP, 1985.

Hahn, H. "Theories and Values: Ethics and Contrasting Perspectives on Disability," in *The Psychological and Social Impact of Disability.* 3rd ed. Ed. R. P. Marinelli and A. E. Dell Orto. New York: Springer, 1991.

Hubbard, R. *The Politics of Women's Biology.* New Brunswick: Rutgers UP, 1990.

Keller, E. F. *Reflections on Gender and Science.* New Haven: Yale UP, 1985.

Kriegel, L. "The Wolf in the Pit in the Zoo." *Social Policy* 13.2 (1982): 16–23.

Lifton, R. J. *The Nazi Doctors: Medical Killing and the Psychology of Genocide.* New York: Basic Books, 1986.

Linton, S. "Reshaping Disability in Teacher Education and Beyond." *Teaching Education* 6.2 (1994): 9–20.

Longmore, P. "Uncovering the Hidden History of People with Disabilities." *Reviews in American History* September 1987: 357–364.

Minnich, E. K. *Transforming Knowledge.* Philadelphia: Temple UP, 1990.

Nichols, R. W. "An Examination of Some Traditional African Attitudes Towards Disability." *Traditional and Changing Views of Disability in Developing Societies: Causes, Consequences, Cautions.* Monograph #53 of the International Exchange of Experts and Information in Rehabilitation, 1993.

Sacks, O. *Seeing Voices: A Journey Into the World of the Deaf.* Berkeley: University of California Press, 1989.

Sacks, O. "A Neurologist's Notebook: To See and Not See." *New Yorker* 10 May 1992: 85–94.

Scheer, J. and N. Groce. "Impairment as a Human Constant: Cross-Cultural Perspectives on Variation." *Journal of Social Issues* 44.1 (1988): 23–37.

Sontag, S. *Illness as Metaphor.* New York: Farrar, Straus and Giroux, 1978.

Tavris, C. *The Mismeasure of Woman.* New York: Simon and Schuster, 1992.

Thomson, R. G. "Speaking About the Unspeakable: The Representation of Disability as Stigma in Toni Morrison's Novels." *Courage and Tools: The Florence Howe Award for Feminist Scholarship 1974–1989.* New York: Modern Language Association, 1990.

Trinkhaus, E. and P. Shipman. *The Neanderthals: Changing the Image of Mankind.* New York: Knopf, 1993.

Wolfensberger, W. *The Principle of Normalization in Human Services.* Toronto: National Institute on Mental Retardation, 1972.

Wolfensberger, W. "The Extermination of Handicapped People in World War II Germany." *Mental Retardation* 19.1 (1981): 15–17.

Afterword

How I Got Started: Student Participation in a (Too) Large Sociology Class
Fred L. Pincus

Editors' Notes: Pincus bring experiments with student empowerment to his large sociology course, Social Problems in American Society. His students codevelop the syllabus with him, voting on which "social issues" to cover. They also codevelop exams by writing short-answer questions. Students also work together in groups for class presentations. With remarkable documentation of his teaching, student evaluations, actual course materials, and student responses, Pincus reports moderate success with this experiment and describes how he would modify his experiment. After thirty years of teaching, Pincus admits that the new methods create more work for him, but he is committed to making his students active learners.

What can we do about the yawns, blank stares, and boredom that seem endemic to large classes (those with more than 60 students)? How can we reach apparently disengaged students?

I've been teaching Social Problems in American Society, a lower-division sociology course, for more than twenty years and have become increasingly frustrated and unhappy with student alienation. In spite of the provocative subject matter, it's difficult to get students to participate. They complain about the lack of discussion in class but refuse to talk when given the chance. They don't ask questions. Students who do poorly on exams don't come for the help that I offer. Finally, the end-of-the-semester student evaluations that I get are mediocre.

As a teacher, I have been dealing with this frustration at the University of Maryland–Baltimore County, a public university in suburban Baltimore. UMBC is a thirty-year-old campus with almost ten thousand students, most of whom are undergraduates. Two-fifths of the students are twenty-one years old or younger, and another two-fifths are between twenty-two and twenty-nine years old. Just more than half of the students are female. Whites still account for 70 percent of the student body, with blacks making up 15 percent and Asians accounting for 11 percent. Only 2 percent are Latino.

Students come from a wide variety of class backgrounds. Only 10 percent to 15 percent of the undergraduates qualify for Pell grants, which are awarded to low-income students, and a much smaller percentage come from wealthy parents. Most of the students, however, work at least part time. One-fifth of the students live on campus and many of the rest still live with their parents. Their academic skills are also quite diverse, although most can read college-level books.

It had become clear to me that the students, most of whom are *not* sociology majors, had no investment in the class beyond getting an adequate grade to fulfill a general education requirement. Many would rather have been taking courses in their major departments. Almost one-third of UMBC students major in one of the social sciences or humanities, while a fifth major in math or science and another fifth in engineering or computer science. There is no single dominant major at UMBC.

Besides acknowledging their lack of enthusiasm for taking a social science requirement, I was also aware that students had no voice in selecting the course topics to be discussed and that they were passive learners. There was no chance for active learning except for when I broke them into discussion groups several times during the semester. Everything else centered around me, the instructor. It was clearly time for a change.

In the fall of 1995, I had begun meeting informally with other social science faculty who taught large classes, some as large as two hundred students. We had good discussions and I learned some helpful techniques, but all of my colleagues taught lecture-based teacher-centered courses. I wanted something different.

To get some new ideas, I turned to the writings of Ira Shor (1996), who tries to empower students by actually giving them more control in the classroom. In his writing and literature classes, students select the books they will read and the topics they will write on and participate as coteachers. They write and grade exam questions in conjunction with Shor. Although this power-sharing principle requires the instructor to give up a certain amount of control over the class, Shor argues that students gain a great deal.

Over the years, I had always thought that Shor's ideas seemed better suited to a small class in which writing and thinking skills could be applied to any subject matter. Out of desperation, I tried to adapt them to a larger disciplinary course with a more specific "body of knowledge." What follows is a description and analysis of a sixty-five-student "social problems" course that I taught in the fall of 1996. The course met for two seventy-five-minute sessions each week. I used *Social Problems: Society in Crisis* by Curran and Renzetti (1996) as my text. My goal was to get students more *involved* in the class in the hope that they would learn more and that they would find the class more enjoyable.

Course Structure

During the first five weeks, I taught the class in a traditional way and discussed the issues of economics, politics, class, and poverty, which were covered in the first four chapters of the textbook. I felt that this teacher-centered opening provided an important context to understanding the other social problems that we would be discussing during the semester. I suppose that I also wanted to retain control over some part of the course. Students took a traditional exam at the end of this section consisting of forty multiple-choice questions and an essay.

There were, however, several important nontraditional elements present during these first five weeks. During the third week of the course, I asked students to vote on which six of the remaining ten chapters of the text they wished to cover. I gave each student six votes and also asked each to indicate which two chapters he or she was most interested in. The "winners" were crime, race relations, education, gender relations, intimate relations, and criminal justice. Although these six are issues that students are typically interested in, I was surprised that the chapter on the environment was one of the losers. Other losers included health care, aging, and population/urbanization. After tallying the votes, I placed each student in a group that was assigned to handle one chapter. Most of the students got to work on their first choice, although some had to settle for their second choice.

The next nontraditional element I introduced was the one entire class that we devoted to "group work" during the fourth week. Since I felt that this group work was essential to empowering students, I required each group to meet for seventy-five minutes to plan its presentations. The room was large enough for each of the groups to form a circle and proceed with its work.

Before going any further, I will explain the structure of the last two-thirds of the semester by quoting at length from the course syllabus. The column on the left contains the actual syllabus. The column on the right, in italics, contains my comments on various parts of the syllabus.

We will discuss six additional social problems to be selected by the students from the remaining chapters of the textbook. Each of the six chapter modules will cover three class periods and will be structured as follows:

Day 1: Class presentation about important issues in chapter by student panel.

Day 2: Class presentation by instructor.

Day 3: 30 minutes—Quiz on chapter and on presentations by students and instructor for that module.

It seemed useful to have some set structure about what was going to happen for each module. I decided to let the students take the lead during the first class. In the second class, I would pick up any loose ends and clarify points that they didn't make clear.

30 minutes—Group work. Some groups will critique the student and instructor presentations and the quiz. Some groups will prepare for future presentations.

15 minutes—Groups doing the critique will share their thoughts with rest of class.

Each group will have two tasks—to prepare student presentations and to formulate test questions. There should be a division of labor in each group with some doing the presentation and others doing the test questions. As much as possible, the division of labor should be based on individual student preferences.

Test Questions No more than two or three students should be assigned to the test questions. They are responsible for constructing eight short-answer questions about the course material in that section. A short-answer question is one that can be answered in a few sentences or a paragraph. This could involve definitions of terms: "What does the text mean by the term 'social class' and provide two examples?" Or, it could refer to causes of social problems. For example, "From the liberal perspective, what is one major cause of poverty? Explain." Or, it could refer to solutions: "List one solution that a conservative might give to solving the problem of poverty. Explain."

Each group is responsible for handing in eight questions along with the answers. These questions may be discussed and shared with the other members of the group but may not be shared with anyone else. They

Since I had never done this before, I decided to make each module independent by ending with a quiz on each. I didn't know what the student presentations would be like, so I wasn't sure if I would be able to construct a second midterm exam at the end of the semester.

Since each group consisted of ten to twelve people, there wasn't enough time for each to make an adequate presentation in a seventy-five-minute class. Shor has discussed involving students in formulating questions and grading tests. I decided to reduce the number of presenters by having two or three members of the group write short-answer questions. Although there is clearly educational value in formulating questions, I would not have done this if the groups were smaller. I would have had all students making presentations on the chapter.

should be handed in to the instructor on the same day that the student presentation is made. The names of the two or three students doing the questions should be attached. The instructor will select three or four of the questions to be used for the quiz.

Student Presentation The remaining students must participate in a panel discussion of the material presented in the chapter. You may want to summarize some of the important points in the chapter. You may want to criticize the text or provide other illustrations. You may want to select an additional short article, which takes a different viewpoint than the chapter or which elaborates on something the chapter says. You may want to select a video that is 30 minutes or less. Each group must decide how to structure its presentations, but everyone must participate. Groups can request to meet with the instructor for assistance. **Each student panelist should hand in a one-page summary of his or her presentation on the day of the presentation.**

This was the heart of my attempt to empower students by making them coteachers. All of those in the group selected that chapter as their first or second choice, so they were interested in the subject matter. I tried to give them a certain amount of latitude as well as guidance in terms of what to say. They also had to do a certain amount of reflection on the chapter as a group, which enabled them to learn from one another.

This summary was to help me in evaluating their presentations. As it turned out, however, it wasn't really that helpful, since I relied more on the notes that I took of their presentations.

Quizzes Each quiz will be worth 30 points and will consist of 16 multiple-choice questions selected by the instructor and 3–4 short-answer questions constructed by the students. The questions will cover the assigned chapter, any other readings, and the student and instructor presentations.

In thinking about quizzes, I was always concerned with making an attempt to do something that was pedagogically sound without being inundated with huge numbers of student papers every three classes. The textbook had a computerized test bank that enabled me to quickly select sixteen multiple-choice questions. The students would then write some short-answer questions that would require a small amount of writing during the quiz.

Group Work on Quiz Days After each quiz, students will work in groups. Some of the groups that have not yet given presentations will get a chance to work on their presentations and/or test questions. They can also meet with the instructor during this time.

Other groups, especially those who have already given their presentations, will critique the chapter, the student and instructor presentations, and the test questions for that module. This includes the group that has just presented. A critique means a discussion of what was good about the presentations, what was bad, what was excluded that should have been included, and what was included that should have been excluded. This is a time for reflection and constructive criticism.

This group work is important. Attendance will be taken in each chapter group and each discussion group. Students who do not stay for the entire 45 minutes of group work cannot get credit for the quiz.

Student panelists will receive their group work grade on the basis of their individual presentations. The instructor will be looking for evidence of understanding the material as well as creativity and articulateness. Remember, each panelist must turn in a one-page summary of his or her presentation. Students who construct test questions will receive a group grade based on the quality of their questions and answers.

This assignment was a result of several different concerns. First, I needed something to do for the forty-five minutes of class that remained after the quiz. Second, I wanted the presenters to reflect on their presentations and feel a sense of closure. Third, I wanted those groups who had not yet presented to have more time to prepare. Finally, I hoped that those who had previously presented could give constructive criticism to others. As I discuss below, this was not a good use of time.

I felt that there had to be some way for me to evaluate student presentations. If two students chose to give a joint presentation, I gave them a group grade. Otherwise, each student was graded on his or her individual presentation.

Afterword

After receiving the above syllabus from me in class, students for the most part passively accepted the course structure and asked very few questions. In fact, they didn't react any differently than other students have reacted to my traditional syllabus. I had expected some students to express apprehension about having to speak in public, and I had hoped that some would tell me how exciting the class sounded.

During the fourth week of class, shortly before the group reports were to begin, I handed out the following elaboration of what I expected for group presentations:

> Begin by introducing yourselves. The first task is to decide who is going to do the presentations and who will formulate quiz questions. Remember, no more than two or three people should be assigned to the questions.
>
> Next, the group must decide how to divide the chapter up into smaller parts and decide who is responsible for which parts. This could be done on an individual basis or it could be done in teams; i.e., one team of 2 or 3 students might be responsible for a certain part of the chapter.
>
> After this division of labor, you must decide what to do. You could decide to summarize the chapter by highlighting some of the main points. You could decide to relate the chapter to current events; i.e., is there something in a newspaper or magazine that has anything to do with the materials discussed in the chapter? It is possible to organize a debate about part of the chapter. You could talk about how the chapter relates to materials in other courses. It would be good if the group members coordinate their efforts so that people are not going off in different directions. If you want to use a video, talk to me well in advance.
>
> Each group should plan to take about 45–50 minutes for its presentation. This means that each group member (except for those who are doing the questions) must make a presentation of 4–6 minutes, depending upon the size of the group. This will leave enough time for questions and comments from the class.
>
> Remember, this is something new and probably frightening to most of you. Hopefully, it is also exciting. Your instructor is available to help. Drop by during office hours or set up an appointment.

During the first group work day, the six groups went about the business of organizing their presentations. Some groups separated into presenters and question writers, while others separated into teams consisting of several presenters and one question writer. I was optimistic after this first day and wrote the following entry in the class diary that I kept:

> Students did not appear to be panicked or anxious. People asked me a few appropriate questions. The crime group asked a few more, but that is normal since they are the first. I circulated throughout the room but groups did not

really need me except to answer a question or two. Can it actually be that this experiment is going to work? That would be incredibly wonderful!

Implementing the New Structure

Student Presentations

Group 1 (Crime) gave its presentation during the sixth week of the course. Each student summarized the section of the book that he or she was responsible for, and the whole thing was fairly boring. Other students did not ask any questions when the presenters were finished, and there was twenty minutes of class time remaining, so I had to try to get a discussion going. Students lacked experience as discussion leaders and I had to fill the gap.

I also ran into the issue of what to do when one of the student presenters was unclear or made an erroneous statement. My first impulse was to correct the student immediately after he or she finished. However, I thought that students might find it too difficult to receive criticisms from the teacher at that point. I also know how teacher interventions often stop any student discussions. So, I decided to make my comments during my lecture period that followed in the next class meeting. Further, I realized that I should not permit students to summarize the book but should have them go beyond the book.

I gave my lecture during the second class of the module and held a quiz during the third class. After the quiz, students met in their groups and discussed the previous week. On the one hand, students—agreeing with me—wanted the presenters to do more than just summarize the book. As a result of these comments, I instructed future groups *not* to summarize and to pause for questions after each individual presentation. In addition, I asked them to prepare some general discussion questions in case there was time left over after the presentation.

On the other hand, students asked me to spend *more* time explaining the book. This was a typical comment that students have made over the years, but I have always ignored it in the past. This time, the class process drove me to alter my own lectures. I wrote the following in my class diary:

> One of the student comments led me to think about my lecture philosophy. Should I stick closer to the book rather than going beyond the book as I usually do. Perhaps I should talk about some of the concepts and give examples rather than go on to new things. This might help to provide students with some anchor. Maybe I should deal with the concepts that the student presenters don't.

This, of course, would take extra preparation time. I felt that my next lecture on the second topic—educational inequality—was a good one, so I decided not to change it. I discussed a number of different explanations of educational inequality, many of which were not covered in the textbook. Here is my diary entry:

> I asked students for feedback; was it better or worse than my previous lecture. Almost all of the students said it was better. When I asked why, a few students said that it went into greater depth. From my perspective, however, it did not go into much detail on *any* of the explanations of inequality! Some of the explanations were discussed in the book and some were not. Maybe "touching base" with the book was an important factor. The struggle continues!

In retrospect, perhaps anything I say sounds important and in-depth to students because of the authority that I have as a teacher.

Throughout the semester, I continually struggled with fine-tuning the new structure. It took a lot of time and I wasn't always happy about it. Consider the following diary entry:

> I spent 4–5 hours today on tasks associated with the course. First, I went over my notes on the student presentations in order to give them a grade. I had to check their presentations with the book to see if they added anything new. Then I went through the students' test questions and found that I could use only two. Then I spent time on the gender lecture. I summarized my old lecture and added a few new things. I think it came out well and it's something I can use again. Finally, I made up the quiz. Is it all worthwhile?
>
> It's a little uncomfortable for me to give up the control that I usually have. Students were talking about some things from the text that I had forgotten about or didn't usually deal with. I guess this is part of the price of student empowerment.

Fortunately, the student presentations got better and better. There was less summary and more creativity as students responded to my instructions and also learned from one another. They made overheads and brought in videos. One student even made a ten-minute video on single-parent families. It wasn't great, but he spent a lot of time on it, and the other students were appreciative.

By the end of the semester, the teacher-student roles occasionally reversed and I was learning from some of the presentations. For example, one woman discussed an empirical study comparing married couples and cohabiting families. I asked her for a copy of the article and integrated it into my own lecture on intimate relations.

One continual problem, however, was that students had uneven skills in their oral presentations. Some were quite articulate and gave excellent talks. Others nervously mumbled while they read their reports, and it was difficult to determine what they were saying. Most fell somewhere in between these two extremes, but virtually all of them came well prepared. I'm not sure how to avoid this situation unless I build a public-speaking component into the class.

If more courses adopted this idea of student coteaching, of course, students would gain more public-speaking skills.

The student presenters reported getting a lot out of their own presentations in a questionnaire distributed during the last day of class. Eighty-eight percent reported learning "a great deal" or "something" as a result of their presentations, while only 12 percent reported learning "a little" or not "learning anything." Students were also reasonably positive in response to the following question: How much did you learn from the other students' presentations throughout the semester? Sixty-five percent said that they learned "a lot" or "something." Twenty-nine percent said that they "only learned a little" and 6 percent said that they "didn't learn anything."

In written comments on the questionnaire and in some informal verbal comments throughout the semester, however, a number of students said that they would rather have me lecture throughout the course in a traditional way. Indeed, student responses on the questionnaire indicated that they learned more from my lectures than from the student presentations. Eighty-nine percent said that they learned "a great deal" or "something" from my lectures, while only 11 percent said that they learned "only a little" or "didn't learn anything."

It takes *less work* and *less responsibility* to just listen to teacher lectures. A participatory course asks students to work harder and take responsibility for their own learning. Many students resent this and would rather listen to the material that will be covered on the exam.

Writing Test Questions

I am more ambivalent about the effect of students writing test questions. Remember that two or three members of each group were to write seven or eight short-answer questions, along with the answers, for the quiz. Here is what I wrote in the first draft of this paper:

> The test question assignment did not work nearly as well. Basically, I could not use most of the questions that the students submitted and those that I did use required rewriting. In retrospect, this task was simply too difficult for students. This was compounded by the fact that the weaker students tended to gravitate toward this assignment as opposed to the presentation. It also took me much longer to make up each quiz. I would not ask students to write questions again.

When Ira Shor read the first draft of this paper, he asked me why I couldn't use many of the questions, so I went back to look at the original student papers again. To my great surprise, thirty-five of the sixty-four questions that students submitted were usable, sometimes with minor modification! Why, then, was I so negative about the assignment?

After some reflection, I would say that my initial negative reaction was caused by my intense dislike of constructing multiple-choice and short-answer quizzes. I had a shortcut easily available to me because the textbook had an accompanying computerized test bank that enabled me to make up a twenty-question quiz quickly. Including the students' short-answer questions took much more time. Then, I had to read and evaluate the answers rather than simply running the scan sheets through the computer to come up with a grade. Although the short answers forced students to write, I'm not sure this was a more effective evaluation measure than multiple-choice questions. I've always preferred essays or papers, but I had sixty-five students in the class. They just don't pay me enough to read that many essays every other week!

In responding to my questionnaire, those students who actually wrote the questions said that it was a positive experience. Eighty percent said that they learned "a great deal" or "something," while 20 percent said that they learned "a little" or that they didn't learn anything. If I were to use this assignment again, I would try to give students more guidance by discussing examples of questions that were good and bad.

Group Work

The group work after each quiz was also a problem. Although the groups that had not yet presented used their time well, the other groups grew bored of the critiques. The reporting students didn't seem interested in doing the critique. Perhaps they needed more instruction about how to do a critique. In addition, I should have been more explicit about how *their* comments were actually being incorporated into the course. For example, I could have mentioned how my lectures began to address the book a little more because of their comments.

After the fourth quiz, I began to give groups various discussion questions in anticipation of the next module. Before the intimate relations section, for example, I asked groups to define the term *family* and list as many forms of the family as they could. In the questionnaire, only 30 percent of the students said that this group work was always or usually enjoyable and worthwhile, compared to the 70 percent who said it was occasionally or never enjoyable or worthwhile. This aspect of the course structure clearly needs some revision.

Finally, I asked students the following question: All in all, how would you evaluate the experimental structure of SOCY 201? Their responses were as follows:

9%	Highly successful
55%	Generally successful but needs some improvement
27%	Generally unsuccessful, with some good points
9%	Highly unsuccessful

I was generally pleased with this response, especially the fact that only 9 percent rated it as a total failure and that there were more students on the positive side than the negative side. I would declare the experiment in student participation to be a "modest" success.

The university also administers a standard student course evaluation questionnaire during the last two weeks of class. Unfortunately, the student ratings on the SCEQ were no different than the mediocre ratings I received for the more traditional class structure that I used in past semesters. To say that I was disappointed is a bit of an understatement. However, I decided to try the new structure at least one more time.

Changes in the Class Structure

The next time I teach the class I am going to change the book. Rather than using a single text, I will use two anthologies (Skolnick and Currie 1997; Finsterbusch and McKenna 1996). Since there are many more discrete topics in an anthology than in a text, I can divide the class into nine or ten two-class modules rather than six three-class modules. This means that the size of each student group will be six or seven rather than eleven or twelve. The smaller group size will enable students to give longer and more in-depth presentations.

I will give each group extensive instructions at the beginning and will be very firm about not summarizing the book. I will also place several additional social problems anthologies and texts on reserve in the library so that a student can consult the relevant articles/chapters and see what additional information he or she can incorporate into the project. Actually, a student suggested this in one of the questionnaires.

I will also incorporate Shor's idea of an "after-class group," a volunteer student committee that meets with the teacher to critique the course. Rather than being in one of the chapter groups, students would have the option of meeting with me once a week to critique the class. This would be my main source of feedback and suggestions for change. I would expect that only students who want to participate in this type of activity will volunteer for the ACG.

Finally, I will drop the quizzes and simply give students three multiple-choice midterm exams. Since some students don't do well on multiple-choice exams, I will provide an optional take-home final exam that can be substituted for one of the midterms.

As the instructor, I was much more involved with the class during this experiment than usual. I had to alter some lectures and create a new one since I did not normally cover the criminal justice system. I also kept a class diary. Finally, I knew more of the students by name than I did in the traditional class structure.

All in all, conducting this experiment was always stimulating, sometimes exciting, and occasionally depressing. I take some comfort in knowing that I can still try new things after thirty years of college teaching in a publish-orperish institution. I look forward to implementing my revised participatory class structure.

Works Cited

Curran, Daniel J., and Claire M. Renzetti. 1996. *Social Problems: Society in Crisis*. 4th ed. Boston: Allyn and Bacon.

Finsterbusch, Kurt, and George McKenna. 1996. *Taking Sides on Controversial Social Issues*. 9th ed. Guilford, CT: Dushkin.

Shor, Ira. 1996. *When Students Have Power: Negotiating Authority in a Critical Pedagogy*. Chicago: University of Chicago Press.

Skolnick, Jerome, and Elliott Currie. 1997. *Crisis in American Institutions*. 10th ed. New York: Longman.

Appendix

An E-Mail Exchange Between Fred Pincus and Ira Shor, One Year Later

Dear Ira:

I just had a wonderful meeting of the "practice" after-class group (ACG) so I thought that I'd do my journal entry in the form of an e-mail to the inventor of the ACG. First, some background.

I have met my social problems class four times so far. As you remember, this is my part of the course and I'm dealing with inequality. They seem like a very good group in terms of asking questions and making comments. Since I haven't done anything too different than last time, I will say that it has something to do with the chemistry of the students.

At any rate, I broke the students down into groups during the regular class. There were fifty students who attended and I formed five random groups. They were to have read two articles on whether inequality was good for society. One, by George Gilder, said that is was and the other, by William Ryan, said that it wasn't. I asked them to first figure out what each author was saying and then asked them who, in their opinions, was right. The groups did very well in terms of figuring out what the authors were saying so they were able to work together to clarify the readings. There were spirited discussions about which author was right. Two groups voted for Ryan and three were split. I'm always amazed how students can enthusiastically get involved in discussions when you give them the right question to discuss.

On the syllabus, I explained what the ACG was all about and said that there would be a practice session after class today so that people could see what it was like. Seven students showed up, and three more said that they wanted to participate but couldn't come today. Remember, being in the ACG is an alternative to being in one of the teaching groups.

I walked into the room and asked the ACG what they thought of today's group discussions. There were all enthusiastically positive and said that it helped them clarify the readings and that it was interesting to see what other people thought. One said that it might have been better if I had given a brief lecture about what the readings said before asking the question "Who was right?" I said that I could have done that in a much shorter time than the class discussion took but that I thought that it was important for students to see that they can also learn from each other. Most of them agreed with me although two thought that the lecture would be more efficient.

Then the issue of some students not doing the readings came up. One or two students in each of the discussion groups said that they hadn't done the readings and the ACG students asked if there was some way to compel them to do the reading. I mentioned my experience with weekly quizzes prior to discussing the readings and most of the students thought that was a good idea. We discussed different ways that this might be done. I also told them that the level of discussion was quite high and was better than in classes where I required weekly quizzes. They still thought some reading evaluation would be a good idea.

As the ACG discussion continued, I knew that I did not want to give quizzes because things were going quite well and because the syllabus was made up; out of principle, I don't like to include new requirements in midstream. If I was using the entire Shor method, I would have said that I would take their proposal up with the rest of the class. However, I am committed to a Pincus-modified version of the Shor method so I said that I would think about it. I also suggested that those who didn't read might have felt left out of the discussion and might do the reading next time. In my heart, however, I know that this will not solve the problem. I wonder how much control I can hold onto and still make the class successful.

At any rate, I just wanted to let you know that things went great! Do you have any sage words?

Fred

Dear Fred:

Hello and thanks so much for your message. I'm so happy to hear the good news of how things went with the practice ACG and the class discussion on inequality.

I suppose that some students will always NOT do the assigned readings and writing and come to class unprepared. If a critical mass of students is motivated to keep up with the work, these non-performers will not necessarily damage the learning process. So, on one hand, it's not essential or even possible to enforce 100 percent compliance or participation. Involved students in my classes have also complained about those who are uninvolved and not doing the work. They are right and have a sense that some folks are not pulling their weight. Sometimes they complain because they have a Utopian ideal of

100 percent participation that emerges from their own enthusiasm with the new kind of course—they want their own eagerness validated by every other student. Non-participating students irk them and unsettle them. I ask students to help get the others involved. I also ask students to write weekly journals one-page long about the readings, to which they attach one or two questions they want to pose for the discussion, so that I announce the expectation that everyone does the reading and everyone comes to class ready to launch the discussion with his or her own questions. Of course, this means I have more to read and respond to (not grade—I don't grade weekly journals but just give credit for doing them and write my comments back to the students). You might think of this weekly journal idea, and might consider asking the ACG to respond to the weekly journals with you as part of its activities, so that you distribute the exercise instead of monopolizing it, sharing with the ACG.

Ira

Acknowledgements for borrowed material (*continued*)

"Human Labor and Literature: A Pedagogy from a Working-Class Perspective" by Janet Zandy. *Changing Classroom Practices: Resources for Literacy and Cultural Studies* edited by David Downing. Copyright © 1994 by the National Council of Teachers of English. Reprinted by permission.

"The Inclusion/Exclusion Issue: Including Students in Choosing Texts" by Christine Sutphin. *Feminist Teacher* 7.1 (1992): 31–34. Reprinted by permission of the Feminist Teacher Editorial Collective.

"Queer Statistics: Using Lesbigay Word-Problem Content in Teaching Statistics" by John Kellermeier. *NWSA Journal* 7.1 (Spring 1995). Reprinted by permission of Indiana University Press.

About the Editors

Ira Shor has a dual appointment as Professor of English at the City University of New York Graduate School and at the College of Staten Island. His *Critical Teaching and Everyday Life* was the first booklength treatment of Freirean literacy in the United States. He worked with Paulo Freire for a number of years and coauthored with Freire his first "talking book," *A Pedagogy for Liberation*. Shor, whose most recent book is *When Students Have Power*, speaks widely around the country. He grew up in the working class of New York City.

Caroline Pari is Assistant Professor of English and Basic Writing Coordinator at Borough of Manhattan Community College, CUNY. She received her Ph.D. from CUNY, specializing in Composition and Rhetoric, Women's Studies, and nineteenth-century women's writing. Pari has contributed to *Teaching Working Class,* edited by Sherry Linkon, and *Attending to the Margins,* edited by Michelle Hall Kells and Valerie Balester. She is a native of Queens, New York, and lives there with her husband.

CALLAHAN LIBRARY
ST. JOSEPH'S COLLEGE
25 AUDUBON AVENUE
PATCHOGUE, NY 11772-2327